Anne Tyler

Twayne's United States Authors Series

Frank Day, Editor
Clemson University

TUSAS 620

Anne Tyler
Photograph courtesy Diana Walker

Anne Tyler

Elizabeth Evans

Twayne Publishers ■ New York

Maxwell Macmillan Canada ■ Toronto

Maxwell Macmillan International ■ New York Oxford Singapore Sydney

Anne Tyler
Elizabeth Evans

Copyright 1993 by Twayne Publishers

All rights reserved. No part of this book may be reproduced or transmitted in any form or by any means, electronic or mechanical, including photocopying, recording, or by any information storage and retrieval system, without permission in writing from the Publisher.

Twayne Publishers
Macmillan Publishing Company
866 Third Avenue
New York, New York 10022

Maxwell Macmillan Canada, Inc.
1200 Eglinton Avenue East
Suite 200
Don Mills, Ontario M3C 3N1

Library of Congress Cataloging-in-Publication Data

Evans, Elizabeth, 1935-
  Anne Tyler / Elizabeth Evans.
    p.   cm. – (Twayne's United States authors series; TUSAS 620)
  Includes bibliographical references and index.
  ISBN 0-8057-3985-8 (alk. paper)
  1. Tyler, Anne – Criticism and interpretation. 2. Women and literature – United States – History – 20th century. 3. Baltimore (Md.) in literature. I. Title. II. Series.
PS3570.Y45Z64   1993
813'.54 – dc20   92-44339
                                                                      CIP

The paper used in this publication meets the minimum requirements of American National Standard for Information Sciences – Permanence of Paper for Printed Library Materials, ANSI Z39.48-1984.

10 9 8 7 6 5 4 3 2 1

Printed in the United States of America.

In memory of

James Penny Smith

and

James Dean Young

Deux qui ont bien vécu

Contents

Preface

A steady and prolific writer since the 1960s, Anne Tyler has published 12 novels, some 50 short stories, and an impressive number of book reviews and occasional pieces, all of which have gained popular and critical renown. Tyler had steadfastly resisted both the media blitz most popular writers covet and the college lecture circuit, choosing instead a quiet and private life as a writer.

A northerner by birth, Tyler spent most of her early years in the South and finds the southern atmosphere hospitable to her writing life. She has frequently said that Eudora Welty's stories showed her that ordinary events and people were, after all, subjects for fiction. So important an influence was Welty in fact that Tyler once considered sending her elder colleague a thank-you note, although, she says, "I imagine she would find it a little strange." Welty has expressed her admiration for Tyler, and these two writers from the South share a gift for creating humor, dialogue, concrete detail, and, most of all, a sure sense for their characters.

Tyler's particular territory is Baltimore, where she has lived since 1967 and where she places her characters, almost all of whom find their primary identity as members of a family. Tyler emphasizes the family situation throughout her work, exploring the quirks and foibles of characters who long for happiness that often remains elusive. Family members suffer disappointments, misunderstandings, and tragedies, yet these families endure. Humor pervades Tyler's fiction as a natural device to help balance life's disappointments. Family members face broken marriages, unhappy children, lost dreams, illness, and loneliness. Through it all these families survive. Tyler is primarily interested in day-to-day endurance; her characters generally succeed through effort.

Tyler's novels are popular and readable, not the characteristics critics generally praise. Some critics chide Tyler for avoiding sexual, political, and social issues in her work and for taking few technical risks; Tyler's novels and stories, however, deal with the problems most people must face every day. Although Tyler cannot be labeled an outspoken feminist, her novels present strong women characters. If these women fail to live independently, they at least attempt to gain a better sense of their lives.

Tyler has established a network of appealing characters who reside in Baltimore, and when a minor character has a cameo appearance in a later novel, we begin to wonder if all these fictional people might really know one another. Tyler looks on her characters as if they were next-door neighbors she cherished. However bizarre or eccentric readers sometimes find her characters, Tyler knows that ordinary people often have within them unique characteristics that set them apart from other "ordinary" people.

Most of all, Tyler *likes* her characters. "I like to think," she has written, "that I might meet up with one of my past characters at the very next street corner. The odd thing is, sometimes I have. And if I were remotely religious, I'd believe that a little gathering of my characters would be waiting for me in heaven when I died. '*Then* what happened?' I'd ask them. '*How* have things worked out, since the last time I saw you?'"

Acknowledgments

I am grateful to Alfred A. Knopf, Inc., for permission to quote from the novels of Anne Tyler. From *If Morning Ever Comes, The Tin Can Tree, A Slipping-Down Life, The Clock Winder, Celestial Navigation, Searching for Caleb, Earthly Possessions, Morgan's Passing, Dinner at the Homesick Restaurant, The Accidental Tourist, Breathing Lessons,* and *Saint Maybe,* by Anne Tyler. Copyright 1964, 1965, 1969, 1970, 1972, 1974, 1975, 1977, 1980, 1982, 1985 by Anne Tyler Modarressi; copyright 1988, 1991 by ATM, Inc. Copyright renewed 1991 by Anne Tyler Modarressi. Reprinted by permission of Alfred A. Knopf, Inc.

The Special Collections Department of the Duke University Library has kindly granted permission to quote from the Anne Tyler Papers.

Judith B. Jones has kindly granted me permission to quote from her letters to Anne Tyler held in the Anne Tyler Papers.

I am grateful to Ernest Morgan for permission to quote from the unpublished "Notes from Memory by Arthur E. Morgan and Grisom Morgan on the Beginnings of Celo Community in North Carolina," 7 October 1957.

I am grateful to Barbara Sutton (yet again) and to Professor Frank Day for diverse and excellent editorial advice.

I owe special thanks to Phyllis Mahon Tyler for permission to quote from her letter (November 1991) to me and for her encouragement of this book.

For permission to quote from materials in the Anne Tyler Papers, Special Collections Department, Duke University Library, and for the work she has given us to read and enjoy, I thank Anne Tyler.

Chronology

1941	Anne Tyler born 25 October in Minneapolis, Minnesota, to Lloyd Parry and Phyllis Mahon Tyler.
1942	Family moves to Coldbrook Farm, Phoenixville, Pennsylvania in June.
1944-1948	Family moves to a Chicago suburb, then back to Duluth, then returns to a different Chicago suburb.
1948	Family moves to the Celo Community near Burnsville, North Carolina, the oldest land trust community in America.
1952	Family moves to Raleigh, North Carolina.
1958	Tyler graduates (at 16) from Broughton High School in Raleigh. Enters Duke University as an Angier B. Duke Scholar.
1959	Publishes "The Lights on the River" and "Laura" in Duke's literary magazine, *Archive*.
1961	Graduates from Duke (in three years) Phi Beta Kappa with a major in Russian (has twice won the Anne Flexner Award for creative writing).
1961	Begins graduate work in Russian at Columbia University; completes course work but not thesis.
1962	Spends summer in Camden, Maine, swabbing deck of schooner and proofreading for a local newspaper.
1962-1963	Works as Russian bibliographer at Duke University library.
1963	Marries Taghi Mohammed Modarressi, an Iranian-born child psychiatrist. First story in national publication, "The Baltimore Birth Certificate," is published in *The*

Critic: A Catholic Review of Books and the Arts. Moves to Montreal, where her husband continues his residency.

1964   First novel, *If Morning Ever Comes*, is published. Works as an assistant librarian at McGill University law library. Visits Iran for three weeks.

1965   *The Tin Can Tree*; daughter Tezh born.

1966   Wins *Mademoiselle* award as one of the country's most promising young career women.

1967   Daughter Mitra born; family moves to Baltimore in June.

1970   *A Slipping-Down Life*.

1972   *The Clock Winder*.

1974   *Celestial Navigation*.

1975   Begins reviews for the *National Observer* and continues to submit until that newspaper ceases publication in 1977.

1976   *Searching for Caleb*.

1977   Receives citation for "literary excellence and promise of important work to come" from the American Academy and Institute of Arts and Letters, which awards her $3,000. Condensed version of *Earthly Possessions* appears in *Redbook*; the novel is published by Knopf in May. Tyler becomes regular reviewer for the *New York Times*, the *Washington Post*, and the *New Republic*.

1980   *Morgan's Passing* is published, nominated for an American Book Award. Tyler receives Janet Heidinger Kafka Prize for fiction by an American woman.

1982   *Dinner at the Homesick Restaurant* is published, nominated for Pulitzer Prize. Tyler wins a PEN/Faulkner Award for Fiction.

1985   *The Accidental Tourist* is published, wins National
             Book Critics Circle Award as the year's most distin-
             guished work of American fiction.

1988   *Breathing Lessons* is published, wins Pulitzer Prize.

1991   *Saint Maybe.*

Chapter One

"Little Threads of Connection between People"

Early Years

Anne Tyler was born on 25 October 1941 in Minneapolis, the daughter of Lloyd Parry Tyler, a chemist for the state of Minnesota, and Phyllis Mahon Tyler, a social worker for the Family Welfare Association of Minneapolis. Three younger children, all boys, completed the family, which in many ways departed from the middle-class model of American life after World War II. Instead of pursuing the American dream of economic and social success, the Tylers led lives far more centered on ethical and moral issues and problems.

Perhaps a fraction of every generation of American youth searches for a life-style that centers on the ethical and the moral in an attempt to counter the prevailing commercial and financial aspirations. Surely the most famous of all experimental undertakings to provide the environment of a "blessed community" was that 200-acre tract of land near West Roxbury, Massachusetts, where on 1 April 1841 Brook Farm Institute of Agriculture and Education was established. Many familiar New England names were drawn to the idealism of Brook Farm: George Ripley, William Henry Channing, Theodore Parker, Margaret Fuller, Charles A. Dana, and, of course, Nathaniel Hawthorne, who would incorporate many of his experiences and memories of Brook Farm into the pages of *The Blithedale Romance* (1852). But this New England experiment was short-lived, collapsing in 1846 and perhaps justifying Ralph Waldo Emerson's calling it the "Age of Reason in a patty-pan." Other experimental communities emerged in the nineteenth century, some founded by Quakers and people in Shaker communities. In their turn and generation and as traditional Quakers, Anne Tyler's parents sought a community where daily living would emphasize the basic values they

1

honored. After several moves in Minnesota and Illinois, the Tylers, in a last attempt to find a "blessed community," moved to Celo in Yancey County, North Carolina, a particularly beautiful valley at the foot of Mount Mitchell. This move came in 1948, and Anne Tyler was not yet seven years old.

Celo Community was founded in 1937 by Arthur E. Morgan, an engineer and educator who was at the time chairman of the Tennessee Valley Authority. According to Morgan, the depression that ended the extraprosperous 1920s brought "some young people, who had felt somewhat like social outcasts in the immediately preceding years, . . . to extricate themselves from the intricate economic relationships in which the current economy was involved."[1] A primary object of this community was to provide families with an environment where "personal integrity, considerateness, and simplicity of taste would be natural" (Morgan, n.p.). Various sites in the mountain areas of Tennessee, Kentucky, South Carolina, North Carolina, and Virginia were considered before the founders settled on a tract of 1,200 acres about 50 miles northeast of Asheville. A clear mountain stream (the South Estatoe River) ran partly alongside the tract and partly through it; surrounding the property were the highest mountains in eastern America. Although the land was not totally ready for agricultural enterprises (a vital part of the livelihood for the community), Arthur Morgan remembers his initial impression was favorable: "I noted when we were looking over the land that dahlias grew and bloomed there of a size and luxuriance I had never seen before, and that a boxwood nursery seemed to have a perfect environment. Blueberries also seemed to be very much at home" (Morgan, n.p.).

Still in operation, the Celo Community, Inc., is the oldest land trust community in America, and, according to Morgan, one of the most successful. The 1,200 acres are owned by the community, and the 30 family units who can reside there purchase "holdings"; during their residence they must use dwellings and land solely for the realistic needs of their families. The community early honored wilderness preservation and has continued to sponsor projects that enhance the quality of life both for its own residents and for people of the surrounding area.

The Tylers lived in one of the original houses built from timber cut on Celo property, and when they began their life at Celo in 1948 there was only one telephone in the community; messages were taken and delivered for modest fees. Home gardens were most important, and a resident still living at Celo remembers that Lloyd Tyler always had an exceptionally fine garden. Anne Tyler's mother, Phyllis Mahon Tyler, recalls those years as extremely busy but pleasurable. On summer nights the family often slept under the stars and frequently gathered at night to read aloud. Because the Tylers' son Seth was allergic to cow's milk, the Tylers kept goats and got their breeding stock from Mrs. Carl Sandburg. Some Celo residents, including Tyler's father, supplemented their incomes with such home enterprises as the machine-knitting of fine socks,[2] a home industry Tyler uses in her 1974 novel, *Celestial Navigation* (Mary Tell installs a sock-knitting machine in her room as one of her many money-making efforts).

In a 1980 interview with the Durham *Morning Herald*, Tyler said her writing career began at the age of three when she began to amuse herself after being sent to bed early: "I pulled my knees up under the blanket and pretended I was a doctor and patients were coming to me with broken legs and arms and they had to tell me how they'd gotten them. . . . And in the day time I drew people on my blackboard and imagined what their lives were like and what unified them. It was a matter . . . of beginning to wonder what it would be like to be other people."[3] Children of the community could attend a two-room log school located at the edge of the property and ironically called Harvard. The Tyler children were educated at home, however, through Baltimore's Calvert Home School Program, which allowed children to proceed with lessons at their own speed. They learned basic arithmetic by working in the community's co-op store. This early training was clearly superior, since all of the Tyler children excelled in public school after the family left Celo in 1952 to make their home in Raleigh. All three of Anne Tyler's brothers earned Ph.D.s (Ty went on to earn an M.D. after his Ph.D. in physics).

In "Still Just Writing" Tyler recalls the differences in the city and the city-school environment from life at Celo. At 11 she emerged from Celo, where she had never used a telephone and could strike a match on the sole of her bare foot. She found the children in the new school as peculiar looking as they perhaps found her.[4] In another autobiographical piece she recalls that life in this community brought her into contact with very few children. As she had done at age three, she whiled away much time by making up stories: "I'd pretend to be various other people – a woman named Delores with eighteen children, I remember, and a girl going west in a covered wagon – and I think of writing as a continuation of that story-telling."[5] Thus far in her fiction Tyler has not resurrected Delores and the 18 offspring or the girl headed west, but the early inclination to be a teller of stories proved auspicious.

Celo provided Tyler with unusual experiences whose influence can certainly be detected in her fiction. The goat-raising period in the lives of Justine and Duncan Peck of *Searching for Caleb* (1976) reflect Celo activities, and the short story "Outside" (1971) portrays a young man who lives in a Celo-like community; as the title suggests he longs to know what the world *outside* is like and ventures into New England for a summer job as a tutor. Perhaps, too, the kind and gentle men in Tyler's fiction – Ben Joe Hawkes, Jeremy Pauling, Ezra Tull, Macon Leary, and Ian Bedloe – share in a minor way the intent of Celo, "a favorable setting for an interesting human adventure lasting through generations, which . . . [is] not a retreat from life, but an adventure in living" (Morgan, n.p.).

Tyler was 16 when she graduated from Broughton High School in Raleigh; the year was 1958, and that fall she would enter Duke University as an Angier B. Duke Scholar. The 1950s – especially in the South – had not yet acknowledged that the women's movement was soon to be a reality, and Tyler recounts in "Still Just Writing" that "it was more important for boys to get a good education than for girls." So rather than going to Swarthmore as she had wanted, Tyler went to Duke with her scholarship. That step, Tyler says, "was the first and last time that my being female was ever a serious issue. I still don't think it was just, but I can't say it ruined my life. After all, Duke had Reynolds Price, who turned out to be the only person I ever knew who could actually teach writing" ("Writing," 13). If Duke had Reynolds Price, Broughton High School had Phyllis Peacock, who early on discerned talent in Anne Tyler – a response, Tyler has said, that "made a huge difference" (Hodges, D3). Years earlier Mrs. Peacock saw the talent in her student Reynolds Price, who praises her in his autobiographical book *Clear Pictures: First Loves, First Guides* (1989) as "the only teacher I've known who simply refused to let a sheep wander."[6]

At Duke Tyler majored in Russian; helped edit the *Archive*, a literary magazine; acted in several productions of the Wesley Players;

twice won the Anne Flexner Award for creative writing; and graduated, in three years, Phi Beta Kappa, twenty-sixth in a class of 271. From Duke Tyler went to Columbia University to pursue an M.A. in Russian; she completed all requirements except the thesis, delayed perhaps by the days in the summer of 1962 when she swabbed the deck of a schooner and proofread for the local paper in Camden, Maine.

Tyler's marriage in 1963 to Taghi Mohammed Modarressi took her out of the South to Montreal, where her husband completed two additional years of residency in psychiatry at McGill University and where Tyler worked in the law library at McGill. A 1965 newspaper article reported that Tyler and her husband planned to move to Modarressi's native Iran, where he would take charge of a psychiatric clinic and its training program. At the time Tyler commented, "It seems so silly to live in Iran and write about a place you came from [the South] 40 years ago, . . . and yet I can't picture writing about a Persian market place."[7] The move did not come until 1967, and then it was, as all Anne Tyler readers know, not to Iran at all but to Baltimore. Here with her husband and two daughters (Tezh born in 1965 and Mitra born in 1967) Tyler has remained and has produced a remarkable number of novels.

From the outset of her career, Tyler says, she has not felt drawn in the least to writer communities, although she admits that the freedom a place like Yaddo affords a writer is tempting – tempting, that is, until the Yaddo residents would gather in the evening to "talk about what they had done that day, which would be writing."[8] When Tyler's husband, also a novelist, talks about how his book is proceeding, Tyler gets uneasy: "It makes me very nervous. I'm afraid that it's going to evaporate; he might just fritter it away" (Lamb, 63). She enjoys, as she says, a measure of luxury as a writer because as the wife of a working husband she can refuse to do an article if the topic does not suit her, can refuse to change a short story if the editorial suggestions seem unwarranted, and can decline to hurry along a book to meet a seasonal market or some other promotion a publisher proposes. On the other hand, as a mother she was the primary caretaker as her children were growing up. Her husband's luxury lies partly in the fact that nobody expected him to drop his professional obligations to care for a sick child. The only person, Tyler says, who enjoys no luxury as a writer is the woman writer who is the sole support of her children. The echo here to the experience of Tillie Olsen (and others, of course) reverberates. And yet even the woman writer like Tyler who has the luxury of a successful working husband still must endure the slings and arrows of people who have little notion of the writing process. In her contribution to Janet Sternburg's *The Writer on Her Work* (1980), Tyler relates this encounter: she was standing "in the schoolyard waiting for a child when another mother came up to me. 'Have you found work yet?' she asked. 'Or are you still just writing?'" ("Writing," 11).

The critical praise that greeted her first novel, *If Morning Ever Comes* (1964), signaled a remarkable talent; yet from the time she began to publish fiction Tyler has shunned the hype and chaos of public appearances, publicity campaigns, and the college lecture circuit, preferring instead to reserve her time and energy for work and family. Anything beyond writing books and raising children, she has said, "just fritters me away," and she describes herself as consciously "narrow. I like routine and rituals and I hate leaving home; I have a sense of digging my heels in" ("Writing," 15). But like so many of the women characters in her novels, there is an inner urge to travel, and Tyler admits the paradox of preferring to *stay* at home and at the same time having a small bag packed and ready to go.

People, of course, often harbor opposing impulses; conflicting opinion and inevitable change simply mark the human condtion. In a short essay for *Vogue* in 1965, Tyler writes from the vantage point of a 23-year-old but does so with the wisdom that marks her mature years. The essay begins with an embarrassing childhood situation: when Tyler was six, her family had a Model A Ford with a radiator that leaked and required frequent stops for water supplies from mountain streams or dripping rocks. This watering stop scene provided roadside comedy for passersby who, Tyler recalls, "always laughed." Even worse than the inefficient radiator was the car's noise, which was "something like a lawn mower, and on bad days the sound of pistol shots came from the rear tires."[9] The laughing cars that sped past emitted a magical swishing sound, and it was that sound from a satisfactory car that Tyler coveted. But when the Model A was gone and another more modern family car had taken its place, Tyler found that the swishing cars could be perceived only when she herself was *outside*, not when she was inside. Tyler ends the piece with a lyric glimpse into maturity and a backward glance at youth, capturing that moment of change when youth transforms experience into understanding. The entire paragraph bears quoting:

> If I ever get truly old, old the way those women on the buses are, so that I am finally certain of things and can sit back, I expect that I will think of being young as a perfect, separate island in time. I will forget what I'm thinking now: that youth is no distinct time at all. I'll look at it, maybe, the way I look at that Model A – picturing my parents, young and dressed up, sitting erect on the seats in front, and my brothers pressing their noses to the cloudy back windows. I'll forget all about the lawn-mower noise and the pistol shots from the tires. (206)

Kinship with the South

Tyler's *Vogue* essay links the life and experience of childhood to the world both of one's parents and of one's own adulthood. Tyler's parents are not southerners by birth, and her own earliest years were not lived in the South. In a 1972 piece for the *National Observer* Clifford Ridley presented Tyler's view of herself as an outsider, as one who was not southern by birth and habit. Tyler told Ridley that she wrote *If Morning Ever Comes* "in a way out of curiosity, out of wondering how it would feel to be part of a huge Southern family. . . . I always felt isolated from the South; I always envied everybody. I used to work at tying tobacco and listen to all the farm wives strung out along a long table, talking all day long; they fascinated me."[10] This sense of isolation, of not quite belonging in and to the South, qualifies Jorie Lueloff's 1965 impression that Tyler "considers herself a Southerner through and through" (Lueloff).

In *One Writer's Beginnings* (1984) Eudora Welty recounts that her mother was not taken with the "talk" of her women friends in Jackson, and after listening "against her will" to such a friend for a long telephone conversation Mrs. Welty responded to her daughter's question, "What did she say?," with "She wasn't *saying* a thing in this world. . . . She was just ready to talk, that's all."[11] But to the writer Eudora Welty this "talk" was the stuff of stories and novels to come. Welty remembers when she shared the back seat of the car on occasion with her mother and a friend out for a ride. As the husbands maneuvered the car along and the women settled back,

Eudora Welty would say as they started off, "Now *talk*" (Welty, 11-12). Anne Tyler's affinity for Eudora Welty is deep and gracefully acknowledged in her review of Welty's *Collected Stories* (1980): "For me as a girl – a Northerner growing up in the South, longingly gazing over the fence at the rich, tangled lives of the Southern neighbors – Eudora Welty was a window upon the world. If I wondered what went on in the country churches and 'Colored Only' cafés, her writing showed me, as clearly as if I'd been invited inside."[12]

In a 1990 review essay for the *Georgia Review*, Fred Chappell raised once again the question, "What does it mean to be a Southern writer?" and quickly rejoined, "It means that interviewers ask you that question more times than you would have thought possible."[13] Chappell goes on to examine in particular what it means to be a southern *poet*, noting that interviewers rarely if ever pose that question, although it used to have a "roundabout, imprecise, but fairly satisfying answer" (Chappell, 698). Chappell suggests that "a Southern poet was someone who ransacked his experience, or searched in familiar history, for stories or specific images that implied a world of significance he could count on his readers – his Southern readers, especially – to share. . . . But that cozy camaraderie has begun to drift from the fireside" (Chappell, 698). There may never have been quite such a cozy camaraderie among southern fiction writers, although perhaps an earlier generation shared distinctive traits that Julius Rowan Raper describes as damaged self-esteem, elevated posture, and dark rage.[14]

"Place," Eudora Welty declares in her familiar and famous essay, "is one of the lesser angels that watch over the racing hand of fiction."[15] With the homogenization of the South in the form of shopping malls, generic radio/television announcers, and the six-lane streets of Atlanta, Charlotte, and Winston-Salem that are overtaking the family farm and the small town, any sense of place – on whose stability, Raper argues, character has depended – "is inevitably doomed by the speed with which modern environments are changed" (Raper, 10). Some declare there is no entity that can safely be recognized and identified as "Southern Literature" because much of the South now looks and sounds like the rest of the country. Still, according to Donald R. Noble, "for every sign of homogenization there is equal evidence that Southern life retains traditions and values, attitudes and accents that will be a very long time in the erasing. For the foreseeable future there is a South, therefore a Southern literature."[16]

Since 1967 Anne Tyler has lived in Baltimore, Maryland, and while generally speaking Maryland may be a Southern state, it is certainly a different environment from Jackson, Mississippi, or Milledgeville, Georgia, or Chapel Hill, North Carolina. (Some 10 years after her move Tyler reflected on this *place*, calling Baltimore "wonderful territory for a writer – so many different things to poke around in. And whatever it is that remains undeniably Southern in me has made it easy for me to switch to Baltimore.")[17] The question of Tyler's relation to the South certainly was a matter of enough interest to the young author that she discussed it with Jorie Lueloff in 1965. While one expects Tyler's views to have modified in the nearly 30 years since the Lueloff interview, it is still useful to review her vision of herself in relation to the South at the beginning of her career and to see how that early view compares with her more recent statements about southern writing and writers.

Tyler told Lueloff that the protagonist of *If Morning Ever Comes*, Ben Joe Hawkes, displays a typical southern fault in his inability to accept the fact that time is changing. Ben Joe, along with his family of womenfolk, continues "to live on the surface as a family – the way it's supposed to be" (22). Tyler declared that "I love the South. . . . I could sit all day and listen to the people talking. It would be hard to listen to a conversation in Raleigh for instance, and write it without putting in color. And they tell stories constantly!" (23). In the North and in northern fiction, Tyler did not find that the conversation had much color – it lacked the quality of southern conversation that Tyler described as "pure metaphor and the lower you get in the class structure, the more it's true" (23). In addition, Tyler found northern writers and readers less tolerant of the family member with quirks and tics, and she remained protective of the "dwarves, hunchbacks, [and] petrified men" who roam the pages of southern writers (23). Most significant in this early assessment was Tyler's defense of the gentle or tactful character, a type that has continued to be a hallmark in her fiction and a type that, in 1965, she identified as primarily southern: "It's the gentle or tactful people . . . who have been ignored by the Northern novelists. There aren't enough quiet, gentle, basically good people in a novel. Usually whole holocausts happen. But this delicate thing where you just walk a tightrope between peo-

ple – that doesn't happen very often in a Northern novel. Most
Southern novelists have concentrated on *these little threads of connection between people*" (Lueloff, 23; my italics).

The phrase "these little threads of connection between people"
so well suggests the intangible quality in fiction that creates the link
between Snowdie MacLain and her irascible husband, King, or
between quite different Welty characters like Laurel McKelva Hand
and the dead of her immediate family, or between Flannery
O'Connor's grandfather and grandson in "The Artificial Nigger," or
the tenuous links between O'Connor's mothers and sons in "The
Enduring Chill" and "Everything That Rises Must Converge." And
certainly in Tyler's fiction the threads between Elizabeth Abbott and
Mrs. Emerson, between Justine Peck and her grandfather Daniel,
between Ezra Tull and his entire family, and between Ian Bedloe and
the children in his life create the dynamics of character but also the
quality of character that defines how one lives and how one does
indeed connect with the people that are near.

More than "Just Writing"

By the mid-1970s Anne Tyler had emerged as a prominent book
reviewer, and her comments on various books by southern authors
indicate that she remains alert to what is *southern*. Of Peter Taylor's
short stories collected in *In the Miro District* (1977) Tyler wrote, "I
suppose this writing is what some people like to call 'Southern':
there's a strong sense of place and of history; the manners are grace-
ful, the confrontations oblique."[18] Reviewing Nancy Lemann's *Lives
of the Saints* (1985) for the *New Republic*, Tyler pointed out definite
southern characteristics: Lemann was particularly mindful of locale;
her characters were clearly southern in being gentle, courtly, funny,
charmingly hopeless, and just the type that "are always falling
apart."[19] Lemann's book succeeds, Tyler wrote, "perhaps because of
its sheer exuberance, its enthusiasm for its characters, its peculiarly
Southern habit of telling us not so much *what* happened as to
whom" (37). Tyler's review of Caroline Gordon's *Collected Stories*
(1981) calls attention to some failures. In particular she noted
"pieces dealing with blacks, where an 'I'se gwine' tone prevails, and
hangings, hauntings, and crimes of passion tend to define the char-

acters."[20] But Tyler also saw in Gordon's stories a precise rendering of locale because her "territory is the South – specifically Kentucky, in that time not so long ago when families still kept track of first cousins twice removed, and when the men spent their days hunting while the women, left behind, sat languorously on the gallery" (16).

It seems an altogether fitting circle of events that Anne Tyler should review Eudora Welty's *Collected Stories*. Welty, Tyler wrote in the *Washington Star,* "is one of our purest, finest, gentlest voices, and this collection is something to be treasured" ("Fine, Full World," D7). Having won the 1991 National Book Foundation award for distinguished contribution to American letters and almost every other award America bestows on its best writers, Welty stands as the most honored of living southern writers. Yet in her review of the *Collected Stories* Tyler suggests that some reader is bound to ask if Welty *is* in fact a southern writer. If such a writer exists, Tyler argues, Welty qualifies by accident of birth, by the speech rhythms she creates for her characters, and by her habit of storytelling that is far less concerned with *what* happens than "with *whom* it happens to and where" (D7; my italics).

The issue of the southern writer and of southern literature continues to ignite sprightly debate here and there, but far more important is the quality of literature that allows it to endure. As distinctive as the southern accent and gesture are in the fiction of Welty and O'Connor, of far greater importance is these writers' ability – and indeed Tyler's ability – to produce fiction that takes into account what Tyler calls "the wealth of enigmas surrounding every human being."[21] After all, "interlocking lives, plots that travel out into space on daring tangents" *are* the stuff of fiction, as they are indeed the stuff of life – southern and otherwise (36).

In her 1976 review of George Plimpton's *Writers at Work: The Paris Review Interviews* Anne Tyler wryly observed that Plimpton's 16 subjects wanted to meet the interviewer's expectations of wise answers about their writing process. She concluded, however, that "their answers often amount to a figurative shrug of the shoulders and 'I don't know; it just happens.'"[22] From the pages of Plimpton's collection Tyler concluded that these sixteen writers view themselves and their work candidly and tell us that a writer "is someone who works hard, treasures his privacy, and often acts a little befuddled from living in too many worlds" (19). Certainly the first two characteristics define Tyler, but although she certainly lives in several fictional worlds, she in no way appears befuddled. Although Tyler has recently said that she intends to stop reviewing books, since the 1970s she has reviewed quite a large number. In her judgments and remarks about the books of others she conveys much about her own sense of style, her notion of successful and of failed fiction, her idea of what a *good* piece of fiction ought to be.

Reading, Tyler says in reviewing Cynthia Ozick's *The Messiah of Stockholm* (1987), fulfills the expectation of an intellectual exercise or of a visceral experience. Tyler votes "for visceral experience myself" and finds that aspect an essential one whether the writing is southern or Third World. Tyler found much of Ozick's writing style laborious and cited a host of infelicities: great clots of turgid phrases that poured out, long sentences that knotted themselves and then devoured their tails; prose that at spots was opaque and drew undue attention to itself; adjective strings that went on for too long; physical descriptions that seemed oddly nonphysical and anatomical descriptions that seemed to be "coined by bemused visitors from outer space."[23] The plethora of stylistic flaws reminded Tyler of the hip advice from a 1960s bumper sticker "ESCHEW OBFUSCATION." While the flaws seem glaring in this book, Tyler argues that a visceral experience occurs nevertheless – Ozick's plot is provocative, and the author, Tyler says, is "intelligent, skilled, and consummately serious" (41).

Tyler faults authors when their prose is long-winded for no reason, when unbroken dialogue goes on in half-page chunks, when the plot takes its center in too much cleverness or is downright obscure. Tyler makes one of her strongest complaints about D. M. Thomas's 1983 novel *Ararat*, whose plot she thinks is not an honest one. "If," Tyler says, "a contract exists between writer and reader that the writer will do his best to draw the reader in and the reader will do his best to follow, D. M. Thomas reneged on his part of the deal."[24]

The skill with which novelists tell their stories interests Tyler, and the traits she most admires are generally those that enhance the pages of her fiction. Tyler looks for and frequently praises a sharp eye for precise detail, as in, for instance, Maxine Hong Kingston's *Tripmaster Monkey: His Fake Book* (1989). Tyler found Kingston's book exhausting to read at times but that carefully chosen the details entered the text precisely when they should. Those passages "remind us how infinitely entertaining everyday life can be when it's observed with a fresh eye."[25] It is such precise details in Janine Boissard's *A Matter of Feeling* (1980), Tyler says, that lets potentially sentimental scenes be "rescued by their particularity, their respectful attention to detail."[26] On the other hand, Tyler's review of Philip O'Connor's *Stealing Home* (1979) pointed out "a scarcity of those gritty details that make people physically visible to us, that separate them from the generalities of 'Pubescent Son,' 'Seductive Divorcée,' 'Suburban Housewife in Mid-Life Crisis.' "[27] This flaw comes because O'Connor generally tells the reader *what* happened rather than emphasizing *who* it happened to. That trait of southern fiction to emphasize the *who* rather than the *what* goes deep.

In fiction, Tyler admires language that is pure and plain and especially direct; she produces such language, heightened at times with a power that enriches a scene with layers of meaning. The final sentence in *Dinner at the Homesick Restaurant* (1982) is a case in point. Cody, the eldest of the three Tull children, has marched through his adult life angry about many things: his childhood, his mother's failures and weaknesses, his sense of unfounded jealousy against his gentle brother Ezra, and especially the loss caused by his absent father. The reunion of the deserted children, now middle-aged adults, with their elderly father comes at the family dinner after they have buried Pearl Tull. Now perhaps a dinner *will* be completed, and Tyler gives the final paragraph to Cody, letting him remember childhood in images of light and at last letting him put to rest the accident long ago when the arrow from the children's archery set had struck his mother's breast. Anger and resentment subside, replaced by images of acceptance. The last sentence reads, "And high above, he seemed to recall, there had been a little brown airplane, almost motionless, droning through the sunshine like a bumblebee."[28] That last sentence, Eudora Welty has said, is a tour de force: "If I had written that sentence, I'd be happy all my life!"[29]

Tyler finds the short story diminished from its former self – "slim and stripped, positively anorexic" – except for the stories of a few writers who still use the genre with extraordinary skill – writers like Peter Taylor, William Trevor, and Alice Munro. A short story, Tyler says, ought to resemble "a child's wooden puzzle" where the end of the story falls into place as precisely and as inevitably as the final wooden piece of a puzzle clicks against the other pieces as it drops to complete the picture that had all along been planned.[30] A good short story exceeds its accepted limitations of length and time span and, Tyler suggests in a splendid image, takes these necessary restrictions and uses them to "dazzle us – like one of those Japanese seashells that, when dropped in a bowl of water, open and branch out and flower, and may even belatedly unfold new flowers so that you feel compelled to keep coming back and giving them another look."[31]

Two important short-story collections were published almost simultaneously – Eudora Welty's in 1980, Elizabeth Bowen's in 1981 – and Anne Tyler reviewed both volumes, finding in each writer distinctive traits and differences. Welty's stories, Tyler suggests, say to the reader, "Step in," and, Tyler continues, you find yourself let into the life and adventures of a traveling salesman named R. J. Bowman, or staring at the mystery of things from a tree with Loch Morrison, or seeing the world from an off-center angle in next-to-the-smallest P.O. in the state of Mississippi with Sister. Bowen's stories, on the other hand, say to the reader, "Stay where you are. Allow me to demonstrate this spinster on holiday, or this woman obsessed by a ghost."[32] Tyler finds that Bowen's approach does not always produce a successful story, and some in the collection she considers "extended epigrams," as if Bowen were "merely exercising her considerable wit and skill, without having much to say" (37). Perhaps no volume of collected stories should be read straight through; certainly Tyler found that reading Bowen's volume in that manner was exhausting. Better instead to treat the volume as "a bedside book – one to be enjoyed frame by frame, then set aside for another evening" (37-38). This method, Tyler suggests, allows the reader time to admire and to reflect so that the power of Bowen's stories comes through, for Bowen's stories do "show the awesome capabilities of the English language, and the surprise and mystery of the human soul" (38).

Among contemporary writers, Tyler thinks that no one surpasses Peter Taylor in producing the short story that is tightly structured, absolutely controlled, filled "with a pure and clear tone."[33] Tyler has high praise, too, for Margaret Atwood, who in *Dancing Girls* (1982) wrote in a style "as precise as cut glass," producing stories, Tyler says, where "entire plots appear to balance upon a choice phrase, and clearly she writes with an ear cocked for the way her words will sound when read back."[34]

If the short-story form is now, as Tyler's image has it, more anorexic than robust, the form still is supple and capable of dazzling results. Bowen's *Collected Stories*, for example, strike Tyler as a positive parade of "exquisitely detailed paintings reflecting, with uncanny vividness, the eras she lived through, from the early part of this century through the 1920s and 1930s, World War II, and the post war years" ("Art of Distance," 36). If paintings on museum walls provide pleasure but also require distance between the work and the viewer, so Bowen's stories "give a sense of an invisible, impenetrable surface between observer and observed" (37). This inevitable distance is not a failing in Bowen's work, however, but "merely reminds us how inadequate is the term 'short story,' covering as it does such a range of approaches" (37). Many things count in a short story – character, tension, precise detail, pure tone, the ear for perfectly reproducing speech – but what matters most, Tyler says, "is that the story enlarge our view of human beings."[35] As a college student, Tyler read the short stories of Hortense Calisher and years later found when she came to read Calisher again that her early enthusiasm was confirmed and sustained because Calisher's stories achieve what the good short story must: each story in Calisher's *Collected Stories* (1977) "manages to alter, in some indefinable way, our perception of the world around us."[36]

Although Tyler has discussed the short-story form in her reviews, her fiction concentrates on the novel, and to date she has published 12. When Tyler's editor at Knopf, Judith B. Jones, sent Tyler the galley proofs for *Earthly Possessions* in 1976, she said, "Don't you find yourself impressed by that growing list on the Also By . . . page?"[37] If Tyler was not impressed then by her list of titles, she and her readers certainly are now. Tyler showed early on that her novels would focus on the intricate relations within family life, a subject at the center of human concerns and one that has no limit to its implications. In several interviews Tyler has described something of her own working habits, and even a glance at her manuscripts in the Perkins Library at Duke University shows that she does indeed write (often prints) in longhand (often on unruled paper), and that she makes meticulous outlines for her novels.[38] In planning *Celestial Navigation*, for instance, Tyler sketched the interior of the Pauling boardinghouse,

identifying the occupant of each bedroom. Her sketch of the front of
the house shows a narrow, three-story dwelling with the definite hint
of companion dwellings on either side – the familiar sight of a Baltimore rowhouse. A worksheet for *Dinner at the Homesick Restaurant* (in the Tyler Papers at Duke University) includes a menu listed
and blocked off, one that Ezra himself might find pleasing even if
family members did bolt before the final course of the meal could be
served:

> Menu:
> A. Curried *eggplant* soup
> B. Minted Leg of Lamb
>   Mushroom Kasha
>   Tossed Salad
>   Wine
> C. Chocolate Mousse
>   Dessert wine
> D. Coffee

For that final (and we hope completed) dinner Tyler draws up work-
sheets for the table seating, a list of 14, eight of whom are children.
All the adult names appear, as do the children's, followed by their
ages and an indication of whose children they are – Cody's or
Jenny's or Joe's or Jenny *and* Joe's. These manuscript details give the
researcher a glimpse of the writer at work – perhaps, as Tyler says of
the subjects in Plimpton's collection, with the writing just happen-
ing, although the meticulous preliminary pages suggest that the process is by no means *that* simple.

Reviewing Judith Rossner's *Looking for Mr. Goodbar* (1975)
Tyler discussed the risk authors take when they allow the trendy
world of advertising and television to invade the novel unduly and
half-seriously wondered "if novelists might be better off living in
whitewashed cubicles. Oh, the cubicles should be comfortable, all
right, and attractively furnished. But windowless. Also soundproof.
And there should be no access to newspapers, radio, or, especially
television."[39] Such isolation, Tyler admits, does have its drawbacks,
since writers simply cannot be totally "out of touch with the rest of
the world"; there are, however, as Tyler insists, "a few surface features of the world – this week's fashionable slogans, political band-
wagons, use or misuse of language – that only get in the way of good

writing" (19). In *Looking for Mr. Goodbar* Rossner might have avoided a trendy tone and lapse into a style that dipped too far into the daily current, Tyler says. She might have retained the strength that Tyler discerned in Rossner's earlier novels – her "private, unique, creative point of view" – had "she been living in a window-less cubicle" (19). In "Because I Want More than One Life" Tyler describes her own writing room as "a stern white cubicle" (1). Obviously she took her own advice.

In one review Tyler reminds readers that the novelist can choose to work at several quite different levels, and once that level is estab-lished, the novel takes its form. "He may simply," Tyler says, "tell what happened, or he may tell what was going on internally as well. Or he may decide that the internal events are the most important of all, treating the external events as mere hooks upon which to hang the true story."[40] Whatever level is chosen, the novelist must accommodate the passage of time within the narrative that is to be told. Tyler finds a model in Gabriel García Márquez who, she says, "has somehow figured out how to let time be in literature what it is in life: unpredictable, sometimes circular, looped, doubling back, rushing through 60 years and then doddering over an afternoon, with glimmers of the past and future just beneath the surface."[41]

It is interesting to discern from Tyler's reviews what she consid-ers a *good* novel. If the short story is difficult to define and the genre difficult to describe, surely the novel is also difficult to define satis-factorily. In reviews of Anita Desai's *Clear Light of Day* (1980) and of Christina Stead's *Miss Herbert* (1976), Tyler declares that the real purpose of the novel has been met. Her views are based less on technical matters than on responses created in the reader. Desai's novel "does what only the very best novels can do: It totally sub-merges us. It takes us so deeply into another world that we almost fear we won't be able to climb out again."[42] And of that remarkable Australian writer Christina Stead and her novel *Miss Herbert,* Tyler says, "We have, at the end, a feeling of breathlessness; we've been through so much so fast. Our lives have been stretched to encom-pass someone else's, someone we never would otherwise have known. At its best that's what a novel is meant to do."[43]

Tyler's Reviewers

Fiction allows readers to glimpse – even to live vicariously – the lives
of other people. Certainly Tyler's novels do just that, and the lives
she presents are in the context of families, for, as Walter Sullivan
notes, "from *Antigone* to *Anna Karenina* and beyond, the sanctity of
family ties has informed much of our greatest literature."[44] Virtually
every reviewer and most critics comment on Tyler's successful pre-
occupation with the family. According to a brief piece in *People*, "No
other American writer has so deftly captured both the details and the
deepest truths of family life – or wrought such quiet beauty from the
everyday."[45] Virginia Schaefer Carroll summarizes quite well the
point that many Tyler critics have made: "The conversations, private
agonies, and rituals in Tyler's work remind us of the primitive ties
that bind, the ways in which, even in a mobile society with few con-
ventionally biogenetic families, we remain fortunately and tragically
allied to our kin."[46] Reviewing *The Accidental Tourist* (1985)
Michiko Kakutani said that Tyler "has claimed as her special
province the family in all its contrary dimensions."[47]

John Updike, who has reviewed several of Tyler's novels for the
New Yorker, notes a frequent theme in her novels: "A fundamental
American tension is felt between stasis and movement, between
home and escape," and that dilemma – in fiction and in
life – reminds us that "home is what we're mired in."[48] In his review
of *Earthly Possessions* (1977) Updike catalogs general strengths and
weaknesses that he sees in Tyler's work. On the one hand he finds
that she is content with her locale, capable of producing a serene
and firm tone, able to draw from her inexhaustible access to the per-
sonalities of her imagination, able to avoid any trace of intellectual or
political condescension. On the other hand he suggests that her one
possible weakness "is to leave the reader just where she found him.
Miss Tyler tends her human flora for each book's season of bloom
and then latches the garden gate with a smile. (Unlike Shakespeare's
tragedies where surviving characters have been chastened)" (130).

Perhaps *any* novelist suffers if the reviewer chooses to compare
their protagonists with Shakespeare's tragic figures. And Updike's
rather Victorian image of the garden gate is unfair. Anne Tyler, after
all, is not writing about tragic heroes or mythic creatures; she writes
about average people, and, as Thomas M. Disch so well pointed out

in his review of *Morgan's Passing* (1980), "because 'average' people don't usually make for large drama or high comedy, they are much less common in fiction than in real life. Perhaps it is Anne Tyler's most striking accomplishment that she can make such characters interesting and amusing without violating their limitations."[49] The strengths Diane Johnson identifies in Tyler are richness of descriptive detail, apt but unaffected diction, engaging characters, high comic tone, and a wonderful ear for small-town language.[50] For Johnson, however, the amelioration episodes of *The Accidental Tourist* allowed the plot to turn a bit into "Reaganesque dream novels where the poor are deserving and spunkiness will win" (17).

These characteristics of the domestic novel put Tyler in an honorable tradition; furthermore, she does not neglect the dismal, the difficult, the tragic that also visit the lives of "average people." Although Tyler does not write political novels, neither does she altogether ignore the political issues of her day. *The Accidental Tourist* and *Breathing Lessons* (1988), Susan Gilbert argues, "though still in the main domestic novels," nevertheless take up some of the "most volatile political issues of the eighties: gun control, crime in the streets, the failure of American public education, and abortion."[51] Certainly Tyler's primary emphasis in fiction is character: she says she would like for her readers "to get lost in my characters' lives for a while."[52] Her own attachment to her characters makes her reluctant to let them go when she completes a novel, their absence creating a real sense of loss. "It's hard enough," Tyler says, "just having to end the book. To send all my characters alone to New York City. (I picture my favorite hero, a shy, pudgy man, waiting hopefully by the railroad tracks with his clumsy little suitcase [Jeremy Pauling, we assume].) For weeks before I finish a novel, I swear I'm going to celebrate the minute I've mailed it off – throw a party, take to strong drink. But when I come back from the post office the house seems so quiet, and I can't believe how white and bleak my study is" ("One Life," 7). Indeed, Tyler somewhat whimsically sketches out a possible retirement plan: taking up residence in a peaceful small town where the houses up and down Main Street are inhabited with the characters from her novels. "After all, they're people I've loved, or I never would have bothered writing about them" ("One Life," 7). To be sure, expressing feeling and sympathy for one's characters is not unique to southern writers. Tyler, like so many southern writers,

creates characters she finds endearing. J. D. Reed reports that a
female interviewer, apparently puzzled by the facets of Gail Godwin's
characters, asked Godwin why she felt "a need to modulate suffering
with sweet reasonableness and humor"; Godwin answered, "Honey,
that's what they call character."[53]

It is true that Tyler does not take social issues as a primary concern and her books barely suggest, as Edward Hoagland has noted,
the racial tension and friction that visit the edges of her fictional
neighborhoods. According to Hoagland, her characters are "eerily
virtuous" and seem "Quakerishly tolerant of all strangers, all
races."[54] Tyler, he writes, "touches upon sex so lightly, compared
with her graphic realism on other matters, that her total portrait of
motivation is tilted out of balance" (44). Be that as it may, there are
still readers who find Tyler's treating sex lightly quite all right.

Tyler's characters give us their lives in conjunction with their
families – warts and all – and to name her characters is to conjure
up their appearances and experiences that are well worth remembering. Devoted Tyler readers find themselves – as Tyler admits to
doing – wondering how Evie Decker's baby turned out, wondering if
Justine and Duncan Peck did finally make a happy life with Alonzo's
Amazing Amusements, wondering if Meg Peck ever left her Caspar
Milquetoast husband, wondering if Ira Moran ever regained his son's
love, wondering if Ian Bedloe and Rita diCarlo lived happily with
their son Joshua. Tyler may not take technical risks, and she does
consistently keep the family unit at the center of her fiction, but she
is more interested in endurance and reconciliation than in alienation
and isolation. She wants her fiction to be *readable* – that is, to be
understood. She has created memorable characters that in her pages
she turns "loose to live as they will, and the choice that each makes
is a testimony to life's infinite variety."[55]

Chapter Two

The Short Stories

Anne Tyler's stories – some 50 of which are in print – have never been collected; indeed, a notation by Tyler in her papers in the Perkins Library of Duke University declares that most are not to be republished or anthologized. Although Tyler clearly prefers the novel form and has said that when she gets a good idea she reserves it for a novel, she is a fine short-story writer, and her work has been included in annual *Best American Short Stories* and has won O. Henry awards.

Elements of Tyler's stories have found their way into her novels: "I Never Saw Morning" (1961) and "Nobody Answers the Door" (1964), for example, are part of *If Morning Ever Comes*; "ReRun" (1988) appears as chapter 2, part 1, of *Breathing Lessons*; and "The Country Cook: A Story" (1982) is chapter 5 of *Dinner at the Homesick Restaurant*. "People Who Don't Know the Answers," chapter 5 of *Saint Maybe*, appeared in the 26 August 1991 *New Yorker*. As such reviewers as John Updike have noted, each of the 10 chapters of *Dinner at the Homesick Restaurant* is rounded like a short story. Indeed, as Doris Betts (quoting Tyler's mother) reports, "each had been designed so it could be published as a separate story."[1]

Some of Tyler's stories focus on situations and character types the author has not chosen to treat extensively in her novels. "A Misstep of the Mind" (1972) relates the violent rape of a teenager who by chance surprises a burglar in her home, a black man who comes to represent the crumbling safety that heretofore had surrounded this young woman's life. Although blacks appear in a number of Tyler's novels – for instance, the tobacco-typing-shed workers in *The Tin Can Tree* (1965) and, of course, Daniel Otis in *Breathing Lessons* – none has been so central to the narrative as Maroon in "The Geologist's Maid" (1975) and Ida in "The Common Courtesies" (1968). The perpetually angry Maroon (she and all of her sisters are

named for colors) rules her professor-employer's sick room and
house, and Ida, another maid, is effective, if more stereotyped: "Ida
was colored, but her heart was in the right place."[2] Powerfully sinis-
ter women – the mother in "A Knack for Languages" (1975) and the
totally selfish Mrs. Brauw in "As the Earth Gets Older" (1966) – are
character types treated in Tyler's stories. Her novels are filled with
strong women, but – except for the disturbing episodes of child
abuse Pearl Tull commits in the early years of *Dinner at the Homesick Restaurant* – she never returns to this unsettling character type.

Tyler's major novels are all closely involved with their geographic setting, Baltimore – a setting she used in the 1963 story "The
Baltimore Birth Certificate," published four years before she made
Baltimore her home. Tyler had used various places for story settings
before claiming Baltimore as her particular place: "I Play Kings"
(1963) begins in Raleigh, North Carolina, but the major action takes
place in New York City; "Dry Water" (1965) takes place in Sandhill,
North Carolina, the setting Tyler used for *If Morning Ever Comes*;
"The Feather behind the Rock" (1967) follows a grandson and his
grandparents through their cross-country drive from their home in
Wilmington, North Carolina, to San Francisco; "The Genuine Fur
Eyelashes" (1967) takes place in the tenant tobacco land of North
Carolina, where the family attend a daughter's graduation from ninth
grade at reform school (they bring the present she had requested – a
pair of "genuine fur eye lashes").

Even though geographic place rings true in Tyler's short stories,
she clearly prefers the detail and presence of Baltimore, which has
figured so prominently in her work since 1972, when she published
The Clock Winder and has her protagonist, Elizabeth Abbott, settle
in Baltimore. Her narrative techniques are evident in the Baltimore
stories: humor, strong characterizations, convincing portrayal of
everyday life. In these stories she occasionally shows her skillful use
of photographs and letters, two major devices in her novels. And in
several stories, including "With All Flags Flying" (1971), she writes
about very old characters and with the same gentle grace she uses to
portray Daniel Peck (*Searching for Caleb*) and Daniel Otis
(*Breathing Lessons*).

From Student Work to the *New Yorker*

Anne Tyler began her writing career in 1959, her second year at Duke University, with two short stories – "Laura" and "The Lights on the River" – published in *Archive*, Duke's literary magazine. The magazine's editorial note astutely and prophetically caught Tyler's essential traits: intellectual intensity and privacy. It reads: "Anne Tyler sits quietly but attractively in most of her courses saying little to demonstrate her intellectual and emotional depth. She is the kind of person who would be lost to all but her closest friends if it were not for her writing."[3] With mature and major work behind her, Tyler obviously has little interest in these first short stories; nevertheless, her early work provides hints of what is to come, lets us see that from the start Tyler took on major themes – initiation, grief, death – and reveals her sure touch for detail and voice as well as her sensitivity to human suffering.

Interest in early work should not center on what the writer has not yet mastered but on the techniques and elements there that will shape the work to come. In assessing the seven stories Flannery O'Connor wrote for her master's thesis at the University of Iowa, Frederick Asals readily acknowledges their "immaturity and general thinness" but values them for showing "the young writer casting about for her own distinctive voice and subject, trying out various modes . . . testing her talents within recognized styles and subjects."[4] While her subject did not narrow as O'Connor's did into the sacramental vision that would dominate all of her work, Tyler's first two published stories engage a serious subject – death and its lingering force. Most of her novels deal with death – from heart attack, from natural causes, occasionally from violent means – as Tyler explores the evolution of ordinary family life in all of its extraordinary dimensions.

Both "Laura" and "The Lights on the River" are filtered through the consciousness of a child who is forced by circumstances into the adult world of suffering and grief. In "The Lights on the River" a father and son go boating, taking along a Sunday picnic, but they do not return at the day's end. Throughout the story the searchlights illuminate the turgid machinery that drags the river until the bodies are at last recovered. The conventional plot is slight – the possibility of an accident and then its reality – but Tyler conveys the mother's acute grief in moving descriptions. Once the fatal news comes, the wife "just sat there with her hands folded in her lap and her face blank."[5] Her eyes – simply reflecting a worried look when the husband and son were merely late – now stared ahead "with nothing in them at all" ("Lights," 6). Tyler ends the story with a minimal yet lyric description, juxtaposing the images of light and dark to underscore the finality of this tragedy: "By night there would be no lights left and the Savannah River would be as dark as it had ever been" ("Lights," 6).

In this tragedy Tyler introduces humor through the neighbor Mrs. Baker, an officious woman whose type appears later in *Searching for Caleb* as the Reverend Arthur Milsom's mother and in *Celestial Navigation* as Amanda. She watches as the men drag the river. Betty Catherine, the child narrator whose father and brother die in the accident, knows that "Mrs. Baker wants to see if there is going to be a double funeral this afternoon. . . . She wants to be the first to find out. When she hears the motors stop at the river she is going to run tell everyone she knows, even my mother who will probably not say anything at all anyway" ("Lights," 5). Hungry to spread bad news, Mrs. Baker is humorous even though her insensitivity is appalling.

"Laura" also centers on a child's facing death. Set in "the Community" (reminiscent of Tyler's early years in the Celo Community), the story tells of Laura, a woman who lives amid the clutter of glazed china souvenirs and a large marble-top coffee table on which rests a sky-blue Bible. The centrality of this gaudy Bible reflects Laura's religious fanaticism. Others in the Community, if they consider the Bible at all, consider it simply as good literature. Laura, however, reads the Bible "as if it were some terrible personal letter which she felt compelled to read to anyone who would listen. She read it tonelessly, loudly, and endlessly."[6] Laura's literal belief that God, if He wished, "could with the thumb and third finger touch both the North and South Pole at once" makes her a symbol of the too literal belief that the Community prefers to discard ("Laura," 37).

Obeying her mother, the child has paid weekly visits to their strange neighbor, taking Laura cookies and enduring her Bible reading. Now Laura's death shows the child that life does continue in all of its banal functions; even in the face of death people continue to stoke fires and go for the mail. People, the child thinks to herself, *"couldn't* just keep going on as if nothing had happened. But apparently they did" ("Laura," 37). And the child, whose uncontrolled smiles rather than tears mark her response to this death, acknowledges her moment of insight: "It was as if I suddenly realized that the smiles were the only way I had of expressing this thing that was bursting out of me – this sudden new feeling of growing up and having things happen to change my life" ("Laura," 37).

"Laura" is one of the rare instances when Tyler overtly uses the Bible as a force in a character's life, and even in this early story religion exerts little direction or power except in Laura's overindulgent ways. The disillusioned Presbyterian minister Arle has turned atheist and literally wrings "his gaunt hands at every mention of the Blood of the Lamb" ("Laura," 36). The King James version, for all its richness of language, cadence, and imagery, has furnished Tyler little as an allusive or metaphoric source, a circumstance also true of Eudora Welty's work. Like Welty, Tyler has a number of ministers emerging in her fiction, but when these figures appear they are – in Welty and in Tyler – objects of satire. The South of the true Bible Belt is not theirs – lines from Psalms and verses from hymns are not on the tongues or in the hearts of their characters. Welty's preachers are generally Baptist, with a Presbyterian here and there. Tyler's clergymen include a wonderfully comic storefront revivalist, Brother Hope, in *A Slipping-Down Life* (1970), as well as Saul Emory, a character Tyler has said she regards with affection, who takes enough training to preach in the Holy Basis Church (*Earthly Possessions*). Saul may be born again (as his biblical name ironically suggests), but he remains as gloomy as ever. Tyler's own view of ministers is not based on general dislike or disregard. "It's not that I have anything against ministers," she has said, "but that I'm particularly concerned with how much right anyone has to change someone, and ministers are people who feel they have that right" (Lamb, 61). Rev. Emmett in *Saint Maybe* does not hesitate, however, to prod people into change.

Tyler published several other stories in *Archive*, but by the mid-1960s her work was appearing in a wide range of national publications, from *Seventeen* to the *New Yorker*.

The Precarious State of Well-Being

When Tyler deals with the ever-precarious state of human safety and well-being, she shows how mysteriously disaster awaits us, whether in the genetic makeup of an infant or in the presence of an dangerous intruder. One of Tyler's best and most moving stories, "Average Waves in Unprotected Waters" (1977), confronts the problem of a mentally deficient child and follows the mother, driven to the limit of her resources, as she commits her son Arnold to the state institution. The disorder of agoraphobia is pervasive in Tyler's fiction, from the severe condition Jeremy Pauling suffers in *Celestial Navigation* to the somewhat lesser form of this disorder that Ira's sister, Junie, suffers in *Breathing Lessons*. Jeremy has not left his Baltimore street block for years; Junie will not step out of the Baltimore apartment unless she has dressed in full disguise, replete with a flaming red wig. As irritating and serious as their conditions are, they do not touch Arnold's severe malady, a tragedy for Bet, the anguished mother in "Average Waves on Unprotected Waters," who "felt too slight and frail, too wispy for all she had to do today."[7]

When Arnold's problem had become evident, Avery, the boy's father, abandoned the family. For a long time Bet agonizes over the reason for Arnold's condition: Was it from a bad gene her husband possessed? that she possessed? Was it because she and Avery married too young and against their parents' advice? No answers, of course, come, and she is left with the arduous daily routine of caring for Arnold and providing a living. On the day the story takes place, Bet dresses the child carefully and frets to keep him neat and clean during the train ride to the state institution – her gesture to show that Arnold *was* special, was cherished. As the nurse locks doors that will keep Arnold inside, Bet hears "a single, terrible scream" – this unearthly sound is the last contact with her child ("Waves," 34).

With few exceptions, Tyler uses her story and novel titles within the texts themselves, thus deepening and layering the titles' significance. The title "Average Waves in Unprotected Waters" comes from Bet's childhood, when she lived with her parents in Salt Spray, Maryland. Her father operated a fishing boat for tourists and could not set out for the day until he received the pertinent weather information: "the wind, the tide, the small-craft warnings, the height of average waves in unprotected waters" ("Waves," 33). So, the title suggests, by arming ourselves we may avoid danger, may ensure safety. Bet, however, cannot protect herself or Arnold from the fate that was his from birth. Precaution cannot always guarantee safety. Tyler suggests by the conclusion of the story that Bet has suffered an extreme loss. As she waits out a 20-minute delay for her train home, local figures scurry about, setting up for the mayor's plan to take "about twenty minutes of your time, friends" ("Waves," 36). Bet watches, sensing that "they were putting on a sort of private play. From now on, all the world was going to be like that – just something on a stage, for her to sit back and watch" ("Waves," 36). Her real self was tied to Arnold, who is hers no longer.

Frequently in Tyler's fiction, characters must face the absurd twists of fate – those inexplicable chance moments that create an Arnold who, locked in his mental chaos, finally goes beyond his mother's reach. Or the irony of time that in "A Misstep of the Mind" causes what the rape victim, Julie Madison, describes as the worst minutes of her life. In this story Tyler exposes several layers of contemporary life in a world where neighborhood safety is no longer a fact and where the violation of rape is made worse by the indignity the police cause the victim, and even by the hapless blunders of neighbors.

Rape, the story insists, implies the total loss of innocence, an episode that opens and closes the story. Tyler begins, "Julie Madison was raped and robbed on a Tuesday, a warm and sunny noontime when you would least expect anything to go wrong," and ends, "Yet what she remembered, after everything else had gone, was the packed feeling that the air has when an intruder lies in wait, the capacity for betrayal in a cheerful world where dust floats lazily in sunbeams, the knowledge that it is possible to die."[8] The private trauma is counterpointed by the public dilemma: the police bombard Julie with questions about the man's physical description and his gun, their concern less over her experience than in their capturing the intruder, "because Baltimore had recently had a plague of burglaries by someone fitting the same description: tall and black, very young, wearing a pale yellow windbreaker" ("Misstep," 118). The old problem of racial tension comes full circle after Julie identifies the man in a lineup (his scar had floated persistently in her dreams), because she must on leaving the police station pass "a black family all dressed up and sternly erect" ("Misstep," 172). If this is the rapist's family, they give a picture of dignity far removed from the crime that has occurred. The racial tension that society endures is manifest in the reality of city life, where each day someone like Julie Madison discovers that "safety had crumbled in a second, as if it had never been more than a myth" ("Misstep," 119).

In concrete detail Tyler describes the plight of a private citizen caught in the world of police investigation. Julie must examine mugshots as a bored policewoman, ignorant of manners, "sighed and cleaned her fingernails with a door key" ("Misstep," 170). Then closed in the booth alone to view the lineup, Julie must obey these instructions: "If you can positively identify any of these men as having done you harm, you have ten seconds to call out his number" ("Misstep," 172). The real world, Julie discovers in this moment, is a far cry from the world of television, where a victim viewing the lineup could, if she chose, just take all the time in the world. This experience has marked Julie's educated, dignified, and sensible family for life, and Tyler's point hits hard: Julie Madison's mother has worked with the Urban League to find better jobs for blacks. Now she can only say of Julie's ordeal, "Oh, it's ironic" ("Misstep," 118). Ironic indeed, and regardless of the complicated social conditions that precipitate such crimes, for Julie Madison, the safety she had assumed and enjoyed had indeed crumbled in a second.

Powerful Mothers and Dutiful Daughters

Two "Grotesques"

In placing Anne Tyler in the context of contemporary American writers, the 1981 *Current Biography Yearbook* described her as "definitely not a member of the Southern Gothic School. Her affectionately realized novels are free of grotesquerie, theological implications, and sudden eruptions of violence."[9] Whether or not Tyler "belongs" to this or any other "Southern School" is of little importance, but the use of the grotesque is not limited to those securely inhabiting the "Southern Gothic School." Characters in Tyler's novels have their share of eccentric and violent behavior, but those in several of her stories transcend the "normal" to become "grotesque" – a type characterized, according to *Webster's New Universal Unabridged Dictionary*, "by distortions or striking incongruities in appearance, shape, manner . . . ludicrously eccentric or strange; ridiculous; absurd." In some Tyler stories grotesque characters loom large – especially in a half dozen or so women who are *fat*. In his insightful study *Art and the Accidental in Anne Tyler* (1989), Joseph C. Voelker overstates when he claims that these fat women "provide Tyler an opportunity to demythologize the Southern theme of inherited guilt."[10] Whatever problems make these various women eat their way into grotesque shapes, the inherited guilt of the South – the condition of slavery in all its social and moral implications that Faulkner explored and that Robert Penn Warren worried about in the Cass Mastern portion of *All the King's Men* (1946) – introduces a topic that matches neither the tone nor the intent of Tyler's work.

Fat women appear in a number of Tyler stories without any particular implication beyond their unsightly appearance. For instance, "The Tea-Machine" (1967) opens with "John Paul Bartlett once knew a girl named Sandra, who was very fat and lazy."[11] And in "Outside" (1971) a young man from a Celo-like community in the North Carolina mountains travels to a small New Hampshire town where he tutors the pudgy son of Mrs. Douglas, who is "fat" and whose attempts at conversation falter hopelessly: " 'I don't . . . Oh, it seems so . . .' There was no way to answer her. Most of her sentences faded before her meaning was clear."[12] But in the stories "The Common Courtesies" and "As the Earth Gets Older" fat women dominate, control, and victimize their families. The tone of both stories is dark, and the virtual immobility of the fat women ironically increases their power.

"The Common Courtesies" gives in Miss Lorna an early version of Lacey Debney Ames, the mother in *Earthly Possessions*, who, as her daughter Charlotte says, is "a fat lady who used to teach first grade."[13] Both women take around a chair stout enough to hold up their weight; Miss Lorna's is "made of wicker, splintered and darkened with age" ("Courtesies," 62). Although Miss Lorna spurns the reclining Strato-lounger Mr. Billy (her husband) presented on her birthday, her loyalty could not keep the wicker chair from splitting. When her maid, Ida, repairs the chair, Miss Lorna declares that Ida's deed "is the kindest thing anyone has ever done for me" ("Courtesies," 62). The chair is an absolute extension of her self, providing a haven and functioning as a throne. Throughout the

month of May Miss Lorna has sat in the wicker chair, steadily eating
the packets of vanilla wafers that Ida hands her.[14] Miss Lorna's activity concentrates on watching her heart, which had received a terrific
jolt when her daughter Melissa had announced that she was pregnant. The slight plot is enhanced by Tyler's humor, which here, as is
so often the case, also carries serious implications.

To Miss Lorna sex, childbirth, and motherhood are alien experiences, events to avoid. Totally opposite Mary Tell in *Celestial Navigation*, who finds pregnancy her natural state and motherhood her
instinctive calling, Miss Lorna associates only shock and displeasure
over Melissa, who was "born in Miss Lorna's middle age, just when
she had finally gotten it through Mr. Billy's head that she didn't hold
with childbearing, arriving at midnight after an ordeal that Miss
Lorna had been trying for thirty years to forget" ("Courtesies," 63).
When it comes time for Melissa to be told the facts of life, Miss Lorna
is content to say, "What with your health and all, I do hope you'll be
careful." With Melissa pregnant, Miss Lorna wonders if she should
have "put it more plainly" ("Courtesies," 63). The humor is a
delight, but the tone darkens when the daily pattern of this small
family unfolds. Mr. Billy – as cheerful as his counterpart, Murray
Ames in *Earthly Possessions* is morose – is beside himself with pleasure as he contemplates his first grandchild. Miss Lorna does not
want to hear anything about the impending birth and indeed exacts
an apology from Melissa for getting pregnant, thus causing Miss
Lorna's heart to take a jolt.

Simply existing in the present, Miss Lorna lives in the past when
her brief singing career made her the center of attention, capturing
particularly her father's praise. Endlessly she repeats her tale of past
glory: "And I would go out on the stage again [for bows] and see my
father, spang in the middle of the very front row, with a huge bou-
quet in his lap and his eyes just as *bright*" ("Courtesies," 116). Now
Miss Lorna's only audience is Ida, whose version of applause is simply to say, "Yes, Ma'am." Miss Lorna neither enjoys nor provides
pleasure and bitterly scorns the happiness that the members of her
family deserve. Tyler's last image of the woman makes her as useless
as she is ludicrous: "a large, ugly woman sinking through the seat of
a wicker chair, chewing vanilla wafers and looking like Andy Devine
in a golfing costume" ("Courtesies," 116).

The plight of a dutiful daughter in "As the Earth Gets Older" ends when Miss Beatrice chooses to perish in a house fire rather than continue to live with her mother, Mrs. Brauw, the fat old lady the firemen rescue. Mrs. Brauw's response to the news that the firemen can do nothing to rescue Miss Beatrice is a simple and controlled, "I understand."[15] Over the years the old woman has thoroughly victimized her tenants who live next door, a mother and daughter who feel obliged to acquiesce whenever Mrs. Brauw summons them to join her and Miss Beatrice in a game of Scrabble. As often as four nights a week they would receive the call – " 'Care for a little game?' she would say, as if it were a new idea that had suddenly come to her" ("Earth," 60). Miss Beatrice and the tenants sit around the table watching Mrs. Brauw who, "fishing for Scrabble letters, cheated, and everybody knew but no one mentioned it" ("Earth," 60).

For the tenants the Scrabble games are to be endured, fearful as they are of offending the landlady. But for Mrs. Brauw and her daughter the game board is a battlefield: "The war was between them really; they played intensely, and watched to see that they did not give each other any opportunities for triple-word scores" ("Earth," 60). The struggle at the game table is nothing more than a surface form of Mrs. Brauw and Miss Beatrice locked in their futile struggle for power and freedom. A broken hip has failed to heal properly, and fat Mrs. Brauw, with her walker and her special chair, rules the house and keeps her daughter close at hand. What Mrs. Brauw says to her tenants after the fire hints at the power she had held and the extreme duty her daughter had assumed: "my only daughter, who gave me her word she would look out for my every need until I died" ("Earth," 64). Now the daughter is dead, and the fat old mother is ensconced next door, again forcing her interminable Scrabble games on her tenants. She expresses no remorse over her daughter's death, experiences no sense of grief. One of Tyler's darkest characters, this fat old lady surveys her surroundings after the fire and calls Miss Beatrice's promise "a cheat from beginning to end" ("Earth," 64). The daughter next door is sure that as the fireman were arriving she saw Miss Beatrice stand in a window where apparently she could have been rescued, but she instantly disappeared. Her fatal choice is perhaps better than the living death she had had with her mother.

Alienation

As selfish as Mrs. Brauw is, the mother in Tyler's 1975 story, "A Knack for Languages," though dead years before the time of the narrative, emerges as vicious. Subject to violent rages, she is an early version of Pearl Tull in the days of her frequent and blind rages in one of Tyler's best novels, *Dinner at the Homesick Restaurant*. In this story Tyler also explores the tension inherent in a cross-culture marriage, here an Italian linguist who teaches at the university where Susan, a graduate student in geology, audits his class. Later they marry. When Mark's two sisters visit, they speak volatile and loud Italian when he is at home, excluding Susan, who thinks to herself, "I am fond of both of them, but when they speak to me so dramatically I find it impossible to rise to the occasion."[16] Thus she is excluded in her married home as surely as she was in the Virginia farmhouse of her childhood, with her shy father and her mother "full of violent moods which she pulled over her face like huge exaggerated masks" ("Knack," 34).

Like so many other hopelessly mismatched pairs in Tyler's fiction, Susan's parents seem extraordinary opposites. The wife is a college graduate whose endless vitality diminishes her farmer husband. Her withering judgments ring out: "'*Some* people,' she announced to her husband, 'dear man, plunge joyfully in, and some dampen a toe first, testing the temperature, and you are one of the latter'" ("Knack," 35). Her cruelest attack comes when she declares that her husband and her daughter must be made of modeling clay: "I could have bought you both in a dime store – father, daughter. Stuck you out in the kitchen in some virtuous pose and *left* you there, I'd never know the difference" ("Knack," 36). Such an outburst is sufficient to determine that this family of three was self-destructive just as the farmhouse is now shabby, reduced to a quintessential grayness, "the color of paper that has been rubbed with a dirty eraser, worn gray and translucent" ("Knack," 33).

Present time in the story covers a Christmas visit Mark and Susan make to her father. Mark is quite obviously out of his element in his new country clothes; his attempts to converse with Susan's father never go anywhere beyond a brief question followed by an even briefer answer. The disparity of the backgrounds continues at the Christmas dinner table as Mark tells "stories about Christmas in Italy, anecdotes involving hordes of fat, merry aunts and uncles, and cousins grouped around the tree" ("Knack," 37). Susan has only to remember the farmhouse front porch, cluttered with "an old wringer washer, a zinc tub of auto parts, a radiator, and a fifty-pound sack of goat chow," to confirm her notion that she and her father "didn't have any stories that would match his" ("Knack," 37).

The exchange of Christmas gifts brings an unexpected turn when the father gives Susan her mother's locket, which contains pictures of husband and wife in their youth, their initials, and the inscription "LOVE FOREVER" ("Knack," 37). Considering the anger of this woman who finally killed herself in the northeast bedroom, taking a poison that is never named, the locket inscription seems to contradict her total way of living. Yet the husband declares to his daughter that he continues to grieve for his wife: "I will miss her till I die. . . . It will never get less" ("Knack," 37). Susan, of course, cannot share her father's past, cannot comprehend this man's love for a woman who was so unlovable. Whatever private understanding her parents had reached in their marriage Susan does not know, but she now sees her own marriage drifting into hopeless separateness. On their return from the Christmas visit, Mark immediately immerses himself in mastering a new language, this time Arabic. As he leans against a windowsill "lined with books in Italian, Middle English, and Old Church Slavonic," Susan knows full well he is moving further away from her and she is to be left behind to realize "there is nothing I can think of to say that will call him back" ("Knack," 37).

The first extended treatment of the family in Tyler's fiction came in 1979, with Stella Ann Nesanovich's dissertation "The Individual in the Family: A Critical Introduction to Anne Tyler." Sharply divided characters are either "homesick" or "sick of home," as Doris Betts describes the situation, the "runaway/stay-at-home conflict" (Betts 1983, 32). In her novels Tyler often lets women characters run away from their homes – by eloping (*A Slipping-Down Life, Celestial Navigation, Searching for Caleb, Dinner at the Homesick Restaurant*), by kidnapping (*Earthly Possessions*), by church weddings (*Searching for Caleb, Dinner at the Homesick Restaurant, Breathing Lessons*), by an aborted marriage ceremony (*The Clock Winder*), and by going away to college (*Dinner at the Homesick Restaurant, Earthly Possessions, Breathing Lessons*). These characters sometimes make a semblance of peaceful compromise by returning to their original home after their runaway experience and establishing a compromised life.

The disruption of a happy family life in "A Knack for Languages" centers on the mother's morose and violent ways. Susan was alienated by her mother while she lived at home, and when she went away to college her mother sent no letters (that traditional link of communication) because "she wasn't the kind of person who could assemble her thoughts that way" ("Knack," 36). This mother had lived, Susan remembers, almost as an enemy: "She plunged into our very souls, stirring and mangling our thoughts" ("Knack," 35). Little wonder that the woman could not marshall her thoughts for the orderly discourse a letter requires. The shy father, however, does write Susan letters, "telling the news about the goats and so forth," a rather sad and touching way to keep the "runaway apprised" ("Knack," 36). Now in the home of her own marriage, Susan's husband is moving away, shutting her out. As he happily turns to his Arabic text, Tyler's image shows the completeness of the isolation Susan now experiences. Taking up the text, Mark "seems touched with gold, enclosed in a bubble of good fortune" ("Knack," 37). The situation promises little hope of change and Susan thinks that "surely he must wish he had married someone with a knack for languages" ("Knack," 32).

Tyler admires the sharp eye for concrete detail and often praises such skill in book reviews, citing that technique in Bobbie Ann Mason's *Shiloh and Other Stories* (1982) as especially successful. "A Knack for Languages" has (as does Tyler's fiction generally) details that match the characters, reflect their daily routine, fit their view of the world. For example, Susan, self-possessed and orderly, completes the clearing of Christmas dinner by cutting up the left-over turkey and leaving it, as she tells her father, "in the freezer in little Baggies" ("Knack," 37). He doubtless has many lonely meals as Susan surmises on her arrival when she sees on the kitchen table the remains of his lunch – "Kellogg's Corn Flakes and an apple core" ("Knack," 34). Susan's Christmas gift to her father is not just a knife but a Swiss Army knife with seven blades, apropos for a man whose usual topic of conversation is "physical objects . . . machines mostly" ("Knack," 35). Susan's father suggests she get her Smith-Corona typewriter repaired; he subscribes to the *Farmer's Almanac*; Susan and Mark drive a Toyota; the Christmas turkey comes from Mrs. Benson's poultry farm. Such details lend to each scene the sense that these characters really do *exist* in Tyler's created world. The story's precise details underscore the very separate lives the characters lead.

Relatives from Afar

One might expect to see in Anne Tyler's novels depictions of the cultural adjustment she likely experienced after marrying Taghi Mohammed Modarressi, an Iranian-born child psychiatrist and novelist, in 1963. Thus far that has not been the case.[17] She has, however, addressed this important and deep experience in other forms of writing. In the 1979 review-essay "Please Don't Call It Persia" she recalls with profound nostalgia her first visit to Iran and the serene atmosphere and routine of her husband's family – a routine that soon would be disrupted because of political changes. The exotic and appealing sound of "Persia" and all of its associations are a memory now sad to recall.

Two of Tyler's stories use a cross-cultural experience and revolve around the same family in Baltimore – the husband, Hassan Ardavi, is a doctor and Iranian by birth; the wife, Elizabeth, is American. "Your Place Is Empty" (1976), which appeared in the *New Yorker* and in the 1977 volume of *Best American Short Stories*, begins early in October when Hassan invites his mother in Iran for a visit and she "accept[s] immediately."[18] Thus begins a family visit fraught with the usual tension of family visits plus the weight of cultural differences that finally bring the visit to an early end. Religion, as one might expect, separates the characters, often in irritating ways. Knowing his mother's religious devotion, Hassan buys a pocket compass so that she can face Mecca daily for her prayers. This ancient custom carries no meaning for Hassan, who has absolutely no idea of the direction of Mecca from his Baltimore house. His failure to observe religious traditions is not a recent move because "he had never said the prayers himself, not even as a child. His earliest memory was of tickling the soles of his mother's feet while she prayed steadfastly on; everybody knew it was forbidden to pause once you'd started" ("Place," 45).

Mrs. Ardavi's religious zeal causes disruptions in the daily routine. Elizabeth and Hilary, the child, have eggs and bacon each morning, and although the mother-in-law longs to know what bacon tastes like, she cannot indulge because it is unclean. Nor can her clothes enter the same laundry because Elizabeth is a Christian. The washer and dryer are unclean because they have "contained, at some point, a Christian's underwear" ("Place," 48). So, she asks the son to buy her a drying rack (ironically, the Christian daughter-in-law assembles it); "then Mrs. Ardavi holds it under her shower and rinsed it off, hoping that would be enough to remove any taint. The Koran didn't cover this sort of situation" ("Place," 48).

The touch of humor that surrounds the drying rack episode fades as the life-style of the Americanized son and his wife clashes with Mrs. Ardavi's habits, beliefs, and routine. The two worlds are hopelessly alien, and Tyler sets down the Iranian mother's bewilderment over the American way of life. For instance, Americans' daily schedule baffles her, "each half hour possessing its own set activity"; in Tehran her sisters spend long hours "drinking cup after cup of tea and idly guessing who might come and visit" ("Place," 46-47). Dining is a problem. Mrs. Ardavi dislikes American food, and even when Elizabeth prepares an Iranian dish, her mother-in-law finds it has an American taste. Little by little Mrs. Ardavi takes over the kitchen for the evening meal, beginning her preparations each day at three in the afternoon, displacing Elizabeth, who eats little when the meal is served. Hassan gains weight. The conflict reaches its climax when Elizabeth finally begins to reclaim her house. Standing in the kitchen she opens a strange tin box with Persian lettering. As if to ensure that the mother-in-law's homeland has invaded this house and will linger, "out flew a cloud of insects, grayish brown with V-shaped wings" ("Place," 53). The visit cannot continue, and Hassan invents an American custom: after a guest has remained three months, she is expected to move into an apartment. That step is never taken, for Mrs. Ardavi claims homesickness for her sisters, and return travel plans go into motion.

The empty place announced in the title remains empty. The mother cannot reclaim her son, and he no longer fits into his place in the Iranian home of his youth. Mrs. Ardavi conveys her deep longing for the past. She had failed to recognize her son in his American clothes when he met her airplane, but she finally recognized his smell – "a pleasantly bitter, herblike smell" – that itself transports her into the past to "the image of Hassan as a child, reaching thin arms around her neck" ("Place," 45). The past, of course, is gone except to memory, and Hassan's place in his mother's home will remain empty.

Mrs. Ardavi's disappointment is real and one that all parents face. The loss of children to adulthood and their own loves is simply a part of life, and Tyler does not make Mrs. Ardavi an especially sympathetic character unless we keep in mind the sadness and the traumas of Mrs. Ardavi's childhood, which had been grim and murky. Her father had had three wives and produced "a surprising number of children even for that day and age" – Mrs. Ardavi had 13 sisters ("Place," 47). Her father was known to chase and trap the servant girls in vacant bedrooms, but an even worse experience came when Mrs. Ardavi was 10: "She was forced to watch her mother bleed to death in childbirth, and when she screamed the midwife struck her across the face and held her down till she had properly kissed her mother goodbye" ("Place," 47).

The cultural differences understandably upset Elizabeth and make a full acceptance of her mother-in-law difficult. Apparently Elizabeth knows nothing of the deep wounds that the woman carries from her youth, painful experiences that might have altered Elizabeth's reaction to her mother-in-law now. The visit ends, and the temporary place Mrs. Ardavi has occupied in her son's home in Baltimore is now empty.

Far more exotic than Mrs. Ardavi is Uncle Ahmad, who comes to Baltimore for a visit with Hassan and Elizabeth and now their two daughters in "Uncle Ahmad" (1977). Larger than life and a millionaire several times over, Uncle Ahmad arrives, "seven feet tall . . . and yellow as an onion. . . . In fact, he reminded Elizabeth of a suntanned Mr. Clean. He even stood like Mr. Clean, when she opened the door to him – arms folded across his chest, feet wide apart between stacks of luggage."[19] When a neighbor happens by to return a casserole dish, she asks Elizabeth, "Why is Yul Bryner sitting in your living room?" ("Ahmad," 78). Such a character invites humor, but the serious aspects of the story dominate. Separated from her son Hassan for 12 years, Mrs. Ardavi could accept his invitation to visit only because she had successfully arranged the wedding of her third son, Babak. The task of finding him a suitable wife had taken her three years: "One was too modern, one too lazy, one so perfect she had been suspicious" ("Place," 47). Uncle Ahmad, on the other hand, observes few of the old customs and apparently conforms least of all to traditional expectations for marriage. The catalog of his roles shocks the women in the family, who disapprove of this "black sheep – the gayest, the loudest, the wickedest, a frequenter of wrestling gyms and gambling joints, a heavy drinker in a Muslim family, an opium smoker, twice divorced, the kind of man who makes his friends' wives tighten their lips and shake their heads." No wonder the "men in the family adored him" ("Ahmad," 76).

Clinging to her strict beliefs, Mrs. Ardavi cannot allow her laundry to mingle in the same machine where a Christian's is routinely going through the cycles. Uncle Ahmad, however, suffers no such hesitation. In hues of "navy and brown and other surprising colors," his ribbed underwear goes in the family wash and, furthermore, "tints everyone else's" ("Ahmad," 79). The colors, like the man himself, invade the territory of others, changing or displacing what they encounter. The pathetic items that tilt Mrs. Ardavi's homeward luggage into 14 pounds of overweight are trivial things for her sisters – "three empty urn-shaped wine bottles, the permanent-press sheets from her bed, and a sample box of detergent that had come in yesterday's mail" ("Place," 54). Uncle Ahmad's tastes are different, and he daily goes on vulgar shopping sprees, heedlessly adding to his possessions. He cannot even wear all the shirts he has bought; his suits come from London, his shoes from Italy. During his Baltimore stay, he drags Elizabeth to Towson Plaza, where his excursions in Hutzler's or Stewart's department stores remind Elizabeth of "those contest winners who are given sixty seconds to gather as many free groceries as possible" ("Ahmad," 79). Finally, exasperated by his insatiable spending and his inexhaustible supply of $10 bills, Elizabeth explodes: "You've got everything. What more do you need?" ("Ahmad," 80).

This first wave of the story subsides only to find Uncle Ahmad veering in another direction, but a self-centered one and still a move that ignores the household routine. Using Hassan's address book (and his telephone charge), Ahmad calls all his other relatives who are scattered in Chicago, Boston, Minneapolis, and New Jersey, inviting them to Baltimore for a weekend reunion. The exasperation over Uncle Ahmad now shifts to Hassan, whose objection centers on what such an influx of family guests will mean for Elizabeth's work schedule. Differences in the two cultures surface in Hassan's questions: "You think we're back home? . . . You think we're in Tehran with twenty servants to make the beds and cook the rice? If you want to see them, go there. Or talk to us first, invite one at a time. Elizabeth can't be expected to manage without notice" ("Ahmad," 80). Hassan's concern, however, is not simply Elizabeth's schedule but equally the telephone bill Ahmad has drastically increased. Since she is at home all day, Elizabeth should watch Ahmad more closely, Hassan implies. But Ahmad has taken all the energy and time she can expend – "How can I? As it is I'm buying his clothes, brewing his tea, following after his opium pipe with a can of Glade" ("Ahmad," 80). For Elizabeth there is no equal time much less equal rights for the woman of the house.

Despite Hassan's displeasure, Ahmad still controls and achieves part of his original plan by failing to uninvite second cousin Hurosh, who appears on Saturday afternoon with his pregnant wife and their two crying babies. Elizabeth finds that even Hassan's alternative of inviting the relatives one at a time exhausts her. She must supply the New Jersey family with makeshift beds (Ahmad has the guest room) and keep in motion by supplying a steady stream of tea, scotch, and mounds of rice. If the demands of married life and in-laws are exasperating Elizabeth now, even more disenchanted is Hurosh's wife, whose marriage had been arranged by proxy. Burdened with her pregnancy *and* her two crying babies, she longs to be still just the bride of their tinted wedding photograph, wherein she is lovely – married, but not yet with the literal day-to-day reality of married life with babies. Like the many failed dinners and reunions and reconciliation attempts in Tyler's fiction, this episode-visit fails. It is not what Uncle Ahmad suggests it is: "the true meaning of life. Food and drink and a pipe to smoke, and your dear ones gathered all around" ("Ahmad," 82). They are all more nearly strangers than cheerful kin greeting kin.

The final episode in the story leads to Uncle Ahmad's departure – a departure that will be final. Caught up in the frantic pace Uncle Ahmad has set, Elizabeth has had no time for the weekly grocery shopping but manages to piece out Friday night dessert with two bowls of ice cream for her daughters. As she comes from the kitchen with the spoons, there is Uncle Ahmad, he who has wealth and utterly superfluous possessions, "lifting Hilary's scoop of ice cream in his fingers" and dripping it across the table cloth as he completes his theft. Both parents react quickly. Elizabeth "rapped a spoon on a glass, sharply like an after-dinner speaker. 'Put it back,' she said." And when Ahmad looks to his nephew for support, Hassan says simply, "back" ("Ahmad," 82). Such a small thing to appropriate – a scoop of ice cream. But Ahmad has for days overstepped the bounds that Elizabeth and Hassan have tried to set. Finally, this trivial act is the one they will not tolerate.

The exotic, bigger-than-life relative departs, leaving indeed an empty place. His commanding presence has been disruptive, yet Elizabeth realizes that such overpowering people gain their power by their wealth and by "consuming chunks of other people's lives" ("Ahmad," 82). And though no one could survive living in Uncle Ahmad's demanding atmosphere for long, when he leaves they miss him "forever afterward like an arm, or a leg, or a piece of a heart" ("Ahmad," 82).

"Your Place Is Empty" and "Uncle Ahmad" present a stage of rich characters, exploring an Iranian-American family's life when relatives come to visit. Regardless of the differences in family background, the longing for ideal family life is strong. The gathering of kin should bring, as Uncle Ahmad falsely declares it does, "the true meaning of life: food and drink and a pipe to smoke, and your dear ones gathered all around." But the dear ones are not collectively content; the runaways sometimes go by choice (Elizabeth in *The Clock Winder*, Caleb in *Searching for Caleb*, Luke in *Dinner at the Homesick Restaurant*), and sometimes a family member is forced to go and leave an empty place like Hassan's mother and like Uncle Ahmad. Disruptions occur, and yet the family continues. As Doris Betts has noted, Tyler's families "break, mend, and persist"; their author "seems in tune with the Moroccan proverb: 'None but a mule denies his family.' "[20] Ahmad, however, might make his family give the proverb a second thought.

Old Age

Tyler's 1971 story "With All Flags Flying" salutes old age through an 82-year-old man who takes charge of his life. He leaves the two-room house, perched on the last scrap of his Baltimore County farm now crowded by the superhighway. Bound for Baltimore, he plans to spurn his daughter's plea to live with her, determined to enter a home for the aged. The old man sets out dressed in the brown suit he bought in 1944 and carries a sack lunch – a hunk of bread and two Fig Newtons. Weaker than he thought he was, he probably would never have reached Baltimore if a shabby young man on a motorcycle "with hair so long that it drizzled out beneath the back of his helmet" had not stopped.[21] He settles the old man behind him on the cycle and delivers him right to his daughter's front door. It was, to the old man, a wonderful ride – "a really magnificent roar, ear-dazzling" ("Flags," 136).

Nothing is more appealing to Anne Tyler the writer than the task of rendering old men, and in this story she is unerring in her description. He plans his physical moves carefully, "giving his legs enough warning to face the day ahead" ("Flags," 137). Installed at his own insistence in a home for the aged, his lyric meditation that ends the story celebrates one man who meets old age with little physical strength but with great courage of spirit: "Let me not give in at the end. Let me continue gracefully till the moment of my defeat. Let Lollie Simpson be alive, somewhere even as I lie on my bed: let her be eating homemade fudge in an overstuffed armchair and growing fatter and fatter and fatter" ("Flags," 140).

Conclusion

Anne Tyler's short stories appear in two forms: those that are later woven seamlessly into a novel and those that remain discreet stories. As I have shown in this chapter, Tyler uses themes in short stories that do not appear in her novels, particularly the important issue of cross-cultural relations, which she explores in stories like "Your Place Is Empty," "Uncle Ahmad," "A Knack for Languages," and "Linguistics."[22]

In several stories Tyler presents the plight of women trapped in domestic routine and limited by society's expectations. These woman are often unable and indeed unwilling to abandon their domestic life. At the same time the tension between fulfilling responsibilities and gaining a sense of self weighs heavy on these women, a dilemma that figures prominently in most of Tyler's novels. In "Under the Bosom Tree" (1977) a recently widowed 67-year-old woman faces her first birthday after her husband's death. Her preoccupied family fails to share her grief or to appreciate her struggle to survive. As she describes the first mornings after her husband's death, she takes her place among Tyler's enduring characters: "I woke up feeling just – oh, elated. I thought, 'Look at me, I made it through the night on my own.' I was proud of that."[23]

In "Laps" the mother of a 14-year-old sees her life as an endless repetition of swimming pool visits for the daughter and the domestic routine of meal preparation and family care. As she gathers her belongings from the poolside to start home, her reflections on past and present show how completely she is paralyzed by her routine: "It occurs to me that I left the breakfast dishes undone. I have spent the day uselessly, wasted it, and see nothing ahead of me but more days to waste the same way."[24]

Tyler's stories need critical attention; her place among contemporary short-story writers has yet to be seriously considered. Intriguing characters and quick humor, as well as societal and family issues, are among obvious aspects that invite critical response. Most of all, the stories need to be read for the good writing and moving experiences. An especially good example is the final paragraph of "Some Sign That I Ever Made You Happy" (1975), a story in which a man discovers the letters his father wrote to his wife after she died. The last letters (written six weeks before the father's death) reveal that the couple missed happiness altogether. Daily the husband had thought of the past, searching "out some sign that I ever made you happy."[25]

Moved by these letters, the son tries to rekindle love in his marriage to avoid the regret he found in his father's letters. His gesture fails because his wife is busy with kitchen chores. As he walks into the living room he experiences an epiphany of cold recognition that reminds one of Gabriel's chilling moment in James Joyce's "The Dead": "So he went. In fact he found that he was even relieved to go. He was looking forward to a quiet half hour with the paper. But just as he was reaching toward the mantel he froze, struck suddenly by an unexpected sorrow, and for several minutes he stood motionless, hoping against hope that the sorrow was the kind that would lessen as time went on" ("Sign," 130).

Tyler's reviews of the stories of Elizabeth Bowen, Eudora Welty, Caroline Gordon, John Cheever, and Hortense Calisher document delight in these novelists' *stories* – the sheer pleasure of having the Calisher volume in hand is "greedy satisfaction" ("Teacup," E1), even though the stories had been available in separate volumes.

Thus far there is no single volume of Tyler's stories, and one would be a welcomed addition to her canon. Readers can hope that eventually *The Collected Stories of Anne Tyler* will appear on library shelves.

Chapter Three

Believable Lies

In an interview conducted in 1981 Anne Tyler said that both her first and second novels, *If Morning Ever Comes* (1964) and *The Tin Can Tree* (1965), "should be burned. . . . They were formless and wandering and should never have been published" (Lamb, 64). She said further that she had recently ditched a book-length manuscript ("Panteleo" [1981]), conjecturing that it shared the flaws of the aforementioned novels – "formless and wandering" (Lamb, 64). "Panteleo" is to date the last of three novels Tyler has chosen not to publish: the other two are "I Know You, Rider" (1961) and "Winter Birds, Winter Apples" (1966).[1]

While not meeting Tyler's expectations (indeed, she refuses to allow these novels-in-manuscript to be quoted), her three unpublished works contain a host of splendid characters, many of whom one hopes may appear transformed in later novels. Early versions of some characters and scenes that appear in Tyler's published novels are clearly present in these novels-in-manuscript. "I Know You, Rider" takes place in an unnamed North Carolina town, where the characters assemble, most having come from the mountain area around Asheville; "Winter Birds, Winter Apples" takes place in a seaside tourist home on the North Carolina coast; "Panteleo" is set in and around Baltimore and has many of Tyler's strongest narrative traits.

"I Know You, Rider" shows us that Tyler had brought to completion a book-length manuscript as early as 1961 – three years before she published a novel. Furthermore, the unpublished novels taken in tandem with the published show us just how extraordinary Tyler's output is from 1961 to 1966: four book-length manuscripts in five years. From the unpublished material we see aspects of Tyler's fiction that have become consistent strengths in her mature work: believable and appealing eccentric characters, good dialogue, a strong sense of place that starts in various real and fictional North Carolina towns and narrows to the effective portrayal of Baltimore and its environs, and a durable humor that is strong and captivating from the beginning. Tyler's major subject matter also dominates from the first novel on: the family in its various configurations and in its inevitable cycle of both banal events and genuine crises.

Most reviewers praised *If Morning Ever Comes* and *The Tin Can Tree*, their effusive words sharply contradicting Tyler's later assessment. Writing for the Raleigh *News and Observer*, Doris Betts (a fellow North Carolina novelist) described Tyler's first novel as "a low-key, sensitive, deftly written book" and found Tyler "unusually skillful with dialogue."[2] Tyler, Betts asserts, "is a young writer who has learned her lessons well, and she has not written some sprawling, overly-philosophical book which would embarrass her later" (Betts 1964, 5). Reviewers voiced far more praise than criticism, and virtually all of them marveled that a 22-year-old produced the novel.

In his review of Tyler's *The Clock Winder* (1972) Jonathan Yardley also remarked on her early work, describing her first three novels as "beautifully realized, quiet, humorous novels, the kind that are too often overlooked in an America eager for sensational fiction."[3] Yardley's comment is still relevant: Tyler has not turned to the experimental or the simply odd but has instead given us nonsensational novels that attract a growing readership. The list of books Tyler has reviewed in various places, including the *New York Times Book Review*, the *New Republic*, and the *Washington Post*, furnishes ample evidence that she reads and reacts to all sorts of "sensational" fiction, from Donald Barthelme's stories to D. M. Thomas's *Ararat*. In many ways her view of fiction can be found in these reviews. What she finds readable is a novel with a plot we can dependably follow, a novel whose characters interest us and has "layers and layers, like life does. *It has to be an extremely believable lie*."[4] And so it is with the novels of Anne Tyler.

If Morning Ever Comes

If Morning Ever Comes was published in October 1964 and reprinted the next month. In May 1981, when reviews of *Searching for Caleb* were coming in, Tyler's editor at Knopf, Judith B. Jones, sent a batch of reviews and also included a copy of *If Morning Ever Comes*, a copy from the seventh edition of that novel.[5] While Tyler now does not welcome this novel into the family of her fiction, there it is, hanging around the edge like a well-meaning great-aunt – marginal and undistinguished but still and all blood kin. It is surprising that in this first novel Tyler's main character is male. Ben Joe Hawkes's life and story, however, emerge from a world of women. The home he has left remains occupied by eight of them: his terse mother, his dotty grandmother, and his six sisters (one moved away to marry but has come home because she left her husband). Many reviewers found Ben Joe a convincing character, though Tyler tends to agree with the reviewer who found him about as interesting as a cucumber sandwich. Nevertheless, he struck the Hartford, Connecticut, *Courant* reviewer as "a reasonable facsimile of a man, who talks and acts like a male, instead of an amorphous androgyne – the usual creation of a young woman novelist's imagination."[6]

Surveying in a 1989 study Tyler's novels through *Breathing Lessons* (1989), Joseph C. Voelker contrasted Tyler's Quakerish reticence with John Updike's Puritan zeal. Though Voelker's argument is fascinating, these two novelists hardly need dramatic labels for their extremely different fictional worlds. More convincing is Voelker's excellent discussion of Tyler's "Southerness," those thematic and technical traits she sees in Eudora Welty and accommodates into her own fictional world. In *If Morning Ever Comes* Voelker sees Tyler's tentative "testing of Southern themes public and private" (Voelker, 27). Alice Hall Petry in *Understanding Anne Tyler* (1990) particularly analyzes three major concerns that Tyler introduces in these earliest novels and later develops and deeply refines in her mature work: those "ambivalent entities" the family, basic communication, and what Petry so very well describes as "the twin exigencies of change and of passing time" (Petry, 33, 39).

If Morning Ever Comes takes us through several days in the family life of Ben Joe Hawkes, beginning with his uneasy and vague feeling that he must go home to Sandhill, North Carolina, and restore stability and order to the house of women he left there when he entered law school at Columbia University. Although Tyler spent some time in New York City as a student at Columbia, that northern metropolitan place does not come to life in the novel (except for the southerner Ben Joe complaining about the city's cold weather). Furthermore, the daily routine and conversation of Ben Joe and the younger student who shares his apartment do not sound convincing. (In the 1963 story "I Play Kings" Tyler depicts New York more realistically, presenting it through the wide eyes of a brother and sister from Raleigh who visit it briefly.) The novel is structured by two train rides: from New York to Sandhill when Ben Joe decides to cut classes and come home and his return to New York with his girlfriend, Shelley Dormer, at his side, ready to settle into marriage with a remnant of the past and Sandhill. Ben Joe's marriage proposal lacks all storybook polish and conveys the flat bored tone that will be heard between most of Tyler's fictional couples. He says to Shelley, "We could . . . hell, get married. . . . Do you want to?" To which Shelley replies, "Well, I reckon so, . . . I just don't know." Somehow Ben Joe's "You won't be sorry?" is a weak hope that this marriage will succeed.[7]

Several reviewers heard echoes of Thomas Wolfe's moving but well-worn words, "You can't go home again," in Ben Joe's return, and Ben Joe's attempt to pick up life back home is disappointing. He discovers that he can do nothing to solve the family problems reported to him through his sister Jennifer's cryptic letters. Indeed, this house of women does not need him at all: his mother and sisters are busy in their individual pursuits, coping well in the aftermath of Phillip Hawkes's death. The notion that the surviving male is the linchpin to maintain household stability is dispelled. In fact, during the brief visit home Ben Joe sleeps an inordinate amount of time or is away from the house carrying on his curious courtship of Shelley. (In his dreams, as Voelker points out, Ben Joe begins to deal with the past of his father's double life and his death.) The marriage of Shelley and Ben Joe is the first of many pairs Tyler creates and sets along a course that Doris Betts describes as a "marriage of opposites" (Betts 1990, 2). Tyler's characters often marry totally unsuitable partners or at least enter marriage with an indifference that baffles, accepting a proposal with "Oh, well, why not" – words Tyler admits she used herself when she decided to marry. She quickly adds, however, that her own marriage – unlike the marriages of so many of her characters – "worked out" (Ridley, 23).

A small-town southern atmosphere pervades the novel, presenting an idyllic and nostalgic picture of the South barely touched by big-city changes. To Ben Joe's mind, Main Street in Sandhill "was wide and white and almost bare of cars; a few shopkeepers whistled cheerfully as they swept in front of their stores. . . . Except for the new hotel, there wasn't a single building over three stories high in the whole town. Above the squat little shops the owners' families lived, and their flowered curtains hung cozily behind narrow dark windows" (*Morning*, 41). Families like Ben Joe's live in a row of medium-sized, medium-aged houses where from the sidewalk you can see people moving behind lace curtains. On a summer night the sounds of television or radio reach the street if not drowned out by the squeaks of a cold porch glider (*Morning*, 93). Blacks still live on the other side of town, and those who shared the train car with Ben Joe from New York disappear at the station with their families. Tyler's description of the train-station waiting room in Sandhill is one window on the South less than a decade into integration: "The waiting room was divided in two by a slender post, with half the room reserved for white people and the other half for negroes. Since times had changed, the wooden letters saying 'White' and 'Colored' had been removed, but the letters had left cleaner places on the wall that spelled out the same words still" (*Morning*, 39). In the early 1960s those words were spelled clean on the walls everywhere a town was big enough for the train to stop.

The action of *If Morning Ever Comes* stretches over roughly a week, as family members intersect in present time and recall shared memories. Family scandals exist in small southern towns but are rarely acknowledged; abandoning his home, Ben Joe's father, Dr. Phillip Hawkes, is the first of several absent husbands in Tyler's fiction. Like Amanda Wingfield's husband in Tennessee Williams's *The Glass Menagerie* (1944) who deserts his family, Jeremy Pauling's father in *Celestial Navigation*, Morgan Gower in *Morgan's Passing*, Beck Tull in *Dinner at the Homesick Restaurant*, and Phillip Hawkes also abandon their families. Phillip Hawkes's involvement with Lili Belle (and the son he has by her) compromises his family, but despite the affair – which, in a small southern town, would certainly be gossiped if not discussed openly – the Hawkeses maintain their position in the community.

Tyler sets the novel's action several years after Phillip Hawkes has gone into his mistress's house (where he has subsequently died) and concentrates on the effect of the man's actions on his legitimate family. The six sisters of Ben Joe Hawkes rarely mention their father, and near the end of the novel readers share Ben Joe's surprise to learn that Jennifer has met Lili Belle. Indeed, rather than mailing the monthly check for Lili Belle's and the child's support, Jennifer takes the check in person and lingers to visit. Ben Joe faces the troublesome fact that, while his father was alive, he had chosen not to deliver a letter from Lili Belle to his father, sensing later that this decision caused his father's death. In great measure the novel focuses on that confrontation during his visit home when Ben Joe confesses to Lili Belle that he intercepted her magenta envelope. But Lili Belle dismisses what had burdened Ben Joe, declaring that 14 letters written and delivered would not have altered the way things turned out. Ben Joe has suffered because of his father's behavior, yet he also learns that in this case the other woman is no monster; she is likable and has made his father happy. He remembers in particular one night he had supper in the mill house where Phillip Hawkes often stayed with his mistress, a supper that reeked of the southern kitchen – "green beans cooked with fat back, hash brown potatoes in a puddle of Mazola, pork chops coated with grease that turned white when they cooled." But he watched as "his father ate more than Ben Joe had seen him eat in years" (*Morning*, 117).

In his 1991 story "The Fare to the Moon" Reynolds Price (Tyler's mentor at Duke) describes the meeting between the teenage Curtis and Leah, his father's nearly white but still black mistress. In a scene with all the potential for anger and hurt, Curtis admits to his friend Cally that "I flat-out liked her. I saw the damned point."[8] Ben Joe has the same experience but, still fighting the complicated family and social issues through his dreams, he cannot share Curtis's candor. Looking at the deserting husbands in Eudora Welty's *The Golden Apples* (1949) and in Anne Tyler's *Dinner at the Homesick Restaurant*, Carol S. Manning notes in particular the difficulty that Snowdie MacLain and Pearl Tull face. While Beck Tull in his dullness pales in comparison to the mythic King MacLain (as almost any character would), Manning suggests that both wives suffer and "in their pride keep close counsel with themselves."[9] And while Snowdie and Pearl have their flaws, they still, Manning argues, keep the house going, maintain order, and raise their children. All these women are in a sense sisters to Homer's Penelope, and even Penelope might well have been justified to greet the long-absent Odysseus with Snowdie

MacLain's consternation over King's return, "I don't know what to do with him" (Manning, 118).

Naturally Phillip's actions affect the women who reside in his house, especially his wife, Ellen, and his mother. Tension abounds with three generations of women under one roof, and unlike the usual case of the *wife's* mother moving in with her married daughter, here the *husband's* mother moves in and remains after her son has died. Furthermore, Ellen Hawkes does not fit the image of the typical southern daughter-in-law or mother. Bewildered that his sister Joanne has left her husband and come home with her baby, Ben Joe turns to his mother for details and explanation. Ellen's tone is matter of fact, and her course of action is simply "hands-off." Chiding Ben Joe for his anxiety, Ellen says, "Well, don't be so dramatic. . . . What's done is done, and it's none of our affair" (*Morning*, 19). Later in the novel Ellen lectures Ben Joe when he tries to encourage Joanne to reconcile the differences with her husband, Gary: "And it's her own business, Ben Joe – nothing we have any right to touch. I don't want to hear about your meddling in it" (*Morning*, 55). There was a time when separation and divorce were conditions a southern family did not mention; at the same time efforts were serious to keep troubled marriages from ending.

Ellen's tough exterior is partly foolish pride (she refused money from Phillip so that Ben Joe could attend Harvard as planned) and partly the reflection of an independence that is unconventional for a small-town southern woman in the 1960s. Ellen regularly has a Tom Collins after supper, sipping the drink one night while she incongruously leafs "through a *Ladies Home Journal*" (*Morning*, 251). Rather than taking full charge after her husband's sudden death, Ellen lets the household financial management go to her daughter Jennifer. In that role Jennifer operates most efficiently and complains to Ben Joe of Gran's expensive and improper shopping. Tyler superbly characterizes the overly serious Jennifer through the letters she writes to Ben Joe, and the letter becomes a consistent device in Tyler's novels as both a means of communication and a vehicle for character revelation. Part of a letter from Jennifer to Ben Joe shows her adult manner (diction from the stuffy business letter) and her dismay over her grandmother's lack of common sense; yet at the same time she asks the absent man of the house to solve the problem. It is quite clear that Jennifer can manage everything and that

Ben Joe, though here deferred to by a female in the family, lacks the power traditionally held by men of the house:

> We received yours of the 12th. . . .
>   I wish you would write a letter to the family suggesting that we go back to a policy of my doing the grocery shopping. Specially since it was me you left in charge of the money. . . .[Gran] gets anything she feels like, minced clams & pickled artichoke hearts & pig's feet & when I ask where are the meat & potatoes she says it's time we had a little change around here. She's ruining us.
>   Enclosed is next month's check for your expenses, etc. I hope you will remember to send a receipt this time as it will make my book-keeping neater. Enc. (*Morning*, 14)

The young Jennifer assumes adult responsibilities early, and her orderly household management makes her sound like an early version of Rose Leary in *The Accidental Tourist*. In fact, distinct traits of the Leary clan are evident in Tyler's first novel. For example, Shelley Dormer "had some sort of phobia about seeing that all the cannisters were neatly aligned along the counter and all measuring spoons were hung in order along on the wall according to their sizes" (*Morning*, 196). When Rose Leary puts away the groceries, the procedure is alphabetical – ant poison goes after allspice. And Ben Joe, as well as Charles, Porter, Macon, and Rose Leary, hates "using the telephone" (*Morning*, 16).

The most volatile confrontation between traditional rivals, a wife and her mother-in-law, occurs during Ben Joe's visit home. Gran, of course, champions her dead son, whose intent, she declares, was for Ben Joe to attend Harvard. Ellen's rejoinder carries controlled anger:

> "Your son could've had his say. If he'd come back he could've had his say and welcome *to* it, but what'd he do instead?" She was sitting up straight now, with one hand clasping her fork so tightly that the knuckles were white.
>   "Who made him like that?" Gran shouted. "Who made his house so cold he chose to go live in another, tell me that!"
>   Ben Joe cleared his throat. . . .
>   "And who didn't give a hoot he left?" Gran shouted triumphantly above Ben Joe. "Answer me *that*, now, answer me – "
>   "That will *do*, Gran," said Ellen Hawkes. (*Morning*, 67)

Gran considers Ellen cold-hearted, a judgment Joanne refutes. But Ellen is not the conventional mother whose love is obvious, whose signals are clear. Indeed, Ben Joe realizes that "you had to be a sort of detective with his mother; you had to search out the fresh-made bed, the flowers on the bureau, and the dinner table laid matter-of-factly with your favorite supper, and then you forgot her crisp manners" (*Morning*, 54).

If she is hurt because Phillip Hawkes lived with another woman, Ellen confides in no one, and this isolation recurs in Tyler's women characters. (Friendship among women in Tyler's fiction is curiously and somewhat disturbingly absent. There are interesting exceptions in *Celestial Navigation* and *Earthly Possessions*, where Mary Tell and Charlotte Emory are for a time close to their respective mothers-in-law; these friendships, however, are not long-lasting ones.) When neighbors attempt to give Ellen Hawkes advice, they fail. Shelley reports to Ben Joe about a fussy neighbor, Mrs. Murphy, who told Ellen all she needed to do was start crying and then "go to . . . um, where your father was at and tell him she wanted him back." Ellen had tossed her head and replied, "Who cared and offered Mrs. Murphy a slice of angel-food cake" (*Morning*, 103).

Ellen's sharp tongue is indeed funny, but it suggests that she will exert little effort to regain her husband. Ironically, this mother of many children does few motherly things. She does not worry about gentlemen callers for her older daughters and finds her son's hovering concern over the family irritating. Late in the novel Ellen announces a theme that Tyler will repeat in her fiction: "Everything," Ellen declares to Ben Joe, "works out on its own, with no effects from what anyone does" (*Morning*, 254). When Tyler published *The Clock Winder* (her fourth novel) in 1972, she discussed the precarious risk the protagonist in that novel takes because she assumes the role of a caretaker. Nearly a decade after she has Ellen Hawkes tell her son that our efforts do little to alter outcomes, Tyler, referring to Elizabeth Abbott in *The Clock Winder*, said, "I must find the idea of taking care of others attractive; there must be a place in life for people who do that. If I have to take a moral stand, though, I feel terribly strongly that nobody should do anything, that you should leave your hands out" (Ridley, 23).

In this first novel Ellen refuses to act or meddle to effect change; in Tyler's eleventh novel, *Breathing Lessons*, Maggie Moran doggedly works to make people change and, except in the most inconsequential ways, fails utterly. For all the delight in Tyler's humor, appealing characters, and interesting plots, it is important to see throughout her novels that characters had better see life realistically, face the fact that many things and most people will not, cannot, change. Ultimately one must endure and do so when husbands desert, wives run away, children die, and family dinners never do last from the soup to the dessert wine.

Although this sobering aspect runs throughout Tyler's fiction, humor also abounds, particularly in eccentric and quirky characters and the skillful use of details and dialogue. We learn that Phillip died at Lili Belle's, what Gran calls "another house," refusing to utter the name of her son's mistress. (Phillip had continued to maintain a presence in both of his "homes.") "Well, he didn't *mean* to go and die there," Ben Joe explains. "He'd just been drinking a little, is all. Went out to get ice cubes and then forgot which home he was supposed to be going back to. Mom explained that to Lili Belle" (*Morning*, 77). The point Ellen stresses is that Phillip died at Lili Belle's simply because he wandered there by mistake, not by choice or preference; to this analysis Joanne sensibly says, "Oh, pshaw."

Later family members vie with each other for the responsibility of Phillip's death. Gran, Ben Joe reports, "blamed herself forever for forgetting to refill the ice-cube trays. Says that's why he died – going downtown to get ice. Though Mom says he could have stepped next door if he'd been sober enough to think of it" (*Morning*, 125). When Lili Belle absolves Ben Joe's guilt over the intercepted letter, she describes her lover's death and underscores the impasse that kept Ellen and Phillip apart. Her words give a tone of sadness to the whole affair: "If your mother'd said one *word* he'd have stayed with her, always would have. He was just wanting her to ask him. But she didn't. . . . Then he came back to me, not even planning to but just drunk and tired, and I took him in" (*Morning*, 126). The narrative balance of the humorous and the serious is impressive; it is a balance Tyler maintains and sharpens in her subsequent work.

In her review of *If Morning Ever Comes* Diane Hobby pointed out the success of Tyler's first of many eccentric characters. Gran at age 80 goes through life wearing black tennis shoes, and during the course of the novel she works away at a project in the attic – she is making a gun belt. To Jennifer's dismay, Gran complicates the household budget: she insists on buying minced clams and pickled artichoke hearts when plain meat and potatoes are needed. Hobby perceptively places Gran in the long tradition of eccentric characters in fiction, a character type particularly accepted in the South. Of Gran, Hobby says, "ODD? NOT AT ALL, nor invented, either. Along with the 18th century English who considered a dotty member of the family no less a member for being dotty, Southern families, in fact and fiction, never imagined that they should be average by anyone else's standards."[10] In reviewing *Morgan's Passing* in 1980 Robert Tower discussed the changing perception of dotty characters. "Twentieth-century psychology," he notes, "has largely tainted the comfortable Victorian enjoyment of eccentric characters in fiction. . . . No doubt there are exceptions, but for the moment I can think of only two first-rate current writers who have successfully evaded the ban on colorfully eccentric characters. One is the octogenarian V. S. Pritchett, who might be regarded (quite wrongly) as a holdover from another era, and the other is the decidedly contemporary Anne Tyler."[11]

The dotty character entertains by willful and odd actions – actions that are incongruous, unexpected, offbeat. When such characters take up a topic, say education, their opinions often are outrageous and may not be taken altogether seriously. So when Gran holds forth outrageous overstatements and little logic abound: "Too much emphasis on brains in this family. What good's it do? Joanne quit after one year of college and the others, excepting Ben Joe, never went. And Ben Joe – look at him. He just kept trying to figure out what that all-fired mind of his was given him for, and first he thought it was for science and then for art and then for philosophy and now what's he got? Just a mish-mash, is all. Just nothing. Won't read a thing now but murder mysteries" (*Morning*, 66). Gran has a point. At this stage of his life Ben Joe has hardly grown up: he goes to law school not because he loves the law but because he thought that path a sure way to prepare himself to support this large family – a family, in fact, that does not need him. And certainly his marriage lacks planning and holds slim prospects for long-term happiness.

To Gran, education is "rubbish," and she considers her granddaughters smart to have avoided college. Ellen disagrees and soon the "Ben-Joe-didn't-get-to-go-to-Harvard" argument ensues. But the issue of education in Tyler's work calls attention to itself – or, I should say, to its relative unimportance. Considering Tyler's precocious and distinguished undergraduate years at Duke, her graduate study, and her insatiable reading as recorded in her published book reviews, it is ironic that her fictional characters – with very few exceptions – do not go to college, take their schoolchildren away without a thought about the math tests the child will miss, never really *read* books. The lack of education – and, worse, the lack of curiosity about books and learning – stunt many of Tyler's women characters intellectually. And the women in her fiction who strike out on their own or run away from home are hopelessly ill-prepared to earn a decent living for themselves much less, as in the case of Mary Tell, provide for a *houseful* of children.

Margaret Morganoth Gullette suggests that, for most of Tyler's women characters, the baby, not the husband, is the true sign of responsible adulthood. But rarely do these mothers give much thought to their children's schooling or to their own intellectual growth. Indeed, these women seem nonintellectual and, to some extent, see themselves as partial failures in parenting. The list extends from Lou Pike in *The Tin Can Tree* (1965), who loses one child and seriously neglects the other, to Maggie Moran in *Breathing Lessons* (1989), who refuses college or even nurse's training for herself, opting to remain a part-time aide in a retirement home. Her son is a high school dropout who cannot keep a job, and although Maggie and Ira's daughter is off to college at the end of the novel, we do not know if education remains significant in her life. Postfeminist readers do not find in Tyler's fiction liberated, independent, self-assured, educated women ready to claim an equal place (and pay) in work and the professional world. Even Jenny Tull in *Dinner at the Homesick Restaurant*, who completes medical school and is a practicing pediatrician, downplays rather than capitalizes on her professional accomplishments. When her brother Ezra points out how well she has done – "Look at you: a doctor" – Jenny is pleased inwardly but brushes the compliment aside, saying, "Oh, shoo, I'm nothing but a baby weigher" (*Dinner*, 200).[12]

Throughout Tyler's fiction the family is central and the various members of these families continually strive to connect and communicate with one another, generally with quite limited success. Their failures do not signal an absence of concern and love but do suggest over and over that even the closest people are still distinct, and in some ways blood kin are also strangers. Tyler expresses this lost connection in various images, and in this first novel Ben Joe describes his family's plight. He "felt confused and uncertain, as if he and his family were a set of square dancers coming to clap the palms of their hands to each other's, only their hands missed by inches and encountered nothing" (*Morning*, 20). The connection is very close but not close enough, and the opportunity is gone, forcing these characters to retreat alone into their private worlds. It is, of course, not a theme unique to Tyler, but it is certainly an effectively rendered part of her fiction.

The Tin Can Tree

Tyler's second novel, *The Tin Can Tree*, stays in North Carolina – in Larksville and nearby Caraway. Place here is much more precise than in *If Morning Ever Comes* primarily because Tyler uses considerable detail about tobacco growing and harvesting, still a major means of livelihood in eastern North Carolina in the 1960s. Tyler is much more ambitious with these characters, bringing forward a host of excellent minor characters and focusing the central action on the activities of tenants in a three-family dwelling. The thinness of the walls all but merges the lives of the Pikes (Roy and his wife, Lou, and Simon, their 10-year-old son, who is an only child now that Janie Rose has died); the Potter sisters; and the Green brothers, James and Ansel. The most vibrant character in the novel is Janie Rose, whose death in a tractor accident plunges her mother, Lou, into deep despair. While Tyler's novel does not have the moving poetic resonances of James Agee's posthumous 1957 novel, *A Death in the Family*, it does portray the tragic loss families suffer when a member dies. Agee presents Knoxville in the summer of 1915, and Tyler creates her semirural setting with impressive details, sharing with Agee the belief "that the life of the individual in the South in the twentieth century is mysterious and complex and a fitting subject for literature."[13]

The plot revolves around the death and funeral of Janie Rose, who had announced to her busy mother that she was going off to play, and Lou, not looking away from her sewing long enough, did not take in what the child had said. Now left to grief and guilt, Lou withdraws to her bedroom, where her cast-off garments lie where she let them fall. Roy Pike, usually a stolidly quiet man, talks softly and incessantly to his wife, trying to help her bear the grief. Their almost-forgotten son, Simon, lingers around the edges of their lives and this house, a lonely and sad little boy. When James Green, a photographer by profession, poses Simon to take his picture, the boy says he thinks he will just move away and board with James's family in Caraway. When James reminds him that his mother would miss him, Simon's reply shows what neglect he suffers: "I think," he says to James, "my mother'd say, '*Who* you say's gone? Oh, *Simon!*' she'd say. 'Him. My goodness. Did you remember the eggs?' "[14] Reconciliation for this part of the plot comes when Lou Pike pulls out of her stupor to ride with James to reclaim Simon. He does run off to Caraway and presents himself to the Green family there. The other plot thread – Joan Pike's frustrating romance with James Green – is not resolved, and Joan is left with a bleak future and slim prospects of a rich life. James will not free himself from his curious brother, Ansel, a most successful hypochondriac who, when he takes the notion, goes on all-night drinking binges.

Within this plot Tyler creates a domestic world of the three families, discreet yet united under one roof, a shared existence that later will be repeated in the boardinghouse of *Celestial Navigation*. The sharp details provide a literal legacy of Janie Rose, dead at age six, and while there is not perhaps the poignancy here that Tyler achieves with Ethan's death in *The Accidental Tourist* much later, the realization of Janie Rose and her childhood world is impressive. Even at age six, Janie Rose had been different and independent. Blond and fat with round pink cheeks and round thick glasses, Janie Rose hated the cold, and even in the middle of the summer, Simon soberly reports, had a 20-pound comforter on her bed. When she did have to wear a dress she refused to draw it down over her head because she was sure that process would make her invisible. And with her chubbiness, stepping into and drawing up a petticoat and a dress took effort.

The book's title comes from a religious phase Janie Rose went through, "a right short one, wouldn't you know," Ansel reports: "But she took this tree out back, this scrubby one she was always drawing flattering pictures of. Dedicated it to God, I believe; hung it with tin cans and popcorn strings. Didn't last but a week; then she was on to something new" (*Tree*, 133). Even though the tree decoration was an elaborate diversion, the flattering pictures she drew of this "scrubby tree" are perhaps more significant. Fat six-year-olds and scrubby trees need other images, and Janie Rose may do little for her own appearance, but through pictures and decoration she at least transforms the tree. It lingers throughout the novel as a reminder of her liveliness and her death. The birds eat the popcorn strings, but the tin cans remain, "still rattling at the ends of the branches when a wind passes through, and Mr. Pike sits out back all day staring at them" (*Tree*, 132).

The history of Janie Rose is captured in the stories of her escapades, such as the time she set fire to a large spot of the yard. It happened while she was crossing the yard dressed "in her mother's treasured wedding dress and holding a lighted cigarette high in front of her with her little finger stuck out" (*Tree*, 190). While her father and a neighbor struggled to stamp out the fire, Janie Rose "sat perched in the tin can tree, crying and cleaning her glasses with the lace hem of the wedding dress" (*Tree*, 191). Perhaps it was the temporary transformation wrought by the wedding dress that later prompted the first-grader Janie Rose to ask, " 'Do you think it's time I should be thinking of getting married?' And then she would smile hopefully, showing two front teeth so new that they still had scalloped edges, and everyone would laugh at her" (*Tree*, 209).

The affinity between brother and sister is extreme, and Simon is positively endearing in his sensitivity. On bad days Janie Rose found comfort in wearing multiple undershirts, sometimes so many that the straps of her overalls "would be strained to the breaking point over drawersful of shirts" (*Tree*, 38). At supper, Simon will quickly pinch the overall strap, testing out his sister's mood, "his way of asking how she was doing. If Janie was feeling all right by then she would just giggle at him, and he would laugh. But other days she jumped when he touched her and hunched up her shoulders, and then Simon would say nothing and fix all his attention on supper" (*Tree*, 38). The connection between these siblings is far stronger and more practical than the parents create between themselves and their children. Yet the parents never seem to acknowledge Simon's loss in the death of Janie Rose.

It is left to Roy Pike's niece, Joan, to pack up the life of the dead six-year-old, and she carries pasteboard boxes to the child's room.

The catalog is as realistic as it is heartbreaking. There was Janie Rose's collection from her jeans pocket still sitting on the edge of the tub where it had been left five nights ago – modeling clay, an Italian stamp, and a handful of peas stashed away during supper (*Tree*, 35). The closet held stacks of overalls, mostly hand-me-downs from Simon, and few dresses, because Janie Rose hated them. Lou Pike had "dreams of outfitting her in organdy and dotted swiss" and the closet held some pink and white things labeled " 'Little Miss Chubby' Mrs. Pike had bought when she wasn't along" (*Tree*, 36). Then the little girl's closet rack is empty, with only "a few hangers and some scattered bubble gum wrappers" (*Tree*, 37). On the shelves were "dolls, still shining and unused, a pack of candy Chesterfields, and an unbreakable plastic record ordered off a cereal box" (*Tree*, 37). On the bed is a teddy bear named Ernest and in the dresser drawer lie sachet bags of lemon, verbena, lavender, rose petals, as well as her mother's empty perfume bottles, an unexpected collection since Janie Rose "had still smelled only of Ivory soap and Crayolas" (*Tree*, 38).

Place in *The Tin Can Tree* reflects the changing South. The little town of Larksville has a main street hidden behind trees, with the post office, the tavern across the street, and the drug store/bus stop within this inviting shady green section. Outside the town limits, however, houses and tobacco fields are exposed to full sun. Economic and population shifts are felt here because the tobacco fields get smaller each year, and the younger people who do go off to college find work elsewhere and do not return to plant and harvest tobacco. It is hot July, and Roy, laid off from his construction job for the entire month, and Joan, whose high school secretary's job ended with the school term, help Mr. Terry gather his tobacco crop. Nearby Caraway is similar, the old small-town image reflected in a barbeque house in the middle of nowhere with pigs chasing each other in the neon lights; newer phases of life appear in the brick ranch houses rising out of North Carolina red clay, drive-in restaurants, a Dairy Queen, and an all-night grill where the bus stops.

It is the summer tobacco work that Tyler renders with particular vividness through several excellent minor characters. The tying-shed work Tyler did briefly in her youth, and she describes it in detail and with immediacy, deftly recording the sounds of women's voices, impressively weaving their conversations in and out, centering on a

black woman named Missouri, who starts out to explain how Mrs.
Pike can recover from her grief and lassitude.[15] Missouri digresses
here and there and must be prompted with the word ("sitting") to
remind her of the point. Interwoven in her analysis (Mrs. Pike has
been sitting too long, and her salvation will be to get up and resume
her sewing for customers) is the process of the women tying tobacco
leaves and the helpers like Joan and Missouri's daughter Lily count-
ing leaves and handing them to the tobacco-tyers, Mrs. Hall and Missouri. Since Mrs. Hall is the fastest tobacco-tyer in the county, two
women hand leaves to her; a third woman and Joan hand leaves to
Missouri, who enjoys the competition.

    Missouri stands "at the end of her rod with her broad bare feet
spraddle-toed in the dust, and first she yanked a handful of leaves
from her daughter Lily and then from Joan, wrapping each handful to
the rod with one sure circling of the twine so that the leaves hung
points-down and swinging" (*Tree*, 93). If Lily and Joan are slow
handing over the leaves, Missouri clicks her tongue in reproach and
holds "the twine taut in her fingers and when the leaves were ready
she would take them with an extra hard yank and bind them so hard
that the twine cut the stems" (*Tree*, 93). Bickering arises because
Mrs. Hall and Missouri tie differently, each claiming her pattern is
better. "What it is . . . ," Missouri says to Mrs. Hall, "I bind *across* the
stick. You bind on the same side, and I declare I don't see how. With
Miss Joan on the left, I take her leaves and bind them on the right,
and backwards from that with Lily. You follow my meaning?" (*Tree*,
93). Mrs. Hall follows all right because Missouri's way is, she
declares, inefficient – it produces three inches of wasted motion
with every bunch she ties. And so on they continue. When Missouri
prepares to start a new stick, "she tie[s] the white twine around the
end farthest from her and then snap[s] it off at a length of five feet or
so, while Mrs. Hall stop[s] tying to watch her. (Mrs. Hall spent every
day of every tobacco season trying to figure out how Missouri
snapped off her twine ahead of time without measuring it)" (*Tree*,
94).

    For their part of the operation, Lily and Joan group the leaves
"together by the stems, a small cluster at a time, so that they lay flat
against each other" and then hold them out for Missouri. Each time
Missouri takes leaves, "there was a funny numb feeling in Joan's finger tips from the leaves sliding across layers and layers of thick

tobacco gum on her skin" (*Tree*, 98). The fingers may feel numb
from the tar, but Missouri is impatient and calls out that Mrs. Hall is
"a stick and a half ahead of me, and you two are poking along. Hurry
it up, Lily" (*Tree*, 100).

A finished stick of tobacco leaves, whichever method of tying is
used, looks, Tyler says, "like one long chain of hanging green leaves,
with the rod itself hidden from sight by the thick stems that stuck up
on every side" (*Tree*, 93). When the last bunch of leaves has been
tied, the tobacco is ready to be transported to the curing barn, a job
the men, not the women, do. Jimmy Terry comes for the finished
rods and "lift[s] the stick from its notched stand and [stands] making
faces because of the weight of it, holding it very carefully so as not to
crush the leaves" (*Tree*, 93-94). Once the wooden sled is piled high
with the tied tobacco leaves, the mule balks at the weight, and the
exchange over the mules and names and owners further adds to this
rural work scene: "'I never,' Missouri went on. 'Jefferson, you no-
good you,' she told the mule, 'you going to keep us waiting all day?'"
Mr. Terry relates that this mule is not Jefferson but his brother's
mule, Man O' War. Missouri may or may not know the famous race
horse that shared this name, but as for the mule at hand, Missouri
does not "care who he is" (*Tree*, 95). And once the men deliver the
last load to the curing barn, they retreat to the house and drink beer
while the women continue tying, a division of labor that no one
questions. But at least Missouri has her say: "In the end, it's the
women that work" (*Tree*, 95).

The tobacco field, tying shed, and curing barn represent a distinct way of life, and a pervasive symbol in Tyler's novel is the
tobacco gum that layers the workers' hands until they are numb. The
tobacco gum covers Joan's forearms as well as her hands, works its
way between the straps of her sandals, and finds its way to the soles
of her feet. When the workday ends her steps homeward leave tell-
tale signs of tobacco – little black marks as tar flicks from her shoes.
The tobacco shed even enters her dreams: there she sees "tables full
of tobacco leaves, stack upon stack of yellow-green leaves with their
fine sticky coating of fuzz and their rough surfaces that reminded her
of old grained leather on book covers" (*Tree*, 98). When Joan relates
details of these dreams, her Aunt Lou retorts sharply, reminding her
of the social stigma associated with tobacco workers: "Nobody
asked you to do it. I even told you, I said it right out. I didn't want

you doing it. Secretaries don't work tobacco, honey" (*Tree* 99). Missouri, Lily, and Mrs. Hall, we assume, will forever tie tobacco leaves, but Joan differs from them and irks her aunt by doing this July work. Work and social status correlate, or at least they are supposed to.

Chapter 5 centers on Missouri's opening remark about Lou Pike's listless state: "I don't believe in sitting. I have never believed in sitting. Minute a person sits his mind gives away" (*Tree*, 92). Mrs. Pike's work is taking in sewing, work Missouri says she must resume. Young Simon will be crucial, she thinks, because he can stay around and make the early conversation with the customer, saving his mother. Missouri declares that Simon is

> "the only one can help now. Not hot tea, not people circling round. Not even her own husband. Just her little boy."
>
> "I don't see how," said Joan.
>
> Missouri made an exasperated face. "*You* don't know," she told her. "You don't know how it would work out. Bravest thing about people, Miss Joan, is how they go on loving mortal beings after finding out there's such a thing as dying. Do I have to tell you that?"

Charlene leans over the tobacco table to say, "Well, I'll be, . . . I never. Was *that* what you did all this talking to say?" And Missouri's sublime answer is a simple "It was" (*Tree*, 106). Missouri's pronouncement dominates and resounds with the authority of truth that cannot be denied. One can only wonder whether Eudora Welty (long an admirer of Anne Tyler's work), pondering character names for *The Optimist's Daughter*, remembered the name of Tyler's splendid minor character. In Welty's quintessential novel of love, loss, grief, and reconciliation she named the clear-eyed, practical, and dependable servant in the McKelva household Missouri.

Joan Pike is one of Tyler's many women characters who have little in common with their parents. Her late-middle-aged parents treat her like a guest and have little idea what to say when she is around. Her mother failed to teach her ordinary domestic skills, and Joan has grown up without ever having learned to keep house. Joan lives with her uncle and his family to escape unhappiness in her own home. She maintains her room as she would a motel room, and although she tries to keep house during the crisis of Janie Rose's death, she remains an outsider. Her attempts to escape her frustrating courtship with James Green and the limited routine with her uncle's family are futile. When she decides to leave, her destination is her parents' home, where obviously she has no real life. When she begins this journey and is waiting for the bus, she "decided she might as well go to a movie first and by the time the movie was over she had changed her mind, and come home again, dragging two big suitcases behind her and hobbling along in her dressup shoes" (*Tree*, 176). Impulse and indecision mark Joan's life, whereas James's inability to act keeps their romance from flourishing. When she presses the question of marriage with James, she argues that they "could be someone besides an old familiar couple that'll be courting when they're seventy and the town's fondest joke"; as she says this she asks James if he is listening. "No" is his reply (*Tree*, 121). And perhaps if they do marry someday, they will find that they have, after all this wait, simply made a marriage of opposites.

Details and speech patterns make even the minor characters in *The Tin Can Tree* lively and appealing. The Potter sisters are the dotty characters here, decked out in hat and gloves when their journey is merely around the side of the porch to the Pikes' or the Greens' door. They will give more than precise detail for trivial concerns – "It was three twenty exactly [when Ansel left their house]," says Miss Faye. "It was my turn to wear the brooch-watch today" (*Tree*, 118). Trying to get factual information from the sisters is a difficult task, as James discovers when he asks them where Ansel went when he left their house. Monologue for them becomes performance: "He didn't say. Well, you know how he is. Some days the world is just too much for him. That's how he put it. 'Miss Faye,' he said, 'some days the world is just too much for me.' He told Lucy that too. 'Miss Lucy,' he said, 'some days the – ' " And to little avail, James asks again, "Did he say where he was going?" (*Tree*, 118). As many readers have noted, Tyler's characters have the speech tag of "Well," a delaying word that holds conversation in abeyance and allows characters time to think what to say next, if anything. A typical example comes in a conversation between James Green and Simon as James tries to provide diversion for the unhappy boy.

    "I almost forgot," [James] said. "You want to see my pictures?"
      "Oh, well I – "
      "They're good ones."
      "Well." (*Tree*, 21)

Sharp detail of ordinary domestic life enhances the realism of character and place. Joan peers "into the glass knob on top of the percolator to see what color the coffee was" and then stirs the coffee "with a kitchen knife that was handy" (*Tree*, 140, 141). The Pikes' kitchen is cluttered. No curtains hang at the windows, whose sills are "littered with lost buttons and ripening tomatoes." Behind the stove some twenty or thirty drawings have been "scotch taped so closely together they might have been wall paper." Those Simon produced show soldiers, knights, masked men with guns; those from Janie Rose are all "the same lollipop-shaped tree with hundreds of tiny round apples on it" and all signed "Miss J. R. Pike" (*Tree*, 42-43). In Caraway the tasteless furnishings in the Greens' house mirror the tension that surrounds the family. When Lou enters this house to recover Simon, Tyler describes the living room: the small fireplace with marble mantelpiece, "the linoleum rug with the roses painted on it, the bead curtains, the turquoise walls made up of tongue-and-groove slats, a Seth Thomas clock on the mantel, a picture of Jesus knocking at the door, and a glass plate that looked like lace" (*Tree*, 251). Lou has eyes only for Simon, but the reader can size up the Greens pretty well by their living room.

The Tin Can Tree is an early novel with much evidence of the talent Tyler readers now take for granted: plots that *are* believable lies, characters that invite the reader's concern, dialogue and detail that reveal and inform, humor that weaves in and out. Most of all this novel is about dealing with grief – grief made especially hard since the death is that unexpected reversal, the accidental death of a young and lively child. The parents must come to terms with the loss and so must young Simon. Thrown in the role of comforter to the family, Joan bluntly admits that she simply has no idea how to go about comforting people. She perhaps knows better than she thinks, or, at least on a walk to town while she and Simon discuss his lost ball, her candor cuts through and helps the child take in and accept the loss. As they walk along, Simon says that about right here "is where I lost that ball. Will you keep a lookout for it?" Joan assures him that she will, and he asks, "Do you reckon I'll ever find it?" Joan replies, "No." And Simon faces the fact by saying, "I don't either" (*Tree*, 54).

The first novels Tyler published indicated that her focus would be on the infinite variety of experiences that families encounter. Her characters face disappointment and often tragedy, and most of them do so with courage and good humor. Her early work impressed reviewers and pleased many readers, a pattern that her mature work has repeated with growing success and recognition.

Chapter Four

Yellow Means Funny

In reviewing *The Accidental Tourist* for the *New Yorker*, John Updike praised Tyler's novels because they stress endurance. Characters survive both trivial and serious events, and some do so with high spirits, good humor, and appealing eccentric ways – Morgan Gower, Justine Peck, Muriel Pritchett, Maggie Moran, to name but four. "If," Updike wrote, "Anne Tyler strikes us as too benign, too swift to tack together shelter for her dolls, it may be that we have lost familiarity with the comedic spirit, the primal faith in natural resilience and the forces of renewal."[1] Certainly Anne Tyler possesses the spirit of comedy; humor glitters on the pages of her work, and her assessment of the humor in the books she reviews serves as a helpful commentary on the humor and comic devices she uses herself. In discussing James Wilcox's *Modern Baptists* Tyler wrote that "every reviewer, no doubt, has methods for marking choice passages in a book. Mine is a system of colored paper clips; yellow means funny."[2] Reading Wilcox's book, Tyler wrote, "I laughed so hard I kept forgetting my paper clips."

The Gamut of Humor

Wilcox, according to Tyler, uses stock comic devices to perfection: "in addition, there's a sense of particularity" by which he endows a quite incidental place or fact or gesture with full individualism ("Lonely," 22). A choice example of Wilcox's success, Tyler noted, is a borrowed car and the oddly named character Burma: "Burma doesn't just drive a borrowed car; she drives a car that's been taken from her nephew as punishment for getting his navel tattooed" ("Lonely," 22). Although the characters in Mary Robison's story collection *Days* (1979) lead bleak lives, humor abounds, and again Tyler sees that humor coming from "particularity, from the absurd

66

irrelevance of individual events and conversations."[3] For example, in Robison's stories, "people cry and trim their toe nails," "study the washing instructions inside their swimsuit bras," "stare at the dishwasher hose" ("Bleak Lives," 13). Tyler assumes – as Robison surely does – that the reader will take in the absurd or ridiculous act – those human foibles that are humorous. To a great extent, humor (as Mark Twain declares in "How to Tell a Story") depends on timing, and in *Days* Tyler finds that "everything is precisely speared, with no wasted motion" ("Bleak Lives," 13), suggesting that the humorous passages come at the right moment and carry only what is needed.

The stories in T. R. Pearson's *Off for the Sweet Hereafter* (1986), Tyler says, contain humor that could be written "only by a Southerner. Certainly the constant straying from 'What Happened' to 'Who Exactly It Happened To' (and 'Who His Grandfather Was,' besides) seems distinctly if not uniquely Southern as does the ambling, wry tone."[4] Tyler finds Pearson's humor as technically the best sort because it "seems organic, built-in, almost unintended, which is as it ought to be." The biggest joke Pearson pulls off, Tyler thinks, is the writing style itself: "the first sentence is 407 words" ("Firesheets," 9). The essential particularity usually rests in a simple detail that juxtaposes two things so as to make humor inevitable. (It is indeed funny to picture someone staring intently at the dishwasher hose or studying those washing instructions for a swimsuit that might still be damp from the pool.) Tyler says that in *Another Part of the Wood* (1980) Beryl Bainbridge writes "like a schoolgirl fighting off the giggles. . . . [She] begins her stories with a determinedly straight face, plods virtuously forward – and then her sharp eye is snagged by some unlikely detail and all is lost. How can I stay serious, she seems to be asking, when people behave so absurdly?"[5] And Tyler finds an unlikely and humorous episode when Bainbridge relates that "a romantic tryst is interrupted by the death of a hamster" ("Wicked Mind," F4). In *Inquiring Time* (1978) Bainbridge shows that "wacky things do happen" and successfully lures the reader into accepting ludicrous details one by one: for instance, absurd as it may seem, there *are* "baked apples behind her refrigerator."[6] Tyler sees Bainbridge's novels confirming "over and over, our lurking suspicion that life may be nothing more than one long pratfall" ("Chaos," G3), generally funnier, however, to the observer than to the victim.

Tyler's review of two volumes by Dame Rebecca West, *The Young Rebecca: Writings of Rebecca West, 1911-1917* and *1900*, is entitled "The Wit and Wisdom of Rebecca West." The humorous and witty passages Tyler cites lead her to observe that West's humor often brought discomfort as well as delight. Writing in 1982 before West died, Tyler identified the English writer's "trademarks" as "a fierce social conscience, a wicked wit, and a stubborn refusal to accept the going fairy tale. Her style is so fresh and vital that it comes as a shock to realize she's been employing it publicly since 1909."[7] Tyler quotes from West's book reviews to illustrate the wicked wit that makes the reader smile, and only after the whole point has sunk in does one feel the discomfort. One writer, West said, has "the solemn yet hiccupy style peculiar to bishops" and another "does not so much split his infinitives as disembowel them" ("Wisdom," 55). West, Tyler says, shows "what the English language can accomplish, when put to proper use," and she has "the liveliest sense of humor imaginable. It creeps up on you. You're dutifully learning about Colonial Secretary Chamberlain, who was the descendant of boot manufacturers, when you're told that 'by a curious coincidence he himself looked like a single, highly polished boot.' Like a *what*?" ("Wisdom," 56).

If Rebecca West's sharp wit often drew blood, it is a reminder that comedy and tragedy lie close together and that often one merges into the other as Tyler thinks Muriel Spark readily shows in *Territorial Rights* (1979). Spark's humor, Tyler finds, derives primarily "from her sharp-eyed, unflinching observation of human frailty."[8] She makes readers laugh, Tyler says, shake our heads, laugh again, and then we're suddenly struck, almost physically, by what has been going on beneath the surface: " 'Why,' we think, 'this matters after all; it's more serious than it looks' " (Spark review, 36). It is true, Tyler says in reviewing Bernice Rubens's *Sunday Best* (1980), "that humor can abruptly change to tragedy."[9]

Humor in fiction seems to draw most reviewers' attention, and certainly it draws the attention of Tyler, who comments on it with pleasure in her book reviews. And the complicated and delightful humor in Anne Tyler's novels mirrors her wry and ironic view of the world and its people. Humor allows her to look at many issues and many types of people (including preachers), and to do so without rancor or bitterness. Tyler's humor, as she has said of Muriel Spark's, runs the gamut from "dry tongue-in-cheek . . . to belly-laugh comedy" (Spark review, 36).

Humor with the Clergy

Seldom in her fiction, so far as I can tell, does Eudora Welty depict a preacher or a church scene without humor abounding. The same can be said of Anne Tyler. When Tyler sets a scene in a church or brings a minister on stage, a sacred atmosphere is not the point. Only with the publication of *Saint Maybe* (1991) does Tyler present the topic of religion in a serious vein. This novel marks a distinct departure as far as religion is concerned.

Tyler's Quaker background perhaps furnishes the starting point for a funny religious scene in *Searching for Caleb*. The novel begins in Baltimore's lovely old Roland Park neighborhood, which Tyler populates with the Peck clan. Their wealth a generation old, the Pecks build sturdy houses, drive sensible black Fords, make money, suspect strangers, and eschew frivolity. The mavericks in the family include Caleb Peck, who disappears one day and is not searched for until decades later when his brother Daniel, retired, nearly deaf, and lonely, undertakes the task. Daniel is assisted in the search by his granddaughter Justine (another maverick), who marries her first cousin Duncan (legal in Maryland, as the lawyer Daniel announces) and leads an existence totally different from the Peck way of life in Roland Park. Justine's restlessness is permanent, and it is ironic that Daniel, with his brushed trousers, high-collar shirt, and symbolic wristwatch, takes up temporary residence with these always-mobile grandchildren. But he does so because Justine will hop on any train with him to follow a lead. He silently overlooks their domestic disorder so that he can search for Caleb.

Humor in the novel takes many forms and uses many subjects. When Tyler is satiric, she bears down on religion, though never in a malicious tone. The peripatetic Justine, for example, takes a Sunday excursion just to be on the go, and she drags her grandfather along to a Quaker meeting even though his religious leanings are not in that direction. Daniel had stopped going to his own church because the minister did not speak loud enough for him to hear. Thus the silence of a Quaker meeting suits him fine, although when a member rises to speak, Daniel loudly whispers to Justine, "What?" On a 3 X 5 memo pad Daniel keeps handy, Justine jots down the speaker's words: "He says that God must have made even Nixon," or "Peace is not possible as long as neighbors can still argue over a lawn mower," to which Daniel exclaims, "*That* took him five minutes?"[10]

Elsewhere in *Searching for Caleb* Tyler presents ministers who lack both conviction and personality. When Justine and Duncan marry, the officiating minister is reluctant to perform the ceremony after Duncan declares that "Christianity was a dying religion. ('It's the only case I know of where *mental* sins count too; it'll never sell,' he said, 'Take it from me, get out while the getting's good')" (*Caleb*, 109). (This notion of Duncan's will find a completely opposite expression in *Saint Maybe*.) The minister goes right on with the ceremony, not from religious convictions but because he could not disappoint "Lucy Hodges Peck, whose family he had known down South" (*Caleb*, 114). It seems altogether fitting that Duncan's courtesy envelope for the Reverend Didicott contains only $50 – in Confederate money.

Far more serious is the humor surrounding the Reverend Arthur Milsom, an assistant minister in Semple, Virginia, whose every move is planned by his Thurberesque mother. (The wordplay in Semple-Simple may well be aimed at Arthur.) This dreadful woman is a self-proclaimed faith healer who cannot – as Duncan points out – heal her own son's sick headaches. The brief courtship of Arthur Milsom and Meg Peck (Justine and Duncan's only child) is ludicrous. Like Evie Decker (*A Slipping-Down Life*) and Mary Darcy (*Celestial Navigation*), Meg marries before she ever gets around to double dates, matching shirts, or the junior-senior prom. Meg surely cannot *love* Arthur Milsom with his anemic demeanor and his subservience to his mother. But marry him she does – elopes, leaving Justine a note that carries along with the marriage announcement the news that Meg will finish high school in Semple.

This subplot reaches its climax when Justine, Duncan, and Daniel pay their first call on Meg after her marriage. Inside the Milsom house Daniel quickly spies pictures of Christ gazing out of gilt frames on every wall, a mark of "poor taste," he had been taught, unless the art is original (*Caleb*, 221). They all settle in for the visit. Arthur is napping, and his mother, not his wife, explains that the extreme pressure of being an assistant minister has brought on another sick headache. Mrs. Milsom had refused to listen when Meg (called Margaret in this house) had explained that Justine could not drink iced tea if sugar has been added. Mrs. Milsom has heaped sugar into the pitcher because she knows that everybody likes it that way. Tea with sugar literally makes Justine gag, but on this occasion she feels she must drink it anyway. Her system immediately cries out for something sour, and relief is literally in front of her – a bowl of sour balls on the coffee table. She seizes a lemon one to counteract the sugar and pops it into her mouth. The sour ball, alas, is a glass marble, an observation everyone else in the room had already made. Justine is left to get the marble out of her mouth and back into the dish on the table while the rest of the room watches. She does so and simply adds another word to the previous banal remarks about the weather. The reader watches the scene acknowledging Justine's discomfort as well as the humor her mistake provides.

Duncan displays a touch of the charm that made him an irresistible child, and Daniel shows his perfect manners, but the visit tells the story of Meg the captive wife, a point that is deadly serious. She says to her mother in a brief moment of privacy, "I live among *crazy* people!" (*Caleb*, 229). At 18 Meg knows her youth is over because Mrs. Milsom will see to it that Meg is trained to be Arthur's helpmeet, his "buffer," not an individual with strong, independent opinions. No part of the young couple's life will be theirs alone. Indeed, Meg reports to Justine, Mrs. Milsom even makes up their bed; it seems Meg did not know how to replicate hospital-bed corners. Little wonder, since Meg's experience was limited to her mother's housekeeping example. When it came to the laundry, Justine waited until every item was dirty and then went off to the laundromat to wash everything save the clothes they wore. Sheets straight from the laundromat dryer to the bed just did not get hospital corners at Justine's hands.

The sharp humor that sparkles from these scenes is counterpointed nevertheless with Meg, who had never enjoyed the vagabond existence her parents lead. As a young child she created her own order: she ironed her clothes and washed her hair according to a schedule; she owned the only alarm clock in the house. When Justine announces yet another of their countless moves, Meg protests: "At least we should consider my schooling. . . . This is my senior year. I won't learn a thing, moving around the way we do."

Justine disagrees and argues that teaching Meg to adapt is the best possible education. Meg thinks otherwise: "Adapt! What about logarithms?" (*Caleb*, 21). At 18 Meg makes a decision that will affect the rest of her days. She leaves her parents' home and marries the silly and spineless Arthur Milsom. Justine and Duncan see what a dreadful mistake Meg has made and are powerless – or, one should say, *choose* to be powerless – to help Meg escape. Justine ends this visit with Meg as surely a prisoner as any captive maiden has ever been, and she gives her daughter no means of escape. Duncan, who usually acts without considering the consequences, tells Meg that she should simply leave Arthur and his dreadful mother. Justine's view is different, and these parents leave their child with nothing more than words. Although Duncan had given Meg strong advice, Justine demurs:

> "Meggie darling, maybe you could just – or look at it this way. Imagine you were handed a stack of instructions. Things that you should undertake. Blind errands, peculiar invitations . . . things you're supposed to go through, and come out different on the other side. Living with a faith healer. *I* never got to live with a faith healer."
> "That's what you're going to tell your daughter," Duncan said.
> "Just accept whatever comes along? Endure? Adapt?"
> "Well – " (*Caleb*, 229)

That tag of Anne Tyler's fiction: "Well – " The character chooses to delay, to defer action, to wait. Justine and Duncan simply can do no better, and they leave Meg to "endure" rather than to engage in a life that might bring her real happiness and satisfaction.

As I noted earlier, Tyler has said she has nothing against ministers per se but simply against ministers (and anyone else) who think they have the right to change other people's lives. As a subject, ministers generally provide Tyler the opportunity for humor, nowhere funnier than in the Brother Hope episode in her third novel, *A Slipping-Down Life*. Brother Hope, a red, knotty-faced man who perpetually looks "like a man swelling with anger but choking it back," is a storefront preacher who discovers his sermon texts in conversations he overhears or in newspaper headlines. Spiritual meditation and growth are not part of his ministry.

Tyler remembered a newspaper story about a Texas girl who carved "ELVIS" in her flesh out of, one assumes, misguided admiration. (In Tyler's 1966 unpublished novel, "Winter Birds, Winter Apples," the character Bridget remembers a classmate named Lola Wilson who carved her boyfriend's name on her wrist with a pocket knife. One only hopes the name was short.) These episodes furnish a starting point for Tyler's character Evie Decker in *A Slipping-Down Life*, who carves CASEY in jagged letters on her forehead and thus begin the events that lead to the marriage of Evie, an overweight high school girl, and Drumstrings Casey, a peculiar and uneducated musician. Because the local newspaper carries the story of Evie's self-mutilation, Drum gains brief notoriety for the Unicorn Club where he performs; it also provides Brother Hope with sermon material. So Evie, Drum, and the drummer-musician David go to the Tabernacle located "on Main Street, an old white clapboard house standing between a pizzeria and a shoe repair shop" (*Life*, 176). A signboard in the Tabernacle yard announces the number of converts every day.

Typically Brother Hope launches into his sermon, telling the 40-odd gathering that they are on a sinking ship. His sermon topics reflect his superficial approach: "One-Way Street," "Do You Have a Moment," and "For Heaven's Sake." The night Evie, Drum, and David attend Brother Hope's sermon the topic is "What Next?" His despair rises as he catalogs the sins of the wayward world: "Today there are women wearing the garb of men, men in the stupors from the fumes of alcohol and the taste of foreign mushrooms, dancers dancing obscenities in public and everywhere, on every corner of the earth, sacrifices made to false gods and earthly idols. What next? What next?"[11] Well, it does look pretty bad, especially the consumption of foreign mushrooms. Then he launches into examples close to home in Pulqua, North Carolina. He recounts a fatal accident caused when a young man's car hit a Good Humor truck. Brother Hope is certain that because marijuana was found in the glove compartment, the young man was a drug addict. Then Brother Hope moves on to Evie Decker's story, telling the gathering that "a young girl living within your own town limits slashed her forehead with the name of a rock-and-roll singer; ruined her life for nothing. If you don't believe me, her name was Evie Decker" (*Life*, 180).

Evie protests by rising rather grandly to challenge this preacher of doom with his ironic name of Brother Hope. Things in her life were not ruined at all, she argues; she married the singer. Evie does not need the likes of Brother Hope, and, as several critics have suggested, she now begins to take charge of her life. Her prospects for the future are limited at best, however, when the novel ends. Her father conveniently dies, leaving his house for Evie. Drum refuses to move there with her, so Evie, a high school dropout, overweight and pregnant, starts her new life alone. Although I find the chances slim for her to rise in the world and to raise the child properly, she at least asserts herself and leaves the preacher hanging.

It is interesting to contrast Brother Hope's preaching scene with a scene in Flannery O'Connor's first novel, *Wise Blood* (1952), where a southern street preacher, Onnie Jay Holy, is another version of Brother Hope. Onnie Jay collects a street crowd just to pass the hat, urging them to join his Holy Church of Christ without Christ where they can interpret the Bible entirely for themselves. No dogma here. Onnie Jay longs for his guitar so that he can sing the crowd to Jesus: everything, he says, is just so much easier with music. This brash, superficial preaching with no spiritual substance darkens in O'Connor's novel to focus on Hazel Motes and his Oedipal confrontation with grace. Brother Hope may be Onnie Jay's fictional kin, but Tyler concentrates on the episode as comedy, as satiric social commentary on the triteness of slick religion. In addition, the Brother Hope episode represents a major Tyler theme: if change is to come, it must come from within the individual, not through the imposition of someone else's influence. In *Saint Maybe*, however, while the drastic change in Ian Bedloe's life does come from within, it is certainly encouraged by strong and precise advice from the Reverend Emmett.

In the South (and perhaps elsewhere) the initials "P.K." stood for "preacher's kid," and those so labeled were by their behavior supposed to reflect their father's serious calling. In *The Clock Winder* the Reverend Abbott suffers because his daughter Elizabeth does not fit the expected mold of a P.K. Elizabeth is not like the Baptist housewives who flock to the front of the church at the call to "Stand Up, Stand Up for Jesus" and are received by Elizabeth's father who "smiled down at them, mentally entering their names on a list that would last forever."[12] Elizabeth wonders what happens if they change their minds in the morning and refuse to join the flock. Elizabeth takes a wide berth from converts like the girlfriend of hers who rushed to the church front "three times before she was fourteen" and thought that religious experience centered in her simply telling fewer lies and loving her mother more and giving up her worldly possessions. Tyler catalogs those possessions with a sharp eye for detail: bangle bracelets and bubblebath, movie magazines, adjustable birthstone rings from Dick Tracy candy boxes. When a visiting minister comes to preach, Elizabeth's friend is completely overcome: "Oh, how could you just *sit* there? . . . With that preacher's voice so thundery and your father so quiet and shining. This has changed my whole life"; the narrator adds, "Although it never did, for long" (*Clock*, 149). Tyler's theme again: forced change is generally shallow and wrong.

The sign outside the Reverend Abbott's church reads, "FAITH BAPTIST CHURCH. THE DIFFERENCE IS WORTH THE DIFFER-ENCE," a phrase Elizabeth never could get straight. Later in the novel when her Baltimore employer, Mrs. Emerson, asks Elizabeth what her father does, she answers, "He's a minister." Mrs. Emerson replies, "Nothing wrong with *that*. Although a lot depends on the denomination. What denomination is he?" When Elizabeth says "Baptist," Mrs. Emerson has no response except "Oh" (*Clock*, 13). The distance between Episcopalians and Baptists in the South has been a matter of humor at least since the encounter of Faulkner's Miss Emily Grierson and the Baptist minister in "A Rose for Emily."

At one point it looks as if Elizabeth may after all take up the role of the minister's proper daughter. She agrees to marry her Sandhill sweetheart, Dommie Whitehill, and the wedding plans move forward. But when the sound of the organ rises to announce the bride, "what it played was not the traditional march but . . . the wedding music from [Prokofiev's] *Lieutenant Kije*," music based on a story whose delightful plot of deception serves as a subtext for Elizabeth's pseudo-wedding (*Clock*, 221; my ellipses). The Reverend Abbott begins the ceremony, the music notwithstanding, with "Dearly beloved" and puts on "a whole new tone of voice in front of a con-gregation" (*Clock* 221). Despite the preparations and the ceremony being under way, when the Reverend Abbott asks, "Do you, Eliza-beth Priscilla . . . " Elizabeth's answer is "I don't. . . . I'm sorry, I just don't." Then she "turned around, and the organ gave a start and wheezed into *Lieutenant Kije* again. Elizabeth came down the aisle slowly and steadily with her nosegay held exactly right and her head perfectly level" (*Clock*, 222). So, Elizabeth Abbott escapes life in the Faith Baptist Church where her sister Polly, newly married and already pregnant, is, as Mrs. Abbott reports, "real active in the Young Wives Fellowship" and will doubtless follow her mother's example of preparing frozen casseroles for the sick and praising her father's sermons.

Unlike Meg Peck, Elizabeth Abbott escapes, and when she does marry it is not to Dommie of Sandhill, North Carolina, but to Matthew Emerson of Baltimore. The novel ends with Elizabeth married and the caretaker for many. It is an ending that Tyler herself sees as not a particularly happy one, since the independent Elizabeth is left in the kitchen tending to the needs of others.

In *The Clock Winder* Tyler presents the Reverend Abbott as a man who enjoys the power of the clergy. In a letter to Elizabeth his wife complains about the women of the church and the superficial activities they revel in. They take *"up all his time for missionary circles and all kinds of lectures and tea-parties and slide-showings and paltry illnesses and so forth, when I tell him he should rest more and behave like ordinary pastors, confine himself to sermons and funerals and maybe a few deathbeds. He eats it all up, I believe. He wouldn't know what to do with himself if they would stop pestering him"* (*Clock*, 37). Yet Mrs. Abbott does not rebel and lives in the new brick ranch house the church built to make the Reverend more comfortable even though she longs for the old Victorian house that had been the manse. Although she sees through her husband and the church ladies' banal busy work, she cooks up "chicken and rice in a pale cream sauce, a dozen portions at once, laid away in the freezer until some church member should sicken or die" (*Clock*, 146). Mrs. Abbott – ever thoughtful – uses casserole pans that do not have to be returned; each Sunday she plays the perfect wife as she nods knowingly and approvingly at her husband's sermons. Proper she is on the surface, but "underneath she was all bustle and practicality, and if she could have deep-frozen her sympathy ahead of time too she probably would have" (*Clock*, 146). If Elizabeth does not play her public role, Mrs. Abbott certainly plays hers.

Quite a different religious experience occurs with the Emerson family of Baltimore, into whose lives Elizabeth steps inextricably. They must endure the suicide of Timothy Carter Emerson. At his funeral Father Lewis "seemed annoyed about something. He was deprived of most of the phrases he liked to use" (*Clock*, 125). Since the occasion is the suicide of a young and promising medical student, Father Lewis can hardly refer to the fulfilled life or, as Tyler puts it, "God's design," and he is left with his "few vague sentences" and silence (*Clock*, 125). When the service is over, Mrs. Emerson (for all the trouble she gives her own children) is refreshingly candid, so different from Mrs. Abbott's religious pretense: "I don't want to disappoint you children in any way," Mrs. Emerson says, "but the fact is that I have never felt all that religious. I just didn't have the knack, I suppose" (*Clock*, 129).

A central part of *Breathing Lessons* is the funeral service Serena stages for her husband, Max Gill, in the Fenway Memorial Church of Deer Lick, Pennsylvania, with her old high school friends gathered to repeat the songs and readings they performed when Serena and Max married in the 1950s. As various characters stumble through verses of "True Love" and "Love Is a Many Splendored Thing" and a passage from Kahil Gibran's *The Prophet*, the "bald-headed minister appeared. . . . He crossed behind the pulpit. He seated himself in a dark wooden armchair and arranged the skirt of his robe fastidiously over his trousers."[13] The minister listens to these love songs of the 1950s as if they were an ordinary part of any funeral service; once the singing stops he says without skipping a beat, " 'Turning now to the Holy Word. . . .' His voice was high-pitched and stringy" (*Lessons*, 67). Lines from pop love songs are juxtaposed to sacred text, and the minister never bats an eye at the difference.

The tone Tyler uses in *Saint Maybe* confronts the reader seriously and thoughtfully with the religious experience of Ian Bedloe who, like many other Tyler characters, had felt embarrassed by religious phrases like "Blood of the Lamb" and "Died for Your Sins."[14] But on a raw January night he stumbles into a storefront establishment called the Church of the Second Chance. The name arches across the storefront in block letters, and at first we expect to find the likes of Brother Hope exhorting the congregation to resist opposite gender clothing and avoid foreign mushrooms. Instead we find a small group of quite ordinary people who address each other as "Brother" and "Sister" and are led by an ex-Episcopal seminarian, Rev. Emmett. As the dust jacket synopsis describes the plot, Ian Bedloe "meddles in his brother Danny's life" when he suggests that Danny's wife, Lucy, is not the honest woman Danny imagined. Slightly tipsy from a stag party, Danny, after hearing Ian's story about Lucy, goes straight out and drives his car into a stone wall and dies in the crash. Lucy dies shortly thereafter from an overdose of pills. From the moment Ian accepts the responsibility for what he has done, the novel (as the dust jacket says) "immerses us in the bewilderments of family life and the surprising complexities of personal salvation." Ian Bedloe literally atones for his deed by altering his life and accepting a great responsibility.

As serious as this religious aspect is, Tyler enriches the Church of the Second Chance – and particularly the Reverend Emmett – by letting them laugh at themselves from time to time. The Caffeine Rule, the Sugar Rule, and the Alcohol Rule turn out to be somewhat futile exercises. After he recovers from a heart attack Brother Emmett tells Ian that of all the rules the silliest was the Sugar Rule. "Truthfully," he says, "I never felt sure that I wasn't merely rationalizing, once I'd seen how hard the rule was to follow." During Rev. Emmett's hospital stay Sister Nell had brought him a book on nutrition in which he discovered that although sugar may be a stimulant for physical energy, "as far as the mental effect: it lulls you." The humor surrounding the members and their homely petitions for prayers, their foibles, and their eccentric ways is minor and subdued. Far more important is their persistent faithfulness for the services they hold and for their Saturday gatherings to carry out Good Works through which they meet the practical needs of others. A central part of their religious life is the Public Amending time that they all take seriously.

The direction and themes of *Saint Maybe* cast in a religious context the gentle and good lives of many other Tyler characters – Caleb Peck, Jeremy Pauling, Ezra Tull, Macon Leary. Unlike these characters, however, Ian Bedloe confronts the process of forgiveness and finds that merely saying "I'm sorry" does not suffice. *Saint Maybe* is a modern rendering of the Scripture's promise that he who loses his life will save it. Ian sacrifices his youth – from age 19 to 42 – as he attends to the daily task of raising three children – Lucy Dean Bedloe's two children by her first husband and the third child, Daphne, who may or may not be Danny Bedloe's daughter. When Ian – who marries the clutter consultant Rita diCarlo – presents his newborn son, Joshua, to the family gathering at the novel's end, we sense that he may now possess the "beatific smile" he had seen on the face of the Reverend Emmett the first time they met.

In her essay "The Priestly Comedy of J. F. Powers" Mary Gordon attributes Powers's great success in recording the daily lives of priests to his sympathy with priests and especially to his "close, hilarious attention to the errors of their lives spelled out by their possessions and their diction."[15] From Arthur Milsom's religious art on the living room walls to Brother Hope's frantic cry, "What Next?," Tyler catches the detail of her fictional clergymen and fixes them in their limited place. Gordon sees in J. F. Powers "the comic possibilities inherent in American religion which Americans nearly always forget" (Gordon, 102). Americans in general may forget these possibilities, but Anne Tyler and a good many other southern writers have not.

The Durable Humor in Life

Besides these humorous treatments of religious acts and characters, Tyler creates many other situations where humor abounds. Often a situation or a descriptive detail is humorous in itself yet at the same time may reveal a callous or insensitive streak in judgmental character. In *Celestial Navigation*, for instance, Amanda Pauling describes her sister Laura's marriage as a failure since she chose a man who "was no more than a boy anyway. A hemophiliac. Dead from a scratch he got opening a Campbell's soup can."[16] The Campbell Soup can (with or without the Andy Warhol paintings) is a familiar sight to any reader. It is ironic, of course, that a simple domestic chore – opening an ordinary can of soup – causes a death. Amanda feels no remorse and just states her opinion that Laura ought to have selected better, if she married at all. She is equally callous in describing her brother Jeremy, the agoraphobic artist of this novel whose eyes, Amanda says, "had an empty look. A man without landmarks, except for the unavoidable ones of getting born and dying" (*Navigation*, 36). Tyler frequently and effectively presents this disparity between what characters say and how their words strike the reader. Amanda simply thinks she is right; the reader, however, finds her bossy and overbearing manner humorous. Small wonder that after Jeremy begins his life with Mary Tell and their children Amanda fades from his life.

Sometimes Tyler's humor is as dark as it is funny. When Amanda prods Jeremy to report any symptoms he noticed before their mother's sudden death, he simply says, "She fell asleep over solitaire a lot" (*Navigation*, 15), obviously failing to see the loneliness of the game she plays or the simulation of death when one sleeps. In *Earthly Possessions* the bank robber, Jake, tells his prisoner Charlotte of a bizarre encounter he had with his brother-in-law, Marvel Hodge, owner of Marvelous Chevrolet. When Jake asked for an auto loan, Marvel not only refuses (Jake *is* a poor risk) but also laughs heartily at him in front of strangers. Jake masks his anger, goes out the door, climbs into his old Ford, and straightens the rear view mirror. Taking careful aim, he hits a new Bel Air, backs up and bears down on a Vega. Then, he tells Charlotte, I "set on down the row of them, crushing everything I come up on. Fenders was crumpled like paper, bumpers curled, doors falling off . . . – Of course my own car got dented some too" (*Possessions*, 93). But Jake keeps protesting as they haul him off to jail that he *had* kept his temper: "I could have mowed down Marvel and his customers as well but I restrained myself" (*Possessions*, 94). The litter of crushed cars to Jake is simply the minor part of his temper's power.

Even though the Emerson clan and their caretaker, Elizabeth Abbott, in *The Clock Winder* create much humor, tragic family events – a suicide and an attempted murder – occur during the course of the novel. Timothy Carter Emerson's suicide forces this fractured family to come together and act. The outspoken maid Alvareen has appeared to prepare an after-the-funeral meal during which the banal conversation sets the stage for a non sequitur that amuses as much as it shocks. One Emerson after the other politely tells Alvareen that the meal is delicious, but Mary goes into detail: "You must give me the recipe for the gravy, Alvareen. Is it onion? Is this something you get from your people?" Taking no offense from Mary's implication about black cooking, Alvareen launches into the recipe with, "All I done was – " until Mrs. Emerson interrupts with an abrupt and chilling question: "Matthew . . . I have to know. Was death instantaneous?" (*Clock*, 130). Alvareen's bad grammar and the absurdity of Mary's asking for a recipe in the midst of such a sad occasion make Mrs. Emerson's serious question all the more intense. The juxtaposition of these disparate things can both amuse and sober the reader.

Andrew Carter Emerson thinks that Elizabeth is responsible for his brother Timothy's suicide, and in his manic-depressive state he sends her many one-line letters threatening her life. Nevertheless, he closes each with the courtesy of a business letter: "Yours very truly." (In *Celestial Navigation* Guy Tell writes his wife, Mary, letters that are wonderfully ungrammatical, threatening her because she has taken the baby and left him. Like Andrew he signs the letters politely: "Sincerely, Guy.") When Elizabeth has had enough of Andrew's one-liners, she fires back, telling him to "lay off" and issuing threats of her own. If his letters do not cease, Elizabeth will put Andrew's name and address on all the magazine coupons she gets and, furthermore, will sign him up with the Avon and the Tupperware ladies. From North Carolina to Canada, she will give every Mormon missionary and every insurance salesman Andrew's name and put his name down for calls when Sears and Montgomery Ward have sales. "When they phone you in the dead of night to tell you about their white sales, think of me, Andrew" (*Clock*, 180). Andrew eventually draws a gun and shoots Elizabeth, luckily inflicting only a superficial wound and bringing himself at last to his senses. Still, the wound must be attended to, and so Matthew (the brother Elizabeth will eventually marry) takes her to the family doctor who has, as he says, "looked the other way quite a few times in my life, but that boy's beginning to bother me." Elizabeth brushes away his concern by saying of Andrew in a sublime understatement, "Oh, well, he's apologized" (*Clock*, 282). We skirt tragedy on the edge of humor in Tyler's pages, and sardonic replies like Elizabeth's reflect many of Tyler's characters, who know that even ordinary life at times must encounter and survive the frightening and the unexpected.

The deadpan manner that Drumstrings Casey exhibits in *A Slipping-Down Life* is a constant source of humor in a rather serious novel. Drum refuses to leave his and Evie's shabby dwelling and live with his pregnant wife in the house she inherits from her father. Early in the novel Drum participates in a radio interview of local rock musicians. Nonplussed by the interviewer's questions, Drum finally says he cannot describe his style because there "*ain't* no style," and with silence ticking away after that bit of information, he adds, "If you don't know what I do, then how come you get me on your program?" (*Life*, 6). Once his mother learns of his marriage to Evie, Drum is no longer the apple of her eye and the hope of the family's future. The proud mother turns into a harridan as she threatens annulments and lawyers and declares, "I'll have your marriage license tore up by the highest judge there is. Oh, where is your father when I need him the most?" Once she has paused to gather her breath and consider her strength, Drum asks – as if he had heard none of her complaints – "Mom, can I have the record player in my room?" (*Life*, 146). Drum disappoints his mother, and later he disappoints Evie when her friend Fay-Jean spends the night with Drum while Evie has been dealing with her father's fatal heart attack. Returning home, Evie discovers the two. Fay-Jean, in her orange lace slip, gropes her way into her black dress, and as she does she asks Evie to "zip me up." Evie does so with a "certainly," as if this dowdy ménage à trois was the most ordinary thing around (*Life*, 208). The exchange shifts, however, when Fay-Jean, teetering in her high heels, wants a ride to the highway to catch the bus. Evie has no more time for this friend and tells her to walk. The tackiness of the place, the clothes, and the timing of the discovery create this parody of the love affair; at the same time the confrontation pushes Evie Decker Casey to act and to act decisively.

Deft Strokes of Humor

Tyler humorously establishes social differences with quick strokes of detail. In *The Clock Winder* the youngest Emerson son, Peter, marries far beneath his mother's expectations. When he introduces his wife, Mrs. Emerson hardly flinches when she learns that the young woman's name is P.J. She takes one look at her tasteless clothes and launches in by asking, "Where are you from, dear?" P.J. answers, "Well, New Jersey *now*. Before it was Georgia." And Mrs. Emerson replies, "Isn't that nice?" (*Clock*, 297). P.J. may not have any social background, but she is smart enough to realize she is no match for Mrs. Emerson. In *The Accidental Tourist* the Leary siblings use a similar one-upmanship to catch anyone who misuses words as Muriel, the vibrant dog trainer and jack of all trades, does constantly and unconsciously. When she describes her old job of copying documents at Rapid-Eze, Muriel says to Macon, "I've never been so disinterested."[17] When Macon says she must mean "uninterested," Muriel, never catching his point, replies, "Exactly. Wouldn't you be?

Copies of letters, copies of exams" (*Tourist*, 190). And when Muriel tells Macon that she can cure his dog Edward because training dogs that bite is her "speciality," Macon says, "Webster prefers 'specialty'" (*Tourist*, 42). To this information, Muriel simply gives Macon a blank look. Macon's sister, Rose, is not sure about Muriel as Edward's trainer, much less Muriel's interest in Macon. Rose describes Muriel to her brothers, Charles and Porter, as "a flamenco dancer with galloping consumption" and shakes her head because when Muriel "talked about her lesson plan she kept saying 'simplistic' for 'simple'" (*Tourist*, 105). The fineness of words intrigues the Learys, but Muriel sees nothing in their passion for exact and correct meaning. To an extent, Muriel's misuse of words is one mirror of her social background. Her small rowhouse on Singleton Street is far removed from the more established neighborhood where the Learys grew up and continue to live. Diction in Singleton Street is terse and sometimes tough, and nobody there really cares that "speciality" is not quite right.

The minor characters that inhabit Tyler's novels are memorable and often very funny. Two of the best appear in *Searching for Caleb* – Justine and Duncan's neighbor, Dorcas Britt, and her daughter Ann-Campbell, who frequently gets kidnapped. The villain, it turns out, is always her father. Dorcas has divorced and remarried Joe Pete Britt three times, always staging a large church wedding. "Lately," though, "relatives had stopped attending and the gifts had thinned out" (*Caleb*, 174). Dorcas comes frequently for Justine to tell her fortune; her daily life and future possibilities make Dorcas a constant source of drama. Even though Joe Britt has fallen six months behind in his alimony payments, he has the nerve to present Dorcas with a bill for $48.95. It seems that while Ann-Campbell was in his care she had dribble-bleached his new emerald ring with a gallon of Clorox (*Caleb*, 174). Dorcas always recovers from these little setbacks and roars up in her baby-blue Cadillac to drive Justine to her engagements – like the Polk Valley Church's April bazaar, where Justine will tell fortunes. Ann-Campbell misses school to come along. Her constant prattle soon makes Dorcas declare, "Ann-Campbell Britt, you are sending a shooting sharp pain right down between my shoulder blades" (*Caleb*, 175).

In *Breathing Lessons* Maggie and Ira's son Jesse marries Fiona, whose mother is the only person at the wedding in the slightest festive mood. Outfitted in "a fuchsia corduroy pantsuit and a corsage as big as her head," Mrs. Stuckey tells one and all that her only regret (never mind that Fiona is pregnant) is that her husband did not live to see this wedding (*Lessons*, 247). She adds, however, that he is "here in spirit" and goes "on at some length about her personal theory of ghosts" (*Lessons*, 247). She holds forth on ghosts and moves next to announce that "to her mind, marriage was just as educational as high school and maybe more so: "I mean I dropped out of school myself . . . and have never once regretted it" (*Lessons*, 247). It is no surprise that daughter Fiona gives her baby girl the outlandish name of Leroy or that Fiona leaves and reconciles and then leaves Jessie again. At the novel's end she takes the greatest pride in a sign that has just been finished to announce her profession: "Fiona Moran, Electrolysis." She is her mother's daughter.

Even the names of these minor characters fit their slightly offbeat existence – Dorcas, Fiona, and in *Saint Maybe* Rita diCarlo (the clutter consultant who marries Ian Bedloe) and her widowed mother, whose name is Bobeen. Perhaps only Bobbie Ann Mason gives characters names that so exactly reflect their taste or lack thereof. Like Eudora Welty, Tyler has a sure knack for the voice, using odd words, incorrect grammar, and homely expressions to let characters reveal themselves. For instance, on one side adventure Maggie and Ira Moran in *Breathing Lessons* stop at a roadside café. When Maggie asks for a salad, Mabel the waitress replies, "The onliest thing I could offer is the lettuce and tomato from a sandwich" (*Lessons*, 28). Mabel then launches into the details of her son's departure. It seems that he complained once too often that she served "foods that are mingled together." With that, Mabel put all his clothes out on the hood of her car, and now he lives on the other side of town with his girlfriend (*Lessons*, 31). Although she appears in just this one scene, Mabel is alive and real; no matter how many women come in and order salads that the café does not have, Mabel will continue to say that she despises "how everybody tries to look like a toothpick nowadays" (*Lessons*, 28). In *The Accidental Tourist* Macon Leary, in a cast from a broken leg, hobbles into a restaurant to meet his estranged wife, Sarah. Here he must deal with the typically officious restaurant hostess and waitress. Helpless without his crutches, Macon battles to keep them but is no match for the hostess who says when he asks if Sarah has arrived, "Not as I know of, hon." Keeping the crutches at his side is, of course, a lost battle. "I'll take these for you, darlin'," she says. Macon protests. "I need to check them up front, sweetheart. It's a rule. . . . They might trip the other customers, honeybunch" (*Tourist*, 130-31). The hostess takes her place with the receptionists and nurses in all the offices of doctors and dentists who think, regardless of age, gender, or status, it is their right to call you "darlin'," "sweetheart," "honeybunch," or all of these terms plus your given name. The menu at Baltimore's Old Bay Restaurant specializes, of course, in seafood, and when Sarah orders "the hot antipasto and the beef Pierre," the put-upon waitress says, "If you say so" (*Tourist*, 133). Tyler's keen ear lets her record the frustration and amusement of our daily battles against life's minor despots.

Tyler often creates a visual image that is extraordinarily humorous once all the details of the scene fall into place. At Max Gill's funeral, several old classmates refuse to participate in the re-creation of the 1950s wedding performance, among them Ira Moran and the Barley twins. Although middle-aged, the Barley twins still act in unison, but the point is not so much their matching dresses as their clip-on sun shades that "stuck out above their glasses like the perky antennas of some sharpfaced, cute little creatures from outer space" (*Lessons*, 83-84). The shades increase the effect of the nods that they produce in unison, suggesting the narrow double life these twins have led.

Sometimes one small habit will be enough to place or pigeonhole a character. For instance, Sarah Leary in *The Accidental Tourist* is judged by a detail: "she was the sort of woman who stored her flatware intermingled" (*Tourist*, 9), and in a Tyler novel, that says it all. Rose Leary's candid remarks go straight to the heart of the issue, making her far more than just an amusing character who organizes *her* kitchen materials in alphabetical order and in the kitchen merrily trills hymn verses that are anything but merry: "I've had trials, I've had sorrows, I've had grief and sacrifice" (*Tourist*, 60). Sarah Leary leaves Macon, and when he finally conveys this news to his siblings, he declares that the last thing he needs is the family gathering to say, "Oh, poor Macon, how could Sarah do this to you." Rose bluntly dismisses his concern: "Why would I say that? . . . Everybody knows the Leary men are difficult to live with" (*Tourist*, 13). Rose surprises everyone by announcing that she will marry Macon's boss, Julian, and plans a garden wedding. Macon checks the sky early on Rose's

wedding day and calls her, alarmed because rain seems imminent.
Rose is undaunted: "Never mind, it will clear." Macon persists that
the "grass is all wet." If the brothers are trying to dissuade their sister from marrying, she will have none of that. She dismisses Macon's
hovering and fretting about the weather with, " 'Wear galoshes,' she
told him. She hung up" (*Tourist*, 267).

Tyler manipulates repartee well, and if the characters involved
are not conscious of their own wit and humor, the reader is. Two
brief episodes from *The Accidental Tourist* show the fun Tyler gen-
erates with this device. As readers of the novel and movie patrons
know, Macon Leary breaks his leg in a bizarre accident caused by the
combination of his Welsh corgi Edward being forced to go down into
the basement, which he fears, Macon's plan to streamline laundry
duties by using a skate board for the basket, and Helen the cat who
forgot that the dryer hose has been reinstalled. Once Macon is moving about in his cast, his boss, Julian, asks how on earth Macon
keeps the cast so white and two grown men discuss the qualities of
shoe polish:

> "I like it white," Macon said. "I polish it with shoe polish."
> "I didn't realize you could do that."
> "I use the liquid kind. It's the brand with a nurse's face on the
> label, if you ever need to know." (*Tourist*, 119)

Having moved back home with Rose, Porter, and Charles, Macon
does not check on his own house (Sarah is now in an apartment),
and his neighbor Garner, sporting a Sherwin-Williams Paint cap,
finally tracks Macon down at Rose's to deliver a carload of papers
and a full complement of the neighbors' opinions and advice. When
Macon explains that he had to leave home because he fell and broke
his leg, a repartee follows worthy of a George Burns and Gracie Allen
radio routine. Garner begins:

> "We didn't see no ambulance though or nothing."
> "Well, I called my sister."
> "Sister's a doctor?"
> "Just to come and take me to the emergency room."
> "When Brenda broke her hip on the missing step," Garner said,
> "she called the ambulance."
> "Well, I called my sister."

"Brenda called the ambulance."
They seemed to be stuck. (*Tourist*, 72)

Any discussion of Tyler's humor must include at least a brief look
at a dog, a Welsh corgi named Edward who, it seems, has now set a
standard for writing about dogs. In his review of Jonathan Raban's
Hunting Mister Heartbreak: A Discovery of America (1991) Justin
Kaplan notes that at one point Raban "shares a rented lakeside cabin
at Polecat Hollow with a borrowed black Lab named Gypsy, as brilliantly portrayed a dog character as Edward in Anne Tyler's novel
The Accidental Tourist."[18]

Edward is not the handsome dog of American lore – Rin Tin Tin
or Lassie – but "very short-legged with a keg-shaped body alert with
expectation." On the other hand, this dog is not named Lassie or
Spot or Inky. His human name – the royal and regal Edward –
signals his humanlike responses and personality. For instance, when
Macon brings Edward home from Muriel's Meow-Bow Kennel, the
dog, eager to rid himself of kennel odors, races to roll on the dining
room rug. But Sarah has taken the rug for her apartment and
suddenly Edward is rolling on the bare floor. He "stopped short,
looking foolish. Macon knew just how he felt" (*Tourist*, 43). No
Edward likes to play the fool. Alert to human foibles, Edward looks
suspicious if Macon's voice creeps into an unctuous tone; generally
when people talk Edward looks as if he follows the conversation and
is prepared to act on what he hears. Active and independent,
Edward has been barred from one boarding kennel because he bit
one of the workers on the ankle; later when Macon moves back
home with his sister and brothers, Edward acts up again: he traps
Charles in the pantry, his barking keeps visitors at bay on the other
side of the front door, and he bites Macon. The Leary siblings press
Macon to do something about Edward.

Edward had belonged to Macon's son Ethan, and Tyler presents
the classic relationship between a boy and his dog without sentimen-
tality. When young Ethan is shot and killed in a holdup at a Burger
Bonanza, Edward remains for Macon the concrete link to his lost
son. And because of his obstreperous behavior, Edward creates the
need for Muriel Pritchett to train him and subsequently to pull
Macon Leary into an unexpected new life. When Edward first stays at
the Meow-Bow Kennel, Muriel reports she and Edward "got on like a

house afire," and indeed Edward seems utterly smitten with Muriel. When she asks Edward if he bites, "Edward grinned up at her and folded his ears back, inviting a pat" (*Tourist*, 29). But Edward's affection for Muriel does not extend to other people, and a long series of misdeeds drive Charles and Porter Leary to make unseemly threats about the dog's future. Macon insists Edward's unmannerly activity is caused by the adjustments he has had to make, but his brothers press for an immediate solution after Edward literally trees Julian. They suggest Macon consider the SPCA, the dog catcher, or a career for Edward as guard dog at a service station. None will do, especially the latter: "Edward alone in some Exxon? He'd be wretched" (*Tourist*, 93). So the dog training with Muriel is the compromise, and the family settles in to await improvement. After several sessions with Muriel, Edward during one evening "chewed a pencil to splinters, stole a pork chop bone from the garbage bin, and threw up on the sun porch rug; but now that he could sit on command, everyone felt more hopeful" (*Tourist*, 105). Edward may sit on command, but he still charges the mailman.

The training of Edward goes forward and backward. Then at long last Edward's finest hour comes after Macon has moved in with Muriel and her sallow-looking little boy, Alexander, whom Macon transforms – from a sickly allergic boy into a rough-and-tumble happy youngster. While neighbor children are teasing and harassing Alexander one afternoon, Macon spies them, drops Edward's leash, and sends the chunky dog to Alexander's rescue.

Some reviewers complained that Edward was singularly missing from the last part of *The Accidental Tourist*, but once Macon establishes himself and Edward in Muriel's Singleton Street apartment, Edward has reached his own apotheosis. Now he lives with Muriel: "There he sat in front of Muriel and grinned up at her. He reminded Macon of a schoolboy with a crush on his teacher; all his fantasies were realized, here he was at last" (*Tourist*, 232). Four-and-a-half-year-old Edward is an endearing creation who leaps to life – "His large, pointed, velvety ears seemed more expressive than other dogs' ears; when he was happy they stuck straight out at either side of his head like airplane wings" (*Tourist*, 93). He is, as Justin Kaplan says, brilliantly portrayed and certainly a source of delight and humor.

In her classic work, *American Humor: A Study of the National Character* (1931), Constance Rourke traces the exuberant origins of humor in eighteenth-century America through the westward expansion and concludes that as the country expanded and developed "the note of triumph [in its humor] has diminished as the decades have proved that the land is not altogether an Eden and that defeat is a common human portion."[19] Since Rourke's study was published American humor has undergone major changes, especially with the advent and universal presence of television – from family sit-coms to the outrageous skits on "Saturday Night Live" – and with a relaxing of social codes that imposes almost no restrictions on subject matter. We are amused by and laugh at the funny and the absurd, the incongruous and the unexpected, the verbal twist and the visual peak. Our verbs that describe laughter – from *giggle* to *smirk* to *guffaw* – suggest in themselves the complexity of humor as well as its endless forms. The various twists that humor takes in Anne Tyler's novels furnish the reader with pleasure and delight; at the same time much of that humor touches the heart. It was Flannery O'Connor who declared that throughout her fiction her way of being serious was a comic one, and that paradox holds for the novels of Anne Tyler as well.

Chapter Five

The Company of Women

In 1980 Mary Gordon published her second novel, giving it the title *The Company of Women*, a solid phrase that suggests the complex relationships that women establish and the variety of those experiences, both brief encounters and friendships that span a lifetime. Many feminist critics have explored this territory, noting differences in the ways men and women establish and maintain friendships and have redefined our perception of gender as well as self. In her essay "Women's Autobiographical Selves: Theory and Practice," Susan Friedman joins other feminist critics in stressing that "women can move beyond alienation through a collective solidarity with other women – that is, a recognition that women *as a group* can develop an alternative way of seeing themselves by constructing a group identity based on their historical experience."[1] It was Simone de Beauvoir who declared that "love affairs between men and women often do not last, by contrast great friendships between women often endure."[2] And Margaret Atwood, in a 1986 piece for the *New York Times Book Review,* suggested that "despite their late blooming, women's friendships are now firmly on the literary map as valid and multidimensional novelistic material."[3]

The women characters who appear in Anne Tyler's novels range from proper and monied Roland Park matrons of Baltimore in Mrs. Emerson (*The Clock Winder*) and the various Peck women (*Searching for Caleb*) to sharp streetwise characters like Muriel Pritchett (*The Accidental Tourist*), Ruth Spivey (*Dinner at the Homesick Restaurant*), and Rita diCarlo (*Saint Maybe*). What is singularly missing in the lives of Tyler's women characters, however, is "the company of women." Her principal women characters are shockingly alone, and when one or two of them do join the company of other women, the experiences are brief and do not represent lifelong friendships at all. For example, Mary Darcy Tell enjoys the company of her husband's brash and cheerful mother, and when her daughter Darcy is born, Mary briefly experiences the rich company of women. As her own mother and Guy's and neighbor women gather to loan baby furniture and give bits of advice, Mary sees that these "women formed a circle that I sank into. I suppose you have to expect that once children come along. The men draw back and the women close in" (*Navigation*, 77). While Mary's husband, Guy, spends hours in cow pastures racing in motorcycle rallies, Mary and other abandoned wives stay at home and take their children to Roy's for hamburgers, "all the women laughing and scolding and mopping spilled drinks, filling every corner of their world" (*Navigation*, 77).

Later, when she moves into Jeremy Pauling's boardinghouse, Mary joins other mothers who bring their children to a Baltimore park for regular outings. But the friendship with Guy's mother and the other neighbors ends when Mary goes off with another man. Brief social visits replace the nurturing times she had enjoyed back home. The boarder, Miss Vinton, observes that the only friends Mary had "were the women [she] sat in the park with, behind a row of strollers. I didn't even know their last names and possibly Mary didn't either" (*Navigation*, 132). Ironically, the only people Miss Vinton might call to say that Mary has yet another baby are these women, who are such casual acquaintances that neither Miss Vinton nor Mary could find their phone numbers in the telephone book.

For a brief time in *Celestial Navigation* Mary takes in the drifter Olivia, and Jeremy realizes as he overhears the inflections in Mary's voice that she is actually teaching Olivia, drawing on the same skills that let Mary coax the baby Rachel into eating her carrots. Jeremy wonders if "this might be a school for women; the thought had often occurred to him. In the old days he had assumed that what women knew came to them naturally. He had never suspected that they had to be taught. . . . Were there no such tutors for men? Was it only women who linked the generations so protectively?" (*Navigation*, 183). Mary does try to draw Olivia into a responsible life, but the episode is short, and finally Olivia nearly destroys Jeremy with complete (and perhaps drug-induced) inertia. Finally, she too abandons him, taking once again to the streets with little prospect of a good and productive life. Mary was willing to try to save Olivia, but in the end she leaves her to her own devices.

In *Saint Maybe* the pregnant Rita has a kitchenful of women, but they are vague and unspecific. Among these women is Rita's mother, Bobeen, who is far more interested in reclaiming her youth as she flirts with Brother Emmett than she is in establishing any meaningful connection with other women. The theme also appears in *Breathing Lessons* – and in a rather interesting version, because Maggie enjoys the company of women. This is not a gathering of her own friends, however, but the cast-off girlfriends of her son Jesse. Even after their time with Jesse is over, these girls still enjoy coming back to talk to Maggie, who in turn enjoys a visit from them. Often Maggie's daughter Daisy would be at home, busy with homework when an old flame of Jesse's would arrive, and as they sat together Maggie "had the feeling they were all three part of a warm community of females, a community she had missed out on when she was growing up with her brothers" (*Lessons*, 224). As important as this association may be, it still does not give Maggie friends of her own age. Maggie had envied Serena Gill's marriage, seeing this couple at a distance appear like "easygoing buddies" who could not have suspected "that dark, helpless, angry confined feeling that Maggie's own marriage descended to from time to time" (*Lessons*, 68). Like Pearl Tull, Maggie tells her deepest agony to no one.

So it is the absence of women's friendships in Tyler's novels that in great part creates the extreme isolation that many of the women characters endure and denies them the network of information and support that women traditionally give each other. It is also true that in Tyler's fiction mothers rarely serve their daughters well, a particular need within the company of women. The mother is often out of tune with the world of the daughter, and only when the daughter does something drastic like eloping does the dramatic unspoken difference emerge. Some mothers in Tyler's fiction are thus oddly indifferent to or unaware of the daughter's true self – Mrs. Darcy in *Celestial Navigation*, Justine in *Searching for Caleb*, Mrs. Abbott in *The Clock Winder*, for example. By contrast, it is interesting to look at the mother-daughter relationship in Edith Wharton's *The House of Mirth* (1905). While Wharton makes it clear that Lily Bart's mother is a managerial and cold woman (she never lets her dying husband forget that his Wall Street losses have ruined them), she nevertheless attends to her duty as a mother. And had the financial setback been avoided, Mrs. Bart would have saved Lily from missteps and misjudgments, would have Lily safely and richly married. To be sure, happiness in marriage is not the point; social status and financial security are. But Mrs. Bart dies, and without her Lily cannot manipulate the course or discipline her own nature; thus she ruins her chances of marriage and ends up with no way out except to die.

While the atmosphere and milieu of Tyler's novels are remote from Wharton's novel of manners, the young women in Tyler's novels often *do* suffer because their mothers neglect them, or fail to guide them, or remain unaware of the lives the daughters lead. In *Celestial Navigation* Mary Darcy says of her imperceptive parents, "What bothered me was not my parents or even their way of living, but the fact that it seemed to be the only way open to me. I would grow up, of course, and go to college and marry and have children, but these were not changes so much as additions. I would still be traveling their single narrow life" (*Navigation*, 63-64). Her path to avoid their single narrow life leads her to marry Guy Tell, who spends his days racing motorcycles and thinks that his sole responsibility for their daughter (a child he thought should be named Guyette) is fulfilled when he occasionally shows her off to his friends. Mary's affair with John comes to nothing but fear of poverty; her years with Jeremy Pauling and their children are not enough, and if her life has increased in complications, it is perhaps still a single narrow life, one circumscribed by the demands of children and the limited opportunity for Mary to become a fulfilled and independent woman.

In *A Slipping-Down Life* Evie Decker's mother is long dead and her quiet father stands by and waits for things to work out. Evie must learn about the world of women from the radio, and from the ads and articles in magazines like *Good Housekeeping* and *Family Circle*. When she musters the energy to leave the small place where she and Drum live, she knows how the scene should be played, because television and movies have shown her exactly how wives leave their husbands. They "laid blouses neatly in overnight bags and had given them a brisk little pat, then crossed on clicking heels to collect an armload of dresses still on their hangers. There was no way she could make a mistake. Her motions were prescribed for her, right down to the tucking of rolled stockings into empty corners and the thoughtful look she gave the empty closet" (*Life*, 211). The movie script is supposed to take the wife through to a happy reunion.

Drum says, as husbands are supposed to, "Evie, don't go," and then the scene should have the husband "changing his mind, saying he would come with her anywhere" (*Life*, 213). But Drum apparently has not watched these television shows, and when Evie asks him to "Come with me, then," all Drum can do is sink down into a chair and say, "No, I can't" (*Life*, 213). The television models do not work in reality, and Evie is left to bury her father and to have a baby that she must raise alone.

For most women characters in Tyler's fiction, marriage or at least the semblance of marriage is assumed. A few women characters pursue education and professions – Jenny Tull (*Dinner at the Homesick Restaurant*) becomes a pediatrician; Maggie and Ira Moran's daughter (*Breathing Lessons*) wins a scholarship to an Ivy League university, completely surprising her mother by wishing to go away from Baltimore to school; and Agatha (Dulsimore) Bedloe (*Saint Maybe*) becomes an oncologist. The majority of Tyler's women characters, however, do not seek professions and generally show little interest in things intellectual. Over and over these women characters are forced to rely on men to provide the money needed to support them and their children. And the marriages often do not appear to be sensible choices.

In her excellent 1985 dissertation, "Anne Tyler's Treatment of Managing Women," Dorothy Faye Sala Brock studies the strong women characters in Tyler's fiction, placing them in two categories: the regenerative managing woman who is at once capable of enduring *and* adapting to the life that is hers and the rigid managing woman who, while she endures hardship and difficulty, makes her family suffer by her inability to adapt, to change. Often, as Brock points out, the rigid managing women are somewhat humorous because of their tunnel-vision view of life. For example, Mrs. Emerson in *The Clock Winder* remains bewildered that her children resent her iron-willed opinion of their actions; in *Searching for Caleb* Mrs. Milsom's bossy manner virtually paralyzes her minister son; Amanda Pauling in *Celestial Navigation* prides herself on meaningless order and routine and thus misses any real human association. But when the rigid managing woman is Pearl Tull, the humor ceases as the latent anger and humiliation over her woman's life results in shocking child abuse – both verbal and physical – a pattern that briefly and terrifyingly reappears in her daughter's adult behavior. On the other hand, the regenerative woman (beginning, Brock argues, in Tyler's first novel, *If Morning Ever Comes*) does not terrify the family but instead nurtures as she adapts and moves through life as do Mary Tell, Justine Peck, Ruth Spivey, Maggie Moran, Bee Bedloe, and Rita diCarlo. And while there is much to admire in the women – both the rigid and the regenerative – there remains the fact that in their individual lives they do not enjoy or foster the company of other women. Their lives may touch the lives of other women as Justine Peck does through her fortune-telling, but what Margaret Atwood calls women's friendship is simply missing.

Perhaps the most poignant example comes in *Dinner at the Homesick Restaurant* when Pearl Tull, abandoned by her husband, refuses to allow herself to confide in her old friend Emmaline. En route to Philadelphia, Emmaline stops by Baltimore, and the visit begins with overtures of the confidential talk that women expect with women; however, Pearl does not share her grief, does not tell her secret. Tyler presents this scene carefully: "Pearl said Beck was out of town; the two of them were in luck; they could talk girl-talk to their hearts' content. . . . They stayed awake half the night gossiping and giggling. Once Pearl almost set a hand on Emmaline's arm and said, 'Emmaline. Listen. I feel so horrible, Emmaline.' But fortunately, she caught herself. The moment passed. In the morning they overslept, and Pearl had to rush to get the children off to school; so there wasn't much said" (*Dinner*, 11). The scene has the vocabulary generally associated with women: "girl-talk" – that is, matters to discuss that one would not talk about if men were present; they "gossip" and they "giggle," ways of communication stereotypically applied to women even though the association now strikes most women readers as belittling. Far more important, however, is Pearl's reluctance to confide. Emmaline's visit is particularly significant because Tyler makes it clear that Pearl has no friends in the neighborhood or at work. So her one opportunity is lost and her tale of disappointment and regret is not relieved by confiding it. The letters Pearl sends to her relatives in Raleigh continue to report that Beck is a loving husband and her marriage is a happy one – all a charade. Ellen Moers pointed out years ago that in Jane Austen's novels the women characters maintained a realistic view of life and marriage and had few illusions about their prospects. Simply put, women had three alternatives: the right marriage, the wrong marriage, or spinsterhood.[4] For a woman like Pearl Tull, the wrong marriage must be made to look like the *right* marriage, regardless of truth.

Pearl expands the myth of the happy family as she encourages her children to consider their small and fractured family sufficient for their existence. Friends, she says, are not needed and only surreptitiously do the children ever bring classmates into their home. But for the eldest of Pearl's children, Cody, the isolated family is not enough. He longs "to have a mother who acted like other mothers! He longed to see her gossiping with a little gang of women in the kitchen, letting them roll her hair up in pincurls, trading beauty secrets, playing cards, losing track of time – 'Oh, goodness, look at the clock! And supper not even started; my husband will kill me. Run along, girls'" (*Dinner*, 59). Cody's daydream is, of course, stereotypic and demeaning: women engage in nonintellectual discussions and their lives revolve around the husband's schedule. This kitchen scene in Cody's mind is static with women busy with rather silly things, and it portrays women's existence as altogether superficial. In reality, the life of Pearl Tull has been as lonely and isolated as perhaps one life can be. Finally, she is blind and alone all day while Ezra is at the Homesick Restaurant, and he assumes she must use up the hours of the day listening to a television whose picture she cannot see. "Certainly," Ezra says, "she saw no friends; she had none. As near as he could recall, she had never had friends. She lived through her children; the gossip they brought was all she knew of the outside world" (*Dinner*, 259).

Even when she took her job at Sweeney's grocery store and obviously had to be pleasant around customers and fellow workers each day, Pearl had nothing to do with any of them: "And now that she had retired, none of her fellow workers came to visit her" (*Dinner*, 259). Never did Pearl realize her own youthful dreams of a happy marriage and a protected family, and never did Cody find the mother of his fantasy. Indeed, Cody becomes as isolated as his mother. After Cody suffers the nearly fatal accident, his New York partner, Sloan, calls to ask about his condition, but no fellow workers bother to visit. In the series of expensive suburban houses Cody rents, his wife, Ruth, laments that "they didn't know any neighbors" and says to her son, "'Everybody needs friends. We don't have a one, in this town. I feel like I'm drying up. Sometimes I wonder . . . if this life is really . . .' But she didn't say any more" (*Dinner*, 222).

Ruth has long ago lost her spontaneous gregariousness and her unselfconscious manner; she strives with little success to be the woman Cody thought he was marrying. Cody repeats his mother's isolation, and in doing so he draws his own wife and child into that same narrow world.

Women and Midlife

Certainly since *Earthly Possessions* Tyler has made her major women characters middle-aged – older than Joanne Hawkes, Joan Pike, Evie Decker, Elizabeth Abbott. (Justine Peck's real middle-age story really begins as *Searching for Caleb* ends.) As her women characters enter their midlife stories, they of course reflect Tyler's own life and age. In her important study of Saul Bellow, Margaret Drabble, Anne Tyler, and John Updike – *Safe at Last in the Middle Years: The Invention of the Midlife Progress Novel* (1988) – Margaret Morganroth Gullette suggests that it is necessary for both character and author to reach that time of middle age before successful midlife fiction can emerge. Gullette celebrates a new kind of novel that she calls "the midlife progress narrative" and points to 1975 as the date when the culture gave "its writers permission to overthrow the traditional decline view that the middle years are a time of devolution, on a spectrum from fatigue through multiplied losses to despair."[5] Gullette assumes that readers have long been skilled in responding to novels whose plots depict loss and despair; she, on the other hand, celebrates novels in which characters are 40 *and* likable and that point to the recovery and gains possible in the middle years.

What Gullette calls "midlife progress narratives" or the midlife bildungsroman serve to remind us that in midlife it is not a matter of becoming "stupidly impervious to tragedy" but instead a matter of recognizing "that even the bleakest event is a 'period' " (41). Gullette argues that generally critics agree that since the mid-nineteenth century "the canon has privileged stories of failure" (152). Unlike these decline novels, the midlife bildungsroman can "tuck in some loss, even the death of loved ones, without losing heart" (80). Midlife teaches all but the most pessimistic that *nothing* lasts "for the rest of [one's] life" (91). Gullette's argument is appealing: when Tyler's midlife women characters must face loss and disappointment, they generally do not totally lose heart. They seem reassured that perhaps the bleakest event *is* only a period and that it can be lived through.

In his review of Tyler's Pulitzer Prize – winning novel, *Breathing Lessons*, Edward Hoagland presents a view of middle age and of Tyler's novel that sharply contrasts with the balance Gullette wants to bring. "The literature of resignation – of wisely settling for less than life had seemed to offer – is exemplified by Henry James among American writers," Hoagland argues (44). "It is a theme more European than New World by tradition, but with the graying of America into middle age since World War II, it has gradually taken strong root here and become dominant among Ms. Tyler's generation" (44). Perhaps then it depends on the reader – on the reader's gender – to decide whether Tyler's middle-aged women (and men) will emerge to face life with the hopefulness of the heroic and comic rather than with the despair of the unheroic and tragic. Tyler does not explore, as does Adrienne Rich, "the anger and helplessness of an artistically accomplished woman who lives in a society that demands that she be selfless and sacrifice her needs to the institution of marriage and motherhood as defined by men."[6] In a discussion of Jane Austen's *Persuasion* (1818) Nina Auerbach makes a point with which many of Tyler's women characters might well concur. "Mrs. Croft's view of women," Auerbach notes, "which her life gives her freedom to practice, is summed up in her cry to Wentworth: 'But I hate to hear you talking so, like a fine gentleman, and as if women were all *fine ladies*, instead of *rational creatures*. We none of us expect to be in smooth water all our days.' "[7] The death of family members, the rejection of women by men, the misalliance of mothers and daughters, and perhaps especially the absence of the company of women make it clear that the lives of Tyler's women characters are by no means easy. Generally these women do survive: Justine Peck is exuberant (if the reader is not) about her and Duncan's future as *Searching for Caleb* ends; Charlotte Emory returns home from her escape in *Earthly Possessions* wiser and probably more self-sufficient; Ruth Spivey in *Dinner at the Homesick Restaurant* knows that the wrong done to Ezra cannot be atoned for but also realizes that her life is so intertwined with Cody's that no separation is really possible; and Maggie Moran in *Breathing Lessons* finally recognizes that her son

Jesse, so golden in his youth, is a failure and in accepting this fact may perhaps better lead her own life in middle age.

Expectations and Assumptions for Women

In the essay " 'Just the doing of it': Southern Women Writers and the Idea of Community" Linda Wagner-Martin looks at the great variety of fiction contemporary southern women writers are producing. She suggests that "what has remained constant in a hundred years of the Southern novel by women is that women characters have been – and still are – drawing much of their sustenance and their wisdom from a female line of ancestry, and thereby creating a true community of women."[8] To many women there is a tradition of collective wisdom and experience to be shared and passed on. In that process the connection between women is made and mutual respect and support assumed. But Tyler's most important women characters seem rather firmly removed from this tradition. Although they do not totally cut themselves off from the older generation of women, they nevertheless seem to lead lives that are individual rather than communal and thus remain outside the circle of women. Carolyn Heilbrun notes that some exceptional career women shun the company of women. In particular, she cites Patricia Bosworth's remark about Diane Arbus, who did not associate with other women photographers in the 1960s and insisted, "Look, I'm a *photographer*, not a woman photographer."[9] And Arbus died, Heilbrun notes, with no network of female support.

In her essay "Through the Looking Glass: When Women Tell Fairy Tales" Ellen Cronan Rose describes the standard version: boys are clever, resourceful, and brave creatures who leave home to slay giants, outwit ogres, solve riddles, find fortunes; girls, however, stay home and sweep hearths while remaining patient, enduring, self-sacrificing. Girls are picked on by wicked stepmothers and enchanted by evil fairies; if they go out, they get lost in the woods where perchance they are rescued by kind woodsmen, good fairies, or handsome princes. Then, of course, they marry and live happily ever after. Rose goes on to suggest that in Anne Sexton's "Snow White" the woman is portrayed as a "plucked daisy," a "dumb bunny," "an Orphan Annie" primarily because "she's never had a real woman to mother her into valuing herself as a person."[10] As we have seen, the presence of a real mother is rare in Tyler's fiction and may to a large extent play a role in the presence of many women characters who lack serious professional and intellectual ambition and of many who take a most inappropriate marriage partner thinking that an available man will lead them to a happier life. Over and over in Tyler's fiction women depend on men, and when they temporarily do not (Mary Tell's abrupt leaving Jeremy Pauling with her houseful of children) the chances for their prosperous and happy survival are no more certain than is the fate of Ibsen's Nora when she slams Torvald's front door. Nora has indeed escaped her doll's house, but to what future does she journey?

The assumption of marriage carries with it a second assumption: brides are beautiful. At least they are supposed to be, and when they are not, the kind woodsmen, the good fairies, and the handsome princes may be scarce indeed. In a rereading of Jean Stafford's fine short novel *The Mountain Lion* (1947) Blanche H. Gelfant looks carefully at young Molly – her chunky figure and her thick eyeglasses. Stafford, Gelfant suggests, knew well that women are judged by their appearance and that ugly ducklings like Molly do *not* always turn into swans.[11] In *Dinner at the Homesick Restaurant* one agonizes with Jenny Tull as she shows up at school wearing her mother's unfashionable old dresses and trudges along in the same style of sturdy brown oxfords her brothers wear. The narrative voice declares that Jenny had real beauty ahead; ironically, when that beauty comes in her young adulthood, Jenny soon has little need of it and baffles her mother by chopping her beautiful hair into irregular and careless shapes.

American advertising rewards and enthrones the beautiful woman who is singularly privileged with clothes, jewels, automobiles, and well-appointed houses. The woman of marginal beauty or, worse, the homely woman does not glance at us from billboards or from the slick pages of *Vogue* and *Harper's Bazaar*. In this regard Caroline Heilbrun calls attention to a moving passage from Catherine Drinker Bowen's *Family Portrait* (1970): "I sometimes wonder why women do not write more about the condition of being born homely. It is something that colors a woman's life, almost from the moment of consciousness. . . . Every girl who lacks beauty knows instinctively that she belongs to an under-privileged group, and that to climb up and out she will have to be cleverer and stronger and more ruthless perhaps than she would choose to be."[12]

Frequently in Tyler's fiction, characters remark on and respond to the presence or absence of beauty in women. At times the longing for beauty includes a domestic scene that is mythlike in its perfection; for several women characters, their less-than-perfect beauty demonstrates Bowen's point that being aware that one is not beautiful affects all of a woman's life. Mary Tell in *Celestial Navigation* feels vulnerable because she has left her husband and gone off with a man named John whose view of a wife is demeaning and stereotypic. Furthermore, he does not have the strength to divorce and fulfill his promise to wed Mary, who knows all too well his notion of a wife: "I wanted a *wifely* wife, someone warm and loving that smells like cinnamon" (*Navigation*, 77). For a time Mary takes comfort in this superficial judgment because John constantly says that *she* smells like cinnamon – the association of cinnamon with baking and the kitchen and women's domestic work creates John's image of woman's role. Food aromas occur again in this novel as Mary, always waiting on telephone calls from John, moves about the miserably unkept kitchen in Jeremy Pauling's boardinghouse. Here she imagines meals: "hot dilled biscuits, roast beef, a fresh green salad. John would open the door and the smells would curl around him and draw him in. We would sit down at a table with a white linen cloth, in a house that was stable, calm, warm, clean, built to shelter us a lifetime. It would never even occur to me to run away again" (*Navigation*, 75). Such images of domestic bliss, however, are the stuff of fairy tales. And to this runaway pair, Tyler gives the classic names of the old radio soap opera lovers – John and Mary. To Mary, John appears the American hero: "square-jawed and handsome, a cigarette ad. Only men like that are comfortable with beautiful women" (*Navigation*, 51). In reality Mary knows perfectly well that she neither meets John's ideal nor fits the American advertising ethos that women must be slim. In a low mood Mary gazes at her mirror and admits "how enormously tall I am and how busty I have grown since the baby and how even if I lost weight, I would never have that chiseled look that models have. I haven't the bones for it" (*Navigation*, 59-60). Although Mary has the chance to remain reasonably secure in this house with Jeremy and the family of children they have produced, she will indeed run away again – this time to the ill-equipped and rundown lake shack belonging to Jeremy's art agent, Brian. Here she will endure until, one has to assume, Brian or another man steps in to take her away and the pattern of a woman dependent on a man for financial security will repeat itself.

In *Dinner at the Homesick Restaurant* Tyler moves the desire for thinness to the serious condition of anorexia nervosa. The problem of women gaining weight is introduced by Jenny Tull's first husband, the cold and calculating Harley Baines, who is obsessed with the fear that Jenny might get fat and constantly orders her to chew food excessively and warns her not to overeat. Yet Jenny is well aware that the women who catch Harley's eye are not thin at all, are in fact "the burgeoning and dimpled ones, blondes, a little blowzy" (*Dinner*, 103). Harley's taste strikes one as yet another form of the double standard: he wants his wife to match the advertising image, yet he is attracted to fleshy women. Later in the novel while Jenny is in divorce proceedings with Harley, she pushes the weight obsession to absurd proportions when she considers herself "perfectly obese" because she gained three pounds in six weeks. To remedy this situation Jenny tells her brother in a letter that she is "living now on lettuce leaves and lemon water" (*Dinner*, 134).

In her awareness that she is not a traditional beauty, Mary Tell is by no means unique in Tyler's fiction, and additional occurrences show how pervasive this presentation of women is. A pivotal moment in *A Slipping-Down Life* occurs during Brother Hope's sermon at the Pulqua Tabernacle when he uses Evie Decker's disfigurement to document the sorry state of contemporary life. (Evie had carved "Casey" on her forehead to prove her admiration of the second-rate singer, Drumstrings Casey.) When Brother Hope uses Evie's gesture as an example of a sacrifice to false gods, Drumstrings Casey calls that interpretation "a bunch of bull" because, as he argues, Evie had hardly any good looks to lose. In a burst of arrogance he makes his point: "It'd been a hell of a lot more sacrifice if she'd been prettier to begin with" (*Life*, 181). The act of Evie's sacrifice then is minimal simply because she had so little beauty to give up. In *The Accidental Tourist* the spikey Muriel Pritchett suffers in adulthood because she had been a lovely baby whose beauty did not last. The baby Muriel had blond hair that instantly curled under her mother's fingers, producing a replica of Shirley Temple, the model of glamour for children of that generation. But as the years passed Muriel's blond hair turned dark, leaving her more homely than beautiful. And in a real way, this change marked Muriel's life: "People thought I'd look that way forever and they talked about me going into the movies. Seriously! My mother arranged for tap-dance school when I wasn't much more than a toddler. No one ever dreamed my hair would turn on me" (*Tourist*, 100). But with the lovely blond curls gone, the beauty too is lost. And for all of Muriel's commendable traits and survival skills, it is clear that she carries regret into adulthood from the loss of early beauty.[13]

Ruth Spivey in *Dinner at the Homesick Restaurant* knows instinctively that Cody Tull's courting her is suspicious. Cody instantly reminds Ruth of those "*smooth*-mannered boys that everything always came easy to, that always knew the proper way of doing things, and never dated any but the cheerleader girls, or the homecoming queen, or her maids of honor at the lowest. Passing me in the halls not even knowing who I was, nor guessing I existed . . . laughing at how poor I dressed and mocking my freckly face and my old red hair" (*Dinner*, 151). The myth of what women and women's lives are supposed to be also provides a sad commentary on Pearl Tull's hard life. Blind and near death, Pearl is dependent on her son Ezra to provide and interrupt information. As Ezra, at Pearl's behest, sifts through old photographs and old diary entries, he has a brief glimpse of Pearl's lonely life. Those old diary entries show Ezra "that his mother had imagined a perfectly wonderful plot – a significance to every chance meeting, the possibility of whirlwind courtships, grand white weddings. . . . Well, nothing had come of it. Nothing came of anything. She married a salesman for the Tanner Corporation and he left her and never came back" (*Dinner*, 268-69).

Unlike Mary Tell and Pearl Tull, Mrs. Emerson in *The Clock Winder* has no financial worries; however, she is one of the most interesting portrayals of women in Tyler's fiction, starting her adult life very much like Ibsen's Nora. Mrs. Emerson was not, Tyler writes, "a stupid woman, but she was used to being taken care of. She had passed almost without a jolt from the hands of her father to the hands of her husband" (*Clock*, 8). Mrs. Emerson does not follow Nora's act of rebellion; instead she capitalizes on her feminine capacities and encourages her daughters to do the same. Coordinated and expensive clothes are essential to Mrs. Emerson, who despairs over her helper, Elizabeth Abbott, for always appearing in

blue jeans yet, to Mrs. Emerson's bemusement, Elizabeth attracts
young men. Elizabeth listens but takes little notice when Mrs. Emerson says, " 'Above all else, be *feminine*,' I used to tell my daughters,
and here you are in those eternal blue jeans, but every time I look
out the window some new boy is helping you rake leaves" (*Clock*,
24).

Mrs. Emerson's logic follows the expectation that the woman
who *is* feminine is the woman who will attract men; Elizabeth Abbott
remains to her an anomaly. On the other hand, Mrs. Emerson herself
is copy for the fashion magazine page. Tyler positions Mrs. Emerson
"at her little spinet desk, wearing a dyed-to-match sweater and skirt
and a string of pearls, holding a gold fountain pen poised over a
sheet of cream stationery. She looked like an advertisement" (*Clock*,
30). Mrs. Emerson is the eternal feminine making her perfect appearance an essential act of every day. To her children Mrs. Emerson
issues criticisms and even forces one daughter to leave the young
man with whom she had eloped. The pronouncements on her children's housekeeping habits, their clothes, and their friends result in
constant friction and make real visits virtually impossible. One tends
to side with the children against this overbearing woman, but
through Elizabeth Abbott (the "handyman") Tyler makes it clear that
Mrs. Emerson is not to be dismissed as merely a lady who dresses
well and wants her daily affairs properly done.

Although she may appear useless in the eyes of her grown children, Mrs. Emerson has looked more closely at her life than they
think. A widow, she admits to Elizabeth that occasionally a terrible
idea floats into her mind: "I think, if he [her husband Billy] was
going to die, then couldn't he have done it earlier? Before I was all
used up and worn out? I could have started some sort of new life,
back then. I would have had some hope. Well, *that's* a stupid thing
to say." But Elizabeth wisely adds, "Oh, I don't know" (*Clock*, 17-
18). Had she only been younger and full of energy when her husband died, she might have pushed forward and made a new life,
finding skills she never knew she possessed. But she never got the
chance to find out if she could be independent and later admits that
perhaps she should after all "have let Billy buy me a lingerie shop on
Roland Avenue, sat there all day the way my friends are doing,
drinking gin and writing up the losses for income tax" (*Clock*, 81).
Here is another version of Cody Tull's image of women gossiping and

rolling their hair on pin curls in one another's kitchens. Mrs. Emerson simply moves in a higher income-tax bracket, and her kitchen is a useless and frivolous lingerie shop where the object is not to succeed in business but to fritter away time sitting and sipping gin.

It is interesting that Elizabeth Abbott does not share the view of Mrs. Emerson that Mrs. Emerson's children hold. Instantly irritated by their mother's ways, the Emerson children ask Elizabeth how she can stand to be around their mother day in and day out: How does Elizabeth manage to put up with Mrs. Emerson with her being dressed for everything, even for breakfast? Her wardrobe contains not a single pair of slacks but many pairs of ultrasheer stockings, and her closet bulges with pair after pair of shoes with heels so spiked they made her arches ache. Looking like an advertisement may appear useless, but such an appearance requires effort and energy. Mrs. Emerson must constantly fight the temptation to "spend her days in comfortable shoes and forget her chin-strap and let herself go" (*Clock*, 6). If her children sense her willpower they never reveal the fact; instead they find their mother's presence and criticism a trial. To their surprise Elizabeth does not find their mother impossible but indeed likes her. "Think," she says to the Emerson clan, "what a small life she has, but she still dresses up every day and holds her stomach in. Isn't that something?" (*Clock*, 110).

Tyler does not cast aside Mrs. Emerson and consider her totally useless, and with this judgment she reminds us of the many women like Mrs. Emerson who may not have had financial worries but who have had to live small lives. (It is interesting to note a parallel of rich women's wasted lives in the 1990 film *Mr. and Mrs. Bridge*, wherein Joanne Woodward portrays the despairing and powerless wealthy wife with little life of her own.)[14] Toward the end of the novel, when Mrs. Emerson struggles hard against the ravages of a stroke, Elizabeth keeps watch and sensitively responds to the effort the woman makes: "She shot Mrs. Emerson a sideways glance, trying to read in her eyes what bottled-up words might be waiting there. But all she saw were the white, papery lids. Mrs. Emerson slept, nothing but a small, worn-out old lady trying to gather up her lost strength" (*Clock*, 261). Her effort might bypass her children, but not the novel's protagonist, Elizabeth Abbott.

Marriage and Myths

From the visual images of advertisements to the titles of fairy tales like "Sleeping *Beauty*" and "*Beauty* and the Beast," the beautiful woman is the one rewarded with the love of the prince. In *Celestial Navigation* the spinster boarder Mildred Vinton thinks of the Pauling boardinghouse as having a front door that "might as well have had a curtain of cobwebs across it, like the Sleeping Beauty's palace gate," suggesting by the image that never will this Sleeping Beauty be awakened to a blissful and happy life (*Navigation*, 140). Even though a novel is not a fairy tale, marriage is often the point, yet that marriage may well be more a cutting off of woman's life than a rich beginning. A blending of fantasy and reality occurs in Charlotte Brontë's *Jane Eyre* (1847), Karen E. Rowe suggests, because Jane Eyre faces the necessity of setting aside childhood dreams so that she can claim not only a woman's maturity but also equality in marriage.[15] It is true that Rochester is both purged and blind, but Jane Eyre's words are not those of the captive maiden released but of a strong woman who is now independent, rich, and her own mistress. Although her precise subject is "Marriage Perceived: English Literature, 1873-1944," Carolyn Heilbrun's observations about marriage apply beyond that geographic and temporal limit. We are, Heilbrun reminds us, fond of noting that happy marriages are not news. And "before the twentieth century brought with it the cold Shavian shower of truth, we all assumed that marriage as a rewarding institution had been continually confirmed by novelists."[16] Heilbrun points to the arrangement of George Eliot and Henry Lewes, that union of extraordinary minds and talents, to note that "George Eliot allows none of her heroines such a union, nor any destiny like her own" (116).

Although Tyler's marriage is one of extraordinary minds and talents, she gives none of her women characters "such a union, nor any destiny like her own." The point, of course, is not that novelists should or should not replicate their own careers in their characters, but in studying the array of women characters in Tyler's fiction one finds women who are basically tied to home and children without the remarkable life and career that Tyler herself enjoys as novelist, short story writer, reviewer, and critic. When her women characters run away their bolt for freedom is often ill-planned or short-lived, and their adventures out into the world usually are circular and brief. (In *Saint Maybe* geography widens: Thomas settles in New York City and Agatha in Los Angeles, but the primary child of the family, Daphne, remains in Baltimore.) Tyler documents in novel after novel the infinitely interesting lives of people who do not achieve fame and fortune, and instead of glorifying success and sharp independence she reaffirms the virtue of enduring. In reviewing Sumner Locke Elliott's *Water under the Bridge* (1977) Tyler might well be praising and describing her own fiction when she writes, "Sumner Locke Elliott has shown himself, once again, to be a master at celebrating the voices of ordinary people – rich, tangential, infinitely varied, murmuring around the edges of life's small and large catastrophes."[17]

On the other hand, many of Tyler's ordinary characters suffer because their illusions – especially about marriage and family – fail to match everyday experience. In *Dinner at the Homesick Restaurant* Cody Tull (that time management consultant) harbors for years his mythic dream of a farm where his wife and children will reside in bucolic pleasure while he flies from consulting job to consulting job on weekdays and becomes the perfect farmer-husband on the weekend. The farmhouse remains in the care of Ezra and his mother, who periodically drive out from Baltimore to pick up the leavings of vagrants and to clean the house. Their efforts are useless, if obligatory, and the reader knows that Cody will never realize his dreams: the comfortable and wholesome American farmhouse where family members are content and ready to comfort and inspire one another. Rather than the vine-covered cottage in the Maryland hills, Cody drags his family along on his series of upwardly mobile job moves, installing them always in a "treeless house barricaded against the elements" (*Dinner*, 181). Ruth was raised on a farm and has little interest or patience with Cody's dream. She knows firsthand that life on the farm is plain hard work, not the pastoral myth of Cody's imagination. And in marrying Cody, Ruth loses the chance to continue working happily and well at the Homesick Restaurant. She loses Ezra as well, the Tull brother she had planned to marry.

Women Alone

In Tyler's fiction some women are alone either because they never marry or because their husbands abandon them. While these particular women are forced to be self-sufficient and independent, their lives are still narrow and limited. They are not, in other words, new women and they do not pursue careers that bring them challenge, great satisfaction, or substantial financial rewards. In reviewing Anita Brookner's *Hotel Dulac* (1985) Tyler noted that the novel's heroine accepts neither of the marriage proposals that come her way and thus is the "first of Miss Brookner's heroines to arrive at a nonromantic, wryly realistic appreciation of her single state."[18] Tyler's women characters who live their lives without men do not appear to have a wry or a realistic appreciation of their single state; instead the unmarried women seem singularly unfulfilled, and the women abandoned by their husbands are forced to hard work and to constant worries about financial security.

Without question, Tyler's most appealing unmarried woman character is Mildred Vinton of *Celestial Navigation*, who supports herself by working in a Baltimore bookstore. She lives in Jeremy Pauling's boardinghouse, smokes, eventually buys an automobile, and suffers few illusions about life. Miss Vinton lives on the edge of Jeremy and Mary's lives, enjoying the birth of each child, basking in her brief part of this domestic drama. Even though she never assumes a role other than that of a boarder, Miss Vinton is aware of the lives and roles others lead. "Never mind that I am an old maid," she says; "I can still recognize a happy occasion when I see one" (*Navigation*, 127). Sensing Jeremy's hunger for art books he will not purchase, Miss Vinton brings new books from the store for Jeremy to pore over, careful to avoid any smudge or stain; then she carefully returns the books before the store owner notices their disappearance. Her involvement in the lives of others, however, is guarded, for, as she says, "I don't like hearing too much of people's personal lives," and certainly the reader learns little about hers (*Navigation*, 130). Perhaps the strongest evidence of Miss Vinton's remaining the outsider occurs after Mary and Jeremy have settled into their living arrangement and have begun to produce a family whose noisy presence brightens the household. This change has made the house warmer, reflected in the many boarders beginning to use each other's first names – all, that is, except Miss Vinton: "I asked them to call me Mildred but apparently that proved impossible. I am doomed to be Miss Vinton forever" (*Navigation*, 135).

For a brief moment Miss Vinton assumes a role reversal – that of the husband when Mary refuses to rouse Jeremy for the late-night hospital trip for her latest delivery. Rather than the husband pacing the small maternity-ward waiting room, it is Miss Vinton who "spent the next hour chain-smoking and reading torn *Life* magazines whose photographs seemed very dim and long ago, the way they always do in waiting rooms" (*Navigation*, 131). Those tired and dim *Life* photographs, which seem here to have little connection to reality, parallel Miss Vinton's role. She faithfully discharges her duties, but she does not belong and will soon enough drop into the background, exerting effort to reconcile Jeremy and Mary but not to make her own life richer. Her habit is to keep silent "when she is moved to speak, keeping out of other people's affairs," and she knows all too well for the shy Jeremy Pauling as well as for herself that "one sad thing about this world is that the acts that take the most out of you are usually the ones that other people will never know about" (*Navigation*, 141). Never does Tyler show Miss Vinton with any women friends, and if romance has ever crossed her life she fails to bring the matter up. Denied a family of her own, Miss Vinton has a dull view of the possibilities of happy families, declaring that "women should never leave any vacant spots for the men to fill; they should form an unbroken circle on their own and enclose each child within it" (*Navigation*, 197). Such an exclusion of men is a bleak picture indeed. And at the novel's end the two old people, Jeremy and Miss Vinton, sadly support each other as they slowly trudge the short distance from house to grocery, their little journey indicative of the small lives they have left to lead.

A far less appealing spinster is Amanda Pauling, Jeremy's insensitive older sister who, despite her self-centered and abrasive ways, knows that her life is narrow and meager. A Latin teacher, Amanda distrusts substitute teachers, dislikes cab drivers who give "out their opinions on politics and the cost of living and crime in the street and other matters I have no interest in" (*Navigation*, 5), and refuses to realize that her agoraphobic brother literally cannot go beyond the short block his house is on. No matter what the circumstance, Amanda prides herself in always taking care that her dignity never wavers and that her basic routine is not altered. Rigid and cold, Amanda nevertheless knows that she has derived little joy in life and speaks perhaps for many hundreds of less vocal spinsters when she says, "There are a thousand jokes about the likes of me. None of them are funny. I have seen people sum me up and dismiss me right while I was talking to them, as if what I *am* came through more clearly than any words I might choose to say. I see their eyes focus and settle elsewhere. Do they think that I didn't realize? I suspected all along that I would never get what comes to others so easily. I have been bypassed, something has been held back from me. And the worst part is that I know it" (*Navigation*, 41). Ugly ducklings do *not* always turn into swans.

In *The Accidental Tourist* Rose Leary is another portrait of the old maid. She attended her grandparents through their last illnesses; now she keeps house for her three brothers as they have drifted into and out of marriage, and she calms her elderly neighbors when they cannot open a child-proof medicine bottle or understand an unpaid bill notice. Her domestic routine is that of the perfect homemaker. For example, while her brother Macon is at home recovering from a broken leg, every day at lunch Rose "cooked a real meal, and served it on regular place mats. She set out cut-glass dishes of pickles and olives that had to be returned to their bottles later on" (*Tourist*, 69). That detail of the pickles and olives, served for a meal only to be returned to their respective bottles until once again they are to be trotted out for the table, is enough to suggest the endless repetition of women's household tasks. Whoever then would have thought that Rose would fall in love with Macon's debonair boss, Julian, and, even more important, challenge her brothers for her right to find happiness. Her unexpected outburst comes ironically at the Thanksgiving dinner table: "You want to drive him off! You three wasted your chances and now you want me to waste mine, but I won't do it. I can see what's what! Just listen to any song on the radio; look at any soap opera. *Love* is what it's all about. . . . You just don't want me to stop cooking for you and taking care of this house, you don't want Julian to fall in love with me" (*Tourist*, 174-75). However unlikely the pairing, Julian and Rose do marry, and Tyler leaves the two at the novel's end with as much or perhaps more chance of happiness than a host of her other characters. Unlike Mildred Vinton and Amanda Pauling, Rose Leary strides forth and claims her right to love.

When men abandon women or refuse to go along with a life change, it is generally the woman who suffers. Evie Decker in *A Slipping-Down Life* is going to leave her irresponsible husband and return to claim her dead father's house. Although Drum is ill-prepared to assume his role as husband and father, he at least questions Evie's decision with, "People don't just take off like this. They think things through. They talk a lot. Like: How will you support that baby, all alone?" But Evie seems to know that Drum will always be just talk, and she declares, "I'll get along" (*Life*, 212). Tyler ends this novel without our ever knowing what kind of mother Evie has turned out to be. We do not know whether her child will repeat its mother's pattern of a limited formal education, a runaway marriage, and a pregnancy far too early in life to promise happiness for either parent or child.

Often in Tyler's fiction when men leave women, financial worry consumes much of the woman's waking hours. For example, in *The Accidental Tourist* Muriel Pritchett's mother-in-law ruthlessly comes after Muriel's husband (in a scene that counterpoints Mrs. Emerson's taking her daughter away from her young husband), leaving Muriel with a sickly infant son and little preparation for earning a living. The ever-resourceful Muriel does not lose heart, but the struggle is real: "I've *had* to be inventive. It's been scrape and scrounge, nail and knuckle, ever since Norman left me" (*Tourist*, 189). Mary Tell in *Celestial Navigation* expresses far more insecurity, reminding herself that *if* things work out with John "I won't be on my own, not if it's up to me. I won't leave anyone else ever. It's too hard. I never bargained for this tearing feeling inside me. I didn't know I would be so confused, as if I were in several places at once and yet not wholly any place at all" (*Navigation*, 73). The imagery here suggests that if a woman is not complemented by a man, she simply is not a whole person.

Powerlessness and Abuse

In their 1988 two-volume study, *No Man's Land*, Sandra Gilbert and Susan Gubar give a telling example to portray the dilemma women face when they are virtually powerless: "The act of infanticide, Barrett Browning implies, is a woman's most potent form of revenge against men because it destroys the patrilineage, but at the same time it is a telling sign of female vulnerability because it reveals that one of the few kinds of power a woman has is destructive power over her child."[19] While none of Tyler's women characters commit infanticide, three of them do commit child abuse. Anxiety over money plays a major role in the abusive behavior of Mary Tell, Pearl Tull, and Jenny Tull; Pearl's acts of violence, however, also stem from her humiliation over being abandoned by her husband, and with Jenny those acts stem from sheer exhaustion from the long hours her medical residency requires and from having to raise a child with little money and her husband gone as well. Whatever the varied motivations, alarming child abuse occurs.

Tyler first uses this subject matter in *Celestial Navigation* when Mary Tell realizes how utterly powerless she is without a man to support her – a realization that leads to frustration and the abuse of her daughter Darcy. For Mary money becomes an obsession. She leaves her husband after the more handsome and far more sophisticated John persuades her to come away with him. Installed in the Pauling boardinghouse and left to wait for John's infrequent calls and visits, Mary worries about her future: "Now I have hours and days and weeks to think: I am entirely dependent on a man I hardly know. I have no money, no home, no family to return to, not even a high school degree to get a job with, and no place to leave Darcy if I *could* find a job. . . . [I]f it works out that John and I are married, I am going to save money of my own no matter what. I don't care if I have to steal it; I will save that money and hide it away somewhere in case I ever have to be on my own again" (*Navigation*, 73). John, of course, has no intention of marrying Mary, and soon he returns to his wife and home. Mary's attempts to earn money are woefully inadequate: she clips magazine and newspaper coupons, sends in household tips for a few dollars of prize money, brings in a machine on which to knit socks at home – a task that proves difficult and earns very little. Cooped up in her boardinghouse room with a restless child, Mary's patience snaps one day when Darcy wants to know where John is and why he does not come to take them out: "Her voice was high and cracked; it tore at my nerves. I can't describe it. I hauled off and slapped her, and for a minute she stared at me with her mouth open. Then she started bellowing. I shook her by the shoulders and said, 'Stop that. Stop it this instant.' So she stopped, but she was trembling all over and I was too. I live in fear that she will remember that day forever" (*Navigation*, 57).

Mary does not again display such violence; however, when Jeremy fails to emerge from his studio for the much-delayed trip to City Hall to be married, Mary – with little money and no more formal education than she had when Darcy was born – loads up all her children and leaves Jeremy and a house where she had established a life for herself. When Darcy challenges the move, Mary does not relent. Like Meg Peck protesting one of Duncan and Justine's many moves, Darcy tells Mary that it is a school day and, furthermore, she has a math test to take that will be half her grade. Mary does not sympathize and merely says, "You can make it up, Darcy" (*Navigation*, 193). Later, when Mary reflects on what hurt she had caused Darcy, the damage is done and not to be forgotten. Darcy "had been yanked out of a school she loved; she had been separated from Jeremy without even telling him goodbye, and in some ways she was closer to Jeremy than any of the others were." Leaving Jeremy and coming to Brian's tumbled-down lake shack was, Mary admits, "the most selfish thing I have ever done" (*Navigation*, 212). Tyler indicates with Brian's line to Mary – "I won't rush you" – that Mary will be rescued from this primitive living condition and once again have the security of a man as well as a home with the standard conveniences. But she is no better equipped to be independent, to earn a living, to cease being powerless. It is interesting that in *The Accidental Tourist* Tyler lets Rose Leary transfer her extraordinary domestic skills and systems into an office environment, replacing Julian's gum-chewing secretary and transforming his haphazard office routine into a model of efficiency and order, and herself into an office manager.

As painful as Mary's treatment of Darcy is, the child abuse in *Dinner at the Homesick Restaurant* is far more disturbing, simply because for many years Pearl Tull frequently abuses her children, verbally and physically. The extent of the abuse is thoroughly alarming, culminating for the youngest of the three children, Jenny, in a double nightmare: her mother as a witch willing to betray Jenny to the Nazis and raising her with the single intent of destroying her. Early in the novel Tyler says that Pearl Tull "was not a tranquil woman; she often lost her temper, snapped, slapped the nearest cheek, said things she later regretted – but thank the Lord, she didn't expose her tears" (*Dinner*, 14). Her pride will not allow her to admit to the children that their father has abandoned her or allow her to show a sign of grief. When Pearl does present her placid exterior, inquiring politely about the children's school friends, Jenny knows that this is not the whole or perhaps even the real mother: "Jenny knew that, in reality, her mother was a dangerous person – hot breathed and full of rage and unpredictable. The dry, straw texture of her lashes could seem the result of some conflagration, and her pale hair could crackle electrically from its bun and her eyes could get small as hatpins" (*Dinner*, 70). There is hardly a more graphic picture of woman/mother as monster.

Pearl's rampages are violent, and the three children know by loud noises – pots thrown about in the kitchen or the contents of Jenny's bureau drawers dumped out – that "Pearl has hit the warpath" (*Dinner*, 49). Often the children are as much mystified by their mother's rampage as they are frightened. The name-calling is extreme: "You upstart," "You wretch, you ugly horror," "Stupid Clod," "Parasites," "serpent," "cockroach," "hideous little sniveling guttersnipes" (*Dinner*, 53, 70). Far worse than these epithets is Pearl's chilling wish: "I wish you'd all die, and let me go free. I wish I'd find you dead in your beds" (*Dinner*, 53). Her physical abuse of the children is equally alarming. She grabs a braid of Jenny's hair so hard she pulls the child off her chair; she throws a spoon in Cody's face and then reaches and slaps his face; she upends a bowl of peas on Ezra's head: "Which of her children had not felt her stinging slap, with the claw-encased pearl in her engagement ring that could bloody a lip at one flick? Jenny had seen her hurl Cody down a flight of stairs. She'd seen Ezra ducking, elbows raised, warding off an attack" (*Dinner*, 70). The abuse does not cease when the three are no longer in childhood.

Cody goes off to college, the passive Ezra unexpectedly proves fit for the army, and Jenny, finishing high school, is left alone with her mother. With her and her siblings grown, Jenny thinks that surely there would be no more violent scenes, but it is here that Jenny relates the nightmare that graphically underscores the psychic suffering Pearl's abuse has caused. The words *witch* and *Nazis* emphasize the imagined and real terror the experiences have caused and hint at the emotional scars that will last a lifetime: "But she never felt entirely secure, and at night, when Pearl had placed a kiss on the center of Jenny's forehead, Jenny went off to bed and dreamed what she *had always dreamed*: her mother laughed a *witch's* shrieking laugh; dragged Jenny out of hiding as the *Nazis* tramped up the stairs; accused her of sins and crimes that had never crossed Jenny's mind. Her mother told her, in an informative and considerate tone of voice, that *she was raising Jenny to eat her*" (*Dinner*, 70; my italics).

Home for a weekend, Jenny visits Ezra's friend Josiah, whose gauntness and excessive height cause some people to consider him a freak. When Pearl sees Jenny give Josiah a light and sisterly kiss, her abuse streams forth. Jenny is consorting with an "animal," "a crazy! A dummy! A retarded person . . . this gorilla, letting him take his pleasure, just to shame me." Jenny is a "piece of trash," a "tramp," a "trashy thing" (*Dinner*, 79). Pearl is incapable of hearing any explanation, and her words send Josiah fleeing in embarrassment and humiliation and leave Jenny remembering the hurts of her childhood now being repeated.

After her years of study, exhausted by excessive hours in her medical residency and struggling to raise her daughter, Becky, alone, Jenny breaks down one night when Becky says "no." Jenny "hauled off and slapped her hard across the mouth, then shook her till her head lolled, then flung her aside and ran out of the apartment to . . . where?" (*Dinner*, 209). Jenny's workdays become a blur from complete exhaustion, and Becky continues to pay a price. Jenny "slammed Becky's face into her Peter Rabbit dinner plate and gave her a bloody nose. She yanked a handful of hair." And with these acts of violence, memories of Jenny's childhood come upon her. She feels her mother's sharp fingernails biting into her and hears "her mother shrieking, 'Guttersnipe! Ugly little rodent!' and some scrap of memory – she couldn't quite place it – Cody catching hold of Pearl's wrist and fending her off while Jenny shrank against the wall. Was this what it came to – that you never could escape?" (*Dinner*, 209). But Jenny recovers from her breakdown, thanks ironically to her mother, who comes and plays the perfect mother/grandmother, fixing nourishing broths and hot tea and entertaining Becky by reading books aloud and taking her for walks in the park. From her close brush with dark impulses, Jenny Tull learns to change. With her third marriage she assumes the responsibility of another woman's children, and her tough and resilient manner of coping with their daily demands and their emotional problems suggests that she and they will survive with fewer problems and scars than one would imagine. Although late in the novel Becky is suffering, as did her mother years before, from anorexia nervosa, the reader assumes that she too will survive this malady and perhaps in her adulthood she will not repeat the abuse she received as a child, as did her mother before her.

Powerlessness and Realistic Choices

Perhaps no one aspect of women's lives has been more discussed and emphasized in the feminist movement than the plight of women against the traditional power of the white male patriarchy. From the repressive legal and social codes under which Edna suffers in Kate Chopin's *The Awakening* (1899) to the wives in Anne Tyler's novels, women struggle for independence and equality. Some of Tyler's women characters struggle but in the end get *and* accept the closed-in life of family and household duties. Charlotte Emory in *Earthly Possessions* is even controlled by the foundling Jiggs, whom she has raised. A natural chairman, Jiggs reminds Charlotte that the PTA meeting begins at eight o'clock, and he wants Charlotte to wear her red dress. It is an event that Charlotte dreads, and she bursts out with, "I have spent my life at the Clarion P.T.A. What's the purpose?" She longs for time alone, telling Jiggs that her "idea of a perfect day . . . is an empty square on the calendar. That's all I ask." The child responds with the coldness of the adult men that Charlotte is obliged to live among: " 'Well, then,' said Jiggs. He adjusted his glasses and ran his finger across the page. 'In the month of March, you'll have three perfect days' " (*Possessions*, 188). This response to Charlotte's needs seems as foreboding as Torvald's insipid and diminishing of Nora by calling her his little squirrel and his little songbird in Ibsen's *A Doll's House* (1879).

Carolyn Heilbrun concludes her essay "Marriage Perceived: English Literature, 1873-1944" with this sentence: "Modern writers have at least established that the unexamined marriage, like the unexamined life, is not worth living, and that Eros alone will not sustain an institution which has lost, or totally outlived, its social and economic justification" (131). In reviewing Ellen Schwamm's *Adja-*

cent Lives (1978) Tyler reminded readers of the time when "marriage provided the Cinderella experience for a novel" – that is, until "readers grew wise and bitter, and marriage no longer did the trick."[20] What replaces marriage, of course, is "the Affair" which allows the woman at long last to be "loved as she deserves to be loved, at long last sexually awakened, free of the trivia of an aging marriage; the heroine sinks into her lover's arms and *now* you can close the book" ("Affair," 1). But the ideal marriage and the ideal affair are probably unexamined experiences, and Tyler reminds readers that the longed-for affair is in reality "a rich, intricate, deeply flawed experience that tends, like most experiences, to thin out as it stretches on, and to finish up with a number of frayed and faded ends" ("Affair," 1).

Most of Tyler's women characters do marry (Mary Tell is the exception in her life with Jeremy Pauling), but the fact of their marriage does not make the reader sigh with satisfaction and close the novel – nor does the marriage relieve the woman's feeling of powerlessness. When Saul Emory proposes to Charlotte, for example, she accepts but knows perfectly well she had not really wanted to marry him. Reflecting on her decision she says, "I should have refused. I wasn't helpless, after all. I should have said, 'I'm sorry, I can't fit you in. I never planned to take a second person on this trip.' But I didn't" (*Possessions*, 69). Ironically, Charlotte does have a means of livelihood in her father's photography studio and could have kept that enterprise going until her sick mother died and gave her the freedom she thought she wanted. Instead she marries Saul and takes on the child they conceive, the foundling Jiggs, sundry homeless folk from the mourners' bench at Saul's church, and eventually one after the other of Saul's brothers. Tyler makes it clear that Charlotte admits there are two worlds: tending to the daily domestic needs of others and taking up a career. "So I survived. Baked their cakes. Washed their clothes. Fed their dog. Stepped through my studio doorway one evening and fell into the smell of work, a deep, rich, comforting smell: chemicals and high-gloss paper and the gritty, ancient metal of my father's camera" (*Possessions*, 183). It is not the smell of bread and cakes baking but the pungent smell of picture-developing chemicals that Charlotte finds "deep, rich, comforting." It is not only earthly *possessions* that Charlotte would like to escape, but too many earthly people as well. Her attempt to leave comes when a young and inept bank robber takes her with him as a hostage, and despite the symbolic message, "Keep on truckin'," that appeared on a cereal box badge, Charlotte's round-trip journey is short-lived and a dead-end escape.

In *Celestial Navigation* when Mary Tell leaves her husband to follow the glamorous John to Baltimore, her affair (and hopes of marriage) are not the stuff of a happy story. Instead of an attractive home Mary and Darcy are stuck in a boardinghouse room, dependent, as Mary bemoans, "on a man I hardly know." Perhaps nowhere in Tyler's fiction do we watch a woman so painfully aware of her powerlessness to change her situation as Mary Tell when she faces her limited resources and options. Her alternative for a number of years is Jeremy. Mary considers pregnancy her natural state, and the children come along in rapid succession. While they enliven the household and bring Mary pleasure, her reaction toward them is mixed. She sometimes feels when she returns from the hospital with yet another new baby that this young life is not a bundle of joy but "another rope, tying me down like a tent. I don't have the option to *leave* any more. I'm forced to depend on him [Jeremy]. He's not dependable" (*Navigation*, 142). And when Jeremy fails to gather the energy for the trip to city hall for the belated marriage ceremony, Mary does leave, but only with the help of Brian, who in the end will again rescue her – but then for himself.

Quite a different woman and a full two generations older than Mary Tell is the quiet and stately Mrs. Jarrett, who is also part of the Pauling boardinghouse and keenly aware of being a widow. Without her husband she feels incomplete, and though she may wonder about her sister's judgment in marrying *four* times, Mrs. Jarrett knows poignantly that a widow is lonely and in many ways vulnerable and powerless. She speaks for many when she says, "We do need someone to lean on. I imagine I'll spend the rest of my life feeling naked on my street side every time I take a walk, and I am sixty-four now and been a widow longer than a wife" (*Navigation*, 122). Her words reflect her time, and perhaps in the 1990s many a young reader may wonder what on earth "street side" even means or why it is of importance to Mrs. Jarrett. Mary is so much younger than Mrs. Jarrett, but no less dependent on men.

As Mary Tell embodies the frustration of powerlessness, Caroline Peck Mayhew in *Searching for Caleb* represents the woman dominated by her father who goes through her short life without a shred of responsible action. Hopelessly immature, Caroline considers herself in absolute exile when her husband, Sam Mayhew, moves her from the security of the Pecks' Baltimore compound to the remote place of Philadelphia when his job necessitates the change. Unable to raise her daughter Justine properly, Caroline manages only brief smothering kisses followed by long periods of neglect while the maid sees to what needs the quiet Justine has. Plump, powdery, and pouchy, Caroline takes to her bed, spending the days reading silly books and magazines while she eats her way through endless chocolates and longs for Baltimore. Nothing but her father's occasional visits can mobilize her into action, but a word from him can get her attention and even make her gasp to hold her stomach in. When Sam Mayhew is called into the army, Caroline joyfully returns to the family bosom in Baltimore, where she remains through his army years. Always effaced, Sam Mayhew finally refuses to be manipulated and goes back to his own people. Years later he bitterly opposes Justine's marriage to her first cousin Duncan Peck, refuses to attend the wedding, and shortly thereafter dies of a heart attack. Caroline finally responds to the uselessness of her life and one night rises from her bed wearing such a billowing night dress that she looks like "a wad of pink bubble gum" and drifts out into the nighttime street: "She had to wait for six cars, all told, before she found one that would run her down" (*Caleb*, 118). *Searching for Caleb* reaches back three generations into a Baltimore family and fortune where strong men rule and women play their roles without question until in Justine and Duncan two people leave for a life of wandering in a marriage where life is carried on more by drifting than by direction.

Tyler's women characters feel the need to depend on men, yet a large number of these women also want to run away, and many of them do. In *Morgan's Passing* Emily never literally runs away, but she takes up walking almost every day and goes for miles. In 1976 she walked "all spring and summer, down alleyways, across tattered rags of parks, through stores that smelled of pickles and garlic. She went in the front doors and out the back, emerging on some unknown street full of delivery trucks, stacked wooden crates, construction workers with pneumatic drills tearing up the pavement."[21] The route is haphazard and tinged with danger because Emily is not following a trail for walkers or a path for joggers. The people she sees are in unexpected places like alleyways and the back doors of stores. As she wanders on these walks, Tyler writes that what goes through her head are "songs about leaving, about women who packed up and left" (*Passing*, 189). The words she sings end with the line "*I know you, rider*"; these words are the title of Tyler's first (and unpublished) novel, in which a character explains that the word *rider* here means a man who willingly lives off a woman's earnings and efforts. At last when Emily and Leon get their puppet show enterprise under way, they soon have more engagements than they can fill. Yet Emily continues to make the costumes, play her roles during the performance, keep up with their child, Gina, and do all the household work as well. Perhaps it is not surprising that on her solitary walks these lyrics move about in her head: "*If you miss the train I'm on, you will know that I am gone. . . . One of these mornings, it won't be long, you'll call my name and I'll be gone. . . . I know you, rider, going to miss me when I'm . . .* Gone, gone, gone" (*Passing*, 189-90). When this ill-matched young couple has no money at all to spare, Emily in an absurd moment of extravagance spends $4.98 for a cosmetic kit, seemingly a useless and most unnecessary item except that the kit is one intended for travel.

In *A Slipping-Down Life* Evie Decker for a time allows herself to be subservient and lets her husband, Drumstrings Casey, treat her as a commodity. Capitalizing on the sensation caused when she carves "Casey" on her forehead, she appears nightly in the tacky Unicorn Club where Drum sings, thinking "of herself as a bait-and-switch ad. People came out of curiosity, bored by the long summer days. They figured they might as well go stare at the girl who had ruined her face" (*Life*, 89). The look at Evie takes no time at all, and the patrons quickly turn their attention elsewhere. The local paper (the *Avalice and Farinia Weekly*) carries a bored review of Drum's performance, but "Evie was not mentioned, any more than the color of his clothes or the brand of his guitar" (*Life*, 90). Evie's worth is thus equated to the shade of Drum's outfit and the guitar make. Drum's manager, David, is irritated when Evie and Drum decide to marry, declaring that "career-wise" for Drum, "marriage is suicide. Look at the Beatles" (*Life*, 139). Once married, Drum shows unexpected domestic skills, installing toothbrush holders and such, but earning a steady income is not part of his agenda. Although Evie has anxious moments fearing Drum will fuss that she has taken a job at the library, she finds that on payday things are fine. Drum picks her up in the old Volkswagen her father had given them, and she hands over her paycheck: " 'Good, I'm out of cigarettes,' he said. She was relieved, but she had a let-down feeling too" (*Life*, 166). Feminists bristle over a woman who must feel relieved that her husband does not fuss because she has a job, sympathize because she feels let down with what happens to her paycheck, and bristle again that she acquiesces without protest. This scene plays its part in preparing Evie for that moment when she leaves Drum, returns to her father's house, and begins what one hopes is a stronger and far more independent life – a life where her sense of power must come from herself if she is to have any at all.

In *Morgan's Passing* Bonny Gower may have her father's money to sustain her when Morgan goes off with Emily, but the grinding routine of household years has molded much of her life. At one point Bonny thinks she will become a writer and plans a short story that will take its subject matter from the tale she can weave by looking at 30 years' worth of check stubs and budget-book entries. The domestic tasks that these women characters take on or willingly accept no doubt deny them careers, and the sheer repetition of tasks that literally never end is a burden that increases the feeling of powerlessness. These various women characters reflect on their lives from time to time and the conclusions they reach while not exact parallels often express the same sharp reality. Neither Charlotte Emory of *Earthly Possessions* nor Mary Tell of *Celestial Navigation* believes at all that things ever end with "and they lived happily ever after." Marooned in her self-exile and living in the damp and dingy lake shack, Mary puts her many children to sleep by telling fairy tales.

These stories from the Brothers Grimm weave their way into her analysis of herself and the prospects that life offers. Looking at herself from the outside, Mary knows that others might well say that she "seem[s] to have been leading a fairly dramatic life, involving elopements and love children and men stretching in a nearly unbroken series behind me, but the fact is that when you proceed through these experiences day by day they are not really so earth-shaking. All events, except childbirth, can be reduced to a heap of trivia in the end" (*Navigation*, 223). The plots of Rapunzel and the Princess and the Pea and Rumpelstiltskin thread their way through Mary's mind, and she presses to think of the ending *beyond* the endings of these tales. These classic endings of joy are not convincing, and what if, after all, the ending *is not* happy: "And after Rumpelstiltskin was defeated the miller's daughter lived in sorrow forever, for the king kept nagging her to spin more gold and she could never, never manage it again" (*Navigation*, 223). The fairy-tale ending does not convince Mary, and the course of her life, the things she has done or wanted to do, end up to her as mere trivial acts – all, that is, except childbirth, the act that defines women as mothers more than it defines them as *selves*. It is a depressing view of the world, and one almost longs for the typical fairy tale and a happy ending.

Trapped by layers of domestic responsibilities, Charlotte Emory in *Earthly Possessions* seems powerless to turn her life in a new direction. Tyler uses a photograph to bring about Charlotte's reconciliation with the past, especially with her grossly overweight mother. The photograph shows a beautiful child, and when Lacey Debney Ames in her final illness orders Charlotte to burn it, Charlotte thinks of the family story that she was not her mother's biological child – some strange hospital mixup. Charlotte cannot part with the photograph, transferring it from pocket to pocket as the days pass. Her mother's illness makes everybody in the household so uneasy they feel compelled to leave the room, but Charlotte works through the past, and even before her mother dies she comes to considerable insight into this ungainly woman's real life. Charlotte sits sewing Girl Scout emblems on her daughter's uniform, and this domestic task of small green stitches allows her, Tyler writes, to fasten "down my mother's foggy memories. I thought about the household tasks – the mending, cooking, story-reading, temperature-taking, birthday cakes, dentist's and pediatrician's appointments – necessary for the rearing of a child. All those things my mother had managed, middle-aged though she had been, crippled with high blood pressure and varicose veins, so clumsy and self-conscious that the simplest trip for new school shoes was something to dread for days beforehand. I had never put it all together before" (*Possessions*, 173).

The mother's rambling mind is now beyond participating in Charlotte's insight, but for the daughter the experience goes deep. Just before she dies, Lacey Debney Ames rallies to identify the child in the photograph that Charlotte has carried in her pocket for days. It was Lacey herself, a beautiful child and not the overweight and unsightly woman of Charlotte's life. The moment lets Charlotte glimpse the inner life of her mother, and near the end of this novel Tyler gives Charlotte an insight that belongs to so many of her characters. Thinking that she must escape and ready to leave, Charlotte turns to bid the dog Ernest good-bye: "Then I straightened and saw the greenish light that filtered through the windows – a kind of light they don't have anyplace else. Oh, I've never had the knack of knowing I was happy right while the happiness was going on" (*Possessions*, 189). It is the lived moment of the present that most people miss, and at least this character in Anne Tyler's fiction sees the greenish light and senses the essential happiness that the moment possesses – even as she holds this moment entirely alone.

Compromise and Endurance, Not Storybook Romance

Doris Betts says that during the past quarter century many readers and critics of novels would agree that "the family has almost died out"; however, the families in Tyler's novels, Betts argues, "break, mend, and persist" (1990, 4). And in most of Tyler's fiction the families who can stay together do so ever mindful of the old Welsh saying that Dorothy Faye Sala Brock so aptly cites in her dissertation on Tyler, "the rent that's due to love." Just as the tenant must pay the landlord the monthly rent if living arrangements are to continue amicably, so the family must constantly contribute to its own daily existence. "Though Tyler is often, and rightly, regarded as a novelist of family life and a traditionalist in the view of what family life is," Brock says, "there should be no suggestion that she closes her eyes to the realities of modern marriages" (1985, 252). Tyler's fictional families, as Brock notes, face divorce, separation, desertion, absurd children, mismatched couples – problems that must be faced and dealt with if the family unit is to survive.

Tyler's realistic view of marriage is evident as she discusses the fiction of other writers. Her review of Iris Murdoch's *The Sea, The Sea* (1978) focuses on the main character, Charles Arrowby. He is a man, Tyler says, "very much set in his ways, and possessed of that special kind of arrogance and selective blindness that you often see in successful men. Moreover, he has never been married. He lacks all understanding of the process of compromise and resignation that can operate in a marriage."[22] There simply are no storybook marriages among Tyler's characters. Near the end of *Earthly Possessions* Charlotte Emory observes the erstwhile bank robber Jake and his pregnant teenage girlfriend, destined now to a risky marriage at best. "I didn't know," Charlotte says, "who I felt sadder for. I hate a situation where you can't say clearly that one person's right and one is wrong. I was cowardly; I chose to watch the parade" (*Possessions*, 131). No one from the outside can make a marriage work when the partners do not understand that process of compromise and resignation.

There is a wide variety of response to marriage among Tyler's characters, responses that reflect much of contemporary life. The "Bride Beautiful" magazines may still take their place on the newsstands, but the facts of marriage and its prospects are less glamorous than the slick photographs such magazines display. Rose, Macon Leary says when his sister enters the garden for her wedding, "looked tense and frayed, as most brides do if people would only admit it" (*Tourist*, 270). In *Breathing Lessons* Maggie Moran listens to a Baltimore radio station as she drives along and pays attention to today's question: "What makes an ideal marriage?" Years ago Maggie's friend Serena had told her that marriage was no Rock Hudson–Doris Day movie, and the female radio caller's answer suggests the sober, if depressing, truth of many a marriage: the ideal marriage means the couple share common interests, says the caller, "like if you both watched the same kind of programs on TV" (*Lessons*, 5).

To Serena, marriage is far more a practical decision than anything romantic movies and slick magazines could portray. Years earlier when Maggie asked Serena if she really wanted to marry Max Gill, Serena echoed the answer Ibsen's Hedda Gabler gave when Judge Brack asked her why she married George Tesman. She had, Hedda said, danced herself tired. Serena is equally blunt: "It's just *time* to marry that's all. . . . I'm so tired of dating! I'm so tired of keeping up a good front! I want to sit on the couch with a regular, normal husband and watch TV for a thousand years" (*Lessons*, 109). Perhaps the caller to the Baltimore radio station had it right after all.

When marriages dissolve in Tyler's novels, it is because the couples simply cannot, or perhaps will not, communicate. In *The Clock*

Winder Mrs. Emerson will not allow her daughter Margaret's elope-
ment to stand and marches into the tiny honeymoon dwelling. The
young husband is no match for her: "Jimmy Joe chewed his thumb-
nail and did nothing, said nothing, allowed Margaret to be taken
away from him and never saw her again" (*Clock*, 199). As Evie
Decker and Drumstrings Casey kiss to confirm their intent to marry,
the failure of that marriage is signaled at this moment. As they kissed
they looked "out over each other's shoulders like drivers meeting on
opposite lanes of a highway" (*Life*, 138). This mismatched pair had
decided to marry during an insufferable heat wave – not a time, Alice
Hall Petry notes in her excellent discussion of this novel, when people are noted for "making intelligent decisions" (1990, 6). True
enough, but the heat wave broke during the three-day waiting period
for the marriage license – broke and pulled "the whole town from its
stupor" (*Life*, 136). The dramatic break in the weather brings relief
to many, but Evie and Drum go right ahead and marry, and their
marriage very quickly dissolves. The experience of this young couple
resembles the impasse that Emily and Leon Meredith reach in *Morgan's Passing*. Their marriage in New York City is as businesslike as
can be. Indeed, Emily declares that there had been more ceremony
"when she got her driver's license" (*Passing*, 69). After several years
of marriage, these two start out each morning with careful courtesies
and hopeful intentions. But things "deteriorated rapidly and [they]
ended up, at night, sleeping with their backs to each other on the
outermost edges of the bed" (*Passing*, 213). And their marriage ends
as Emily takes up life with the eccentric Morgan Gower, and Leon,
that rebel in his youth, returns to his parents and Richmond to take
up the staid banker's life his father had planned for him all along.

Other pairs show how carelessly people marry. Morgan and
Bonny Gower's daughter Carol, for instance, "got divorced before
she'd finished writing her thank-you notes," and their daughter Amy
is marrying a young man named Jim who, Morgan says, "had the flat,
beige face of a department-store mannequin. . . . Morgan couldn't
think of a thing to say to him" (*Passing*, 130, 97). Even without
Norman's selfish and heartless mother, Muriel and Norman Pritchett's marriage is doomed because they simply were playing house.
And in *Breathing Lessons* Fiona did not marry Jesse Moran for love
but, she says, "for that cradle" which Maggie claimed he was making
for the baby (*Lessons*, 269).

Perhaps Mary Tell in *Celestial Navigation* gives the sharpest and most realistic statement, though not one that all Tyler women characters would accept. It is one thing to compromise in choosing a marriage partner and have things work out reasonably well, as Serena and Max Gill's marriage apparently has; it is another thing when married life is unbearable. When Mary Tell has the chance to leave the motorcycle-racing Guy, she does so and takes full responsibility for that decision. She knows that the choice is a hard one, but, she says, "I don't know which takes more courage: surviving a lifelong endurance test because you once made a promise or breaking free, disrupting all your world. There are arguments for both sides; I see that. But I made my choice" (*Navigation*, 75). Many wives in Tyler's fiction are in less-than-happy marriages, but they choose to stay, to endure – Charlotte Emory, Mrs. Billy Emerson, Justine Peck, Pearl Tull, Maggie Moran. But others do not choose to stay and in leaving do disrupt their world. Charlotte Emory (*Earthly Possessions*) is cheated out of college. Her father dies suddenly and she is obliged to come home to look after her mother who is so overweight every movement requires effort. Charlotte's days are dull, and she says she "felt locked in a calendar." Her mother's conversations center on her dead husband, who had been given to black moods and little kindness. "I married him out of desperation," she tells Charlotte. "I settled for what I could get. Don't ever *settle*, Charlotte" (*Possessions*, 61). Charlotte declares to her mother and to herself that she will never do that, but her life with Saul Emory suggests that she does, although her ability in the process of compromise and resignation seems successful. That ability to compromise remains a strong force in Tyler's fiction, and those who run away eventually find that staying at home is, after all, what they must do.

Chapter Six

Family Matters:
"We Make Our Own Luck"

In his review of *Saint Maybe* Brad Leithauser argued that this novel – as do her others – places Tyler within "the comedy of manners – a genre nearer to the English literary tradition than the American. . . . For decades now the sort of amiable social comedy she embodies has been largely set aside by our best writers, who have arguably conceded it to Hollywood."[1] Although Tyler's work is indeed laced with a humor that delights, it is "beautifully suffused" – as Leithauser so well puts it – "with melancholy" (1). And perhaps this blending of humor and melancholy is best shown in the family situations and dilemmas her novels explore.

Reviewing *Dinner at the Homesick Restaurant* Benjamin DeMott found the novel a "border crossing" for Tyler because she "edges deep into a truth that's simultaneously (and interdependently) psychological, moral and formal – deeper than many living novelists of serious reputations have penetrated, deeper than Miss Tyler herself has gone before."[2] In this novel, as we have seen, Tyler boldly depicts serious incidents of child abuse and at the same time depicts the survival of those children in their varied and reconciled lives as adults. It is certainly true that the presence of melancholy hangs directly over this novel even though there are moments of bittersweet comedy – Cody's childhood practical jokes, the rigid and ridiculous Harley Baines and his library shelving system, Jenny Tull's interview with her stepson's young and jargon-laden school teacher, for example. From her first novel on, Tyler forces readers to take into account the family whose individual members are inevitably marked by "the subtle, inescapable ways in which certain family traits reappear."[3]

Family Life: Illusion and Reality

Often Tyler's characters long for the family to appear as it *should be*, and that illusory ideal haunts young Ben Joe Hawkes in *If Morning Ever Comes* as indeed it does old Mrs. Emerson in *The Clock Winder*. As Cody Tull (*Dinner at the Homesick Restaurant*) in his teenage years longed for his working mother to stay home and gossip in her kitchen with other women, so Ben Joe Hawkes from his New York City student apartment conjures up an ideal image of home. The picture of Sandhill, North Carolina, "comes drifting toward me – just the picture of it, like some sunny island that I have got to get back to. And there's my family. Most of the time I seem to see them sort of like a bunch of picnickers in a nineteenth-century painting, sitting around in the grass with their picnic baskets and their pretty dresses and their parasols, and floating past on that island" (*Morning*, 199). The picnicking family in the painting is perfect, unable to quarrel or disappoint – but also unable to respond or to live. What keeps families at odds in Tyler's fiction is a never-ending array of tense moments and often a desire for the ideal rather than an acceptance of reality.

In *The Clock Winder* Matthew (one of the seven Emerson children) had wanted a Swiss army knife for Christmas, but his mother paid no mind and gave him what suited her image of his wishes: a violin, a record player, and a complete set of the Brahms symphonies. Little wonder that in their adulthood these children *work* hard at moving away from their mother. Old and in need of daily assistance to run her house, Mrs. Emerson tells her "handyman," Elizabeth Abbott, of the past – why when the children were young and the family piled into the car they surely must have given the neighbors cause for envy as they drove off on an outing: " 'There go the Emersons,' people would say, and never guess for an instant that behind the glass it was all bickering and arguing, scenes and crises." The young and realistic Elizabeth simply replies, "I reckon *most* families work that way" (*Clock*, 18). It is the same message Victor Apple delivers to Emily and Leon Meredith in *Morgan's Passing*: "Other people's mothers always look so nice. Up close, they're strict and grabby and they don't have a sense of humor" (*Passing*, 78). And Charlotte Emory in *Earthly Possessions* certainly expresses this theme in a bleak way after the exotic and enviable Alberta (her husband's mother) throws caution, convention, and family obligations to the wind, leaving what Charlotte had thought was her happy "nuclear" family to elope with her father-in-law. Charlotte explains her new understanding of Albert's life: "What I mean to say is, I was easily fooled by appearances. Maybe all families, even the most normal-looking, were as queer as ours once you got up close. Maybe Alberta was secretly as sad as my mother" (*Possessions*, 65). Later in the novel Charlotte's husband, Saul, has retreated into his own world, preoccupied with his good works as preacher at the Holy Basis Church. His distance leads Charlotte to describe one of the bleakest prospects for family happiness that Tyler expresses anywhere in her work: "'Remember, we're a very unhappy family. I don't know why it should come as any surprise.' I think, 'It feels so natural. It's my luck, I'm unlucky, I've lived in unhappy families all my life. I never really expected anything different'" (*Possessions*, 137). And Saul offers not a word of protest to this declaration.

In *Searching for Caleb* Tyler provides the most complex family history in any of her novels, tracing the Peck clan from the mid-1880s through three generations. The acquisition of houses and automobiles as well as the self-contained society of this family protects it from neither tragedy nor dissolution. In 1911 Margaret Rose Bell, who had married Daniel Peck and borne his children, wants to visit her family in Washington for the celebration of her mother's birthday. To Daniel's mind, the Bells are "an undisciplined, frivolous, giggling lot," and he will allow Margaret Rose to go – provided she is back in time for Sunday church services – but he forbids her to take the children. She goes, and when she fails to return, Daniel makes no effort to reclaim her. Fairly soon, the children no longer ask for her at all. Even before news of her early death arrives, Margaret Rose has been expunged. In the present time of the novel, the entire family line approaches dissolution: "the aunts and uncles were old, the grandfather wore a hearing aid, and the cousins (Sally divorced, the rest unmarried, all childless) were developing lines and sags in their curiously innocent faces like aging midgets" (*Caleb*, 148).

The occupations and preoccupations of Justine and Duncan's five cousins ironically mirror their fading lives. Having no children herself, Esther supervises a nursery school, and Alice is a librarian (once a stereotypic job for an "old maid"). Sally, quickly subdued after her month-long marriage ended, now sedately teaches piano lessons in her great-grandmother's parlor. Besides Duncan, the only Peck men of this generation are Richard, who has left the cluster of family houses to live in a high-rise apartment in downtown Baltimore, and Claude, who lives over the garage and "spent all his money on steel engravings that nobody liked" (*Caleb*, 256). There will be no more "Pecks," and if any part of the family line continues it must be through the female side – through Justine and Duncan's only child, Meg (named for the runaway Margaret Rose), who has married so unwisely. This large extended family – who must have looked to its Roland Park neighbors in Baltimore like the ideal wealthy family who delighted in the company of each other – now faces the end of this generation and the end of the family name.

In *Dinner at the Homesick Restaurant* Cody Tull for a long time harbors resentment over his childhood, his bitterness evident to his young son Luke. Tyler entitles one chapter "This Really Happened," the tag line Cody always uses when he repeats the stories of his childhood, keeping his hurt and anger alive. Although his mother had abused the children, she had also raised them and supported them, and had done so with very little help from her husband, who deserted because life with her had grown too gray to bear. At last Pearl takes stock, weary of complaints about the past, and says to herself, "Honestly, . . . wasn't there some statute of limitations here? When was he [Cody] going to absolve her? He was middle-aged. He had no business holding her responsible any more" (*Dinner*, 22-23). Psychotherapists and psychiatrists might analyze the problem differently from Pearl, but Tyler's treatment of children and parents throughout her fiction suggests that she may, to a great extent, share Pearl's view. In her article "Family and Community in Anne Tyler's *Dinner at the Homesick Restaurant*" Paula Gallant Eckard asserts that "Tyler resists the temptation to indict parents, particularly mothers, for the transgressions of the past and for the ultimate shaping of offspring. Maternal ambivalence is a not uncommon thread in the fabric of human experience."[4] (In *The Clock Winder* Elizabeth Abbott reiterates the point that parents are often slighted. She says to her employer, Mrs. Emerson, "Isn't that surprising? People you wouldn't trust your purse with five minutes, maybe, but still they put in years and years of time tending their children along and they don't even make a fuss about it. Even if it's a criminal they turn out, or some other kind of failure – still, he managed to get grown, didn't he? Isn't that something?" [*Clock*, 274]. Mrs. Emerson does not answer, but considering her children's harsh judgment toward her, she must take some comfort in Elizabeth's words.)

In many of her book reviews Tyler pays particular attention to the working of family life and implies here, as she does so often in her novels, that perhaps people simply expect too much. Tyler reviewed Margaret Logan's *Happy Endings* (1979), an autobiographical account of a mother who proposed that she and her daughter undertake a 45-day bicycle trip, crossing the Alps from Paris to Rome. Never mind that this journey will be the longest time they have spent in each other's company since the child's birth: Tyler wonders whether the daughter can "keep her soul together in the face of colossal, all-encompassing maternal intrusion."[5] The book operates, Tyler suggests, "on that most modern of notions: That parents and children must by rights share their deepest inner life . . . earnestly invading each other's private space" ("Feathers," D8). An invasion, after all, involves a conflict that produces a victim and a victor. The sheer risk in family relations means that failure is always possible and that what is *supposed* to be a happy family situation is not always so.

The zany adventures in *Breathing Lessons* never completely dominate the melancholy that its characters experience. Serena Gill stages an unusual funeral for her husband, Max, and that service is surely one of the funniest episodes in Tyler's fiction. Serena, however, has few illusions. She had married Max not out of breathtaking love but because she was so tired of keeping up the pace and appearance that dating required. And Maggie Moran remembers that "it was Serena who'd said that motherhood was much too hard and, when you got right down to it, perhaps not worth the effort" (*Lessons*, 54). Now Max is dead and Serena's overweight daughter Linda has children of her own. When Maggie asks if Serena will get an apartment to be near Linda and her family, Serena's reply suggests that even grown children are not necessarily a pleasure: "Well, I'm not sure. . . . Seems anytime we spend a few days together I begin to realize we haven't got a thing in common" (*Lessons*, 79). The mention of grandchildren is supposed to be the irresistible pull, but not to Serena: "Oh, well, grandchildren. I've never felt they had all that much to do with me" (*Lessons*, 79). Maggie thinks that parents and children should be close, but despite her constant efforts to make things work, her own children are as distant as the stars.

The bleakness of the novel persists. Maggie's husband, Ira, "was just as sad as Maggie was, and for just the same reasons. He was lonely and tired and lacking in hope and his son had not turned out well and his daughter didn't think much of him, and he still couldn't figure where he had gone wrong" (*Lessons*, 280). Ira turns on his son Jesse, that boy who was so golden in his youth, and coldly cites the failures: never husband material, Jesse drifts from girlfriend to girlfriend, unable to keep any job more than a few months. "Everyone in Jesse's acquaintance," according to Ira, "by some magical coincidence ends up being a jerk" (*Lessons*, 310). Tyler ends the scene with Jesse leaving his parents' house, and one detail lingers to haunt. Jesse does not storm away from his accusing father and slam the front door but instead leaves without a word, letting the door "click very gently behind him" (*Lessons*, 310). That final and unexpectedly gentle click is powerful. Throughout the novel Maggie has tried and failed to reconcile her family members; now Jesse's departure signals a loss that probably is final.

The most balanced response to complicated family life in Tyler's fiction comes, I think, through Jenny Tull (*Dinner at the Homesick Restaurant*) and Ian Bedloe (*Saint Maybe*). Certainly Jenny Tull endured and survived serious child abuse as well as an unwise first marriage and a heart-breaking second one. Later, as a medical resident, the pressure of long hours and of raising a child alone pushes her over the edge and into a breakdown. Her recovery leads her to readjust her life, which eventually includes a third husband and his houseful of children. Joe's eldest son, Selvin, misses his mother and finds the new household routine hard; his grades at school plummet, and Jenny answers the teacher's summons for a conference. Taken aback that the teacher – who is tiny and not out of her twenties – can intimidate so quickly, Jenny listens for a bit to the jargon modern society uses so freely. Selvin's trouble, the young teacher explains, is his "experiencing emotional problems due to the adjustments at home" (*Dinner*, 195). Jenny struggles a moment to keep her composure when the baby's pacifier falls out of her purse; then she speaks to the young teacher, her words coming out of more experience than this young woman may ever know: "I don't see the need to blame adjustment, broken homes, bad parents, that sort of thing.

We make our own luck, right? You have to overcome your setbacks. You can't take them too much to heart. I'll explain all that to Selvin. I'll tell him this evening. I'm certain his grades will improve." Then Jenny "bent to pick up the pacifier, and shook hands with the teacher and left" (*Dinner*, 196). Tyler does not carry the novel on to reveal what Selvin is like as an adult, but the reconciling epiphany that Cody experiences at the novel's end suggests that Jenny's words hit the mark: we do overcome our setbacks or at least we had better.

In *Saint Maybe* Ian Bedloe in middle-age looks at the three adults he gave up his youth to raise, observing now how they have shifted and evolved out of the difficult stages of their growing up. If ever the ideal relation between parent (or surrogate parent) and child exists, Ian describes what that should be: "He enjoyed them the way he would enjoy longtime best friends who found the same things funny or upsetting and didn't need every last remark explained for them" (*Saint*, 254).

Tyler does not spare her fictional families their troubles, yet most of them endure, and some face the future with optimism. As *Breathing Lessons* ends, for instance, Maggie and Ira Moran prepare to drive their daughter to begin her college career, a sign of promise, particularly since she has won a full scholarship.

The Family Dinner

Sometimes in Tyler's fiction naive and young characters start out hopeful and starry-eyed, sure that marriage will bring promised bliss. In *Breathing Lessons* Maggie Moran reminds her friend Serena of their early dreams. Why, Maggie says, "we promised we wouldn't wash the dishes right after supper because that would take us away from our husbands; remember that? How long since you saved the dishes till morning so you could be with Max? How long since Max even noticed that you didn't?" (*Lessons*, 23). In Tyler's fiction the family dinner stands as a major image, serving as a paradigm for family expectations that come so often to disappointment. Maggie's disillusionment probably began during supper, not with dishwashing.

From 13 to 15 November 1990 the *New York Times* and CBS News conducted a telephone poll of 1,370 people around the continental United States, asking, "Did most of your family eat dinner together last night?"[6] A vast majority (80 percent) reported that on a typical weeknight their family did indeed eat dinner together. Although "dinner" varied for these families from a formal meal at home to a quick meal in a fast-food restaurant, the occasion was obviously important. The *Times* quoted Thomas S. Weisner, a professor of anthropology at UCLA, who said that "even though it may not be enacted every day, the family dinner is still there as a cultural ideal" (*NYT*, C6). Historically, the American family dinner was the midday meal, but, the *Times* article noted, when the Industrial Revolution radically shifted working habits during the mid-nineteenth century – with the result that a vast number of men worked outside the home and ate the midday meal away – the principal meal for the family became the evening one: "Dinner became a celebration of the breadwinner's return and it took on great ceremony" (*NYT*, C6). Poll respondents had to be pressed to concede any deviation in observing family dinner and "talked about these occasions differently, as if these more haphazard meals did not count and certainly did not represent their family traditions" (*NYT*, C6).

The 1950s immortalized "Mom" in a frilly apron and happy in the kitchen; millions of Americans – those people in circumstances of divorce, poverty, and unconventional work hours, as well as those in a stable family situation – saw the ideal American family at dinner in the weekly episodes of "Ozzie and Harriet" and "Father Knows Best" (*NYT*, C6). By the 1960s and 1970s a vast number of women had joined the work force, and unless there was a division of labor in the home, the woman faced preparing the evening meal *after* a day's work outside the home. Despite these obvious cultural changes, the *Times*/CBS staff found one thread constant among the 31 families interviewed after the November poll: "the passion with which they embraced the concept of eating dinner together. Respondents spoke of dinner as the linchpin for the day, a respite from the chaos and separation in daily life" (*NYT*, C6). Although American family life in the 1990s seems especially fragile and frayed, evidence suggests that "dinner together is one of the absolute critical symbols in the cohesion of the family" (*NYT*, C6). Indeed, one person interviewed declared, "without it [the family dinner] they would no longer feel as though they were a family" (*NYT*, A1).

That most distinguished writer about food in American, the late M. F. K. Fisher, took a less optimistic view of the happy family dinner.

In Fisher's *An Alphabet for Gourmets* "F" stands for family, and Fisher's expectations for the family having pleasant dinners are limited. The cover on an old *Saturday Evening Post* featuring the American family at Thanksgiving dinner – idealized by Norman Rockwell – does not impress Fisher. "The cold truth," she declares, "is that family dinners are more often than not an ordeal of nervous indigestion, preceded by hidden resentment and ennui and accompanied by psychosomatic jitters."[7] Perhaps the only successful family dinner, Fisher speculates, occurs when a will is about to be read – an occasion for which one could presuppose "good manners during the meal, if the lawyer is not scheduled to appear until after it" (Fisher, 37). Occasionally, Fisher concedes, an amiable family dinner may occur, but probably only so by happy accident. Why, "brothers and cousins and grandparents who may have been cold or even warlike suddenly find themselves in some stuffy booth in a chophouse, eating together with a forgotten warmth and amity." A successful routine family dinner, Fisher insists, is possible but "rare. Most often it must be prearranged with care and caution" (Fisher, 40).

The use of the family dinner in Tyler's fiction is most obvious, of course, in *Dinner at the Homesick Restaurant*, where Ezra Tull strives to make his patrons feel at home even though they are dining out and where he repeatedly tries – with care and caution – to gather his own family for dinner. Growing up, Ezra had few models of happy family dinners. His mother, Pearl, would return from her day's work at Sweeney's Bros. Grocery and Fine Produce and, without taking off her hat, start banging pots and pans in the kitchen, mumbling with complaints as she did so. The meals were grim: strange combinations like leftover pineapple in mashed potatoes; gravy appeared eternally as undiluted cream of mushroom soup. Pearl created no pleasurable experience with food except when the children were sick. Then her nourishing broths and hot tea were a welcomed change to the usual family dinner.

It was Ezra who prepared hot milk laced with cinnamon to comfort his sister, Jenny, after an encounter when Pearl was on the "warpath," as the children described it. When Ezra begins his career at the restaurant, his passion is to bring the family together at dinner to celebrate important occasions. His best plans fail because a member of the family (usually Pearl) behaves badly, bolts, and refuses to

return to the table. The abrupt move to disrupt the family dinner
ruins the event, and finally Pearl admits that in storming away from
the table at Ezra's Homesick Restaurant she "acted badly. Very
badly" (*Dinner*, 140).

At one point in the novel Pearl tries hard to analyze why she acts
badly, spoils Ezra's careful plans, makes the family uncomfortable. It
is a painful look at herself, as if she stands as two people – one
watching the poor behavior of the other and powerless to intervene.
In a long and moving interior monologue addressed to Cody, Pearl
Tull looks at her life, insisting that she had not always been a difficult
old woman and wondering *why* she keeps spoiling Ezra's dinners:
"So then, why, I went and made a scene that caused the dinner to be
canceled, exactly as if I'd planned it all ahead of time, which of
course I hadn't. . . . I know when I'm being unreasonable. Sometimes I stand outside my body and just watch it all, totally separate"
(*Dinner*, 140). In *Breathing Lessons* Ira Moran and his two sisters
are neglected as children. Mrs. Moran "had never shown much of a
talent for mothering"; she was far more interested in radio evange-
lists and the pamphlets door-to-door missionaries passed out. Food
simply did not interest her, and it never crossed her mind that the
family might derive pleasure from savory dishes: "Her idea of a meal
was saltines and tea, for all of them. She never got hungry like ordinary mortals or realized that others could be hungry" (*Lessons*, 140).

If the titles of Anne Tyler's novels drift by in order, readers can
remember in virtually every one of them a distinct use of the family
dinner, and usually the occasions are disappointing in quality and
ambiance. In *A Slipping-Down Life,* for instance, Evie Decker sits at
dinner with her widowed father to eat the "baked beans and frank-
furters, lukewarm rings of canned pineapple and instant mashed
potatoes" that the maid, Clotelia, had left. Once she and her father
had finished the sherbet glasses of Jell-O, "they were free" (*Life*, 62).
For them the evening meal has been an ordeal to endure and from
which to escape, not a time for conversation and visiting. The one
extended family dinner Evie Decker prepares as a newlywed shows
that she has far more backbone than her earlier actions would suggest; the occasion also depicts the strain a family dinner can create.
Her mother-in-law, displeased over the marriage, at first refuses
Evie's Sunday dinner invitation with, "Thank you, but we'll not
trouble you by coming" (*Life*, 154). Determined to bring this occa-

sion off, Evie calls Mrs. Casey right back on the drugstore telephone and insists, "we were *expecting* you" (*Life*, 154). So the three in-laws arrive to dine on a main dish of tuna fish and canned peas. Anxious because her mother-in-law might well arrive with a "parchment announcing an annulment," Evie fears a verbal fight. Instead her guests "circulated serving dishes, spoon side outward; they leapt to pass the butter to whoever asked for it and they filled silences with hopeful questions" (*Life*, 154). The only contest was for the best behaved, everyone carefully avoiding the serious topics that promise disagreements. At three o'clock, they all got ready to leave, and Mr. Casey delivered that proper and dispirited word of thanks, " 'joyed it," and left (*Life*, 155).

In *The Clock Winder* a particularly important family meal occurs after Timothy Emerson's funeral. The circumstances are difficult, and the menu is a bit bizarre because the maid, Alvareen, has included mashed potatoes and baked potatoes and sweet potatoes. When she emerges from the kitchen with a hot apple pie for dessert, Mary Emerson pipes up: "We won't be needing dessert. . . . Now, aren't you an optimist. Have you ever known this family to make it through to the end of a meal?" The blood kin may not be able to enjoy each other throughout a meal, but the surrogate family Mrs. Emerson has formed with her "handyman," Elizabeth Abbott, can. Alvareen quickly retorts, "Your Mama and Elizabeth always did" (*Clock*, 133). Many other episodes in Tyler's novels focus on meals during which arguments or indifference cause the meal to fail: the sharp disagreements between Gran and Ellen Hawkes in *If Morning Ever Comes*, the parodies of proper meals in the boardinghouse kitchen of *Celestial Navigation*, the awkward meals Macon and Sarah Leary attempt at the Old Bay Restaurant in *The Accidental Tourist*, and Maggie Moran's frantic attempt to cook a supper that will help reunite her son and his estranged wife in *Breathing Lessons*. Hopeful meals begin with promise and end in failure. In reviewing Irene Handl's *The Sioux* (1985) Tyler noted a single-family supper quite different from the ones her characters have: it lasted for 31 pages – 40 "if you count the coffee in the salon."[8]

In *The Rituals of Dinner* (1991) Margaret Visser says that "researchers into the dynamics of family relationships assure us that most quarrels in the home take place at the table."[9] Be that as it may, the family dining table (or kitchen substitute) "has for centuries been the locus of the typical household's daily meals, and represents, as no other piece of furniture can, the family as a whole" (Visser, 82). As parents and children and perhaps remnant relatives gather about it, the table bears the food for the meals of a family. Years pass and children grow up and leave their places empty; parents by deserting or dying leave an empty place. As the decades pass, the table "is haunted by memories of the dramas that have certainly taken place round this symbol of the family itself" (Visser, 82). The existence of a family does not guarantee happiness any more than care and caution can guarantee a successful and palatable family dinner. Living is – as M. F. K. Fisher has said of eating – an art. And to do it well requires skill and effort, care and caution.

Feminist Issues after All

In an interesting piece published in 1972 in the *National Observer*, Clifford Ridley conveyed a number of Anne Tyler's preferences. She acknowledged that if there were influences on her, they came primarily from Eudora Welty. Tyler also noted that she really did not "care for writers who write about people they don't like" and expressed what is so obvious in her fiction – a great affection for the elderly ("I'd like to spend the rest of my life writing about old men"). She also made what at the time looked like an extremely reactionary response to the novels by "liberated" women: "I hate 'em all" (Ridley, 23).

Anne Tyler and her work do not readily suggest association with strong feminist positions, and generally, as Dorothy Faye Sala Brock notes, Tyler's "works are largely free from feminist grievances against society. As a rule, Tyler's books do not concern themselves very much with either sex or politics, nor with sex as politics" (1985, 21). Tyler's position is perhaps not so much an indifference to the issues that confront women *and* men as it is a constant emphasis, as Brock suggests, to center her attention on ordinary people caught up in the daily efforts of family life. People caught in ordinary life, of course, need to be aware of shifting gender roles and responsibilities. And if many of Tyler's women characters disappoint us by refusing to become strong, competent, and independent, Tyler's views on feminist issues are not altogether confined to the lives her women characters choose to lead. Nevertheless, issues that touch feminist nerves thread their way through Tyler's novels and show characters who react to these issues. For example, Maggie Moran very much wants her erstwhile daughter-in-law, Fiona, to have her baby even though Maggie's son has no apparent desire or ability to take his role as father. Maggie is not intimidated by the anti-abortion protesters who have gathered in front of the clinic. One of the protesters takes it on herself to announce to Fiona as she prepares to enter the clinic, "All the angels in heaven are crying over you," to which Maggie Moran – who too often is dismissed as a slight Lucille Ball (a character type Maggie says she dislikes) – retorts, "Just because *you've* got too many children is no reason to wish the same trouble on other people." It is a brave stand for Maggie, who is anything but political. And Maggie's argument to Fiona about the abortion is realistic: "Fiona! Just think it over! That's all I ask of you" (*Lessons*, 240).

The encounter with the protesters who picket the abortion clinic is one of the few political issues that Tyler treats outright, and, as several reviewers have noted, neither party at the abortion clinic can claim victory. There simply is something to be said for each side if one is honest enough to say it. Maggie (like Mrs. Emerson) wants her son to match the image she cherishes, and in encouraging the picture of the happy family she fails to acknowledge that Jesse is not apt to assume the responsibility of being a parent. She offers only vague and slim promises to assure Fiona that Jesse not only wants to marry her but also will be a dependable provider. Neither Fiona nor the reader is convinced.

A look again at Tyler's book reviews shows that feminism is an issue she frequently takes note of. In "The Wit and Wisdom of Rebecca West" Tyler dwells on Dame Rebecca's choice were she to become an animal. A tiger is her choice – one escaped from a menagerie and destined to "liven up a rural district" ("Wisdom," 55-56). Tyler finds that this sharp intent toward disorder goes to the very soul of Rebecca West. "Notice," Tyler writes, "that she hardly glances at the possibility of being an uncaged, jungle-variety tiger. She automatically assumes – as any woman might who was born in the 19th century – that she'll have to face certain restrictions. But unlike most of her contemporaries, she's downright gleeful at the prospect of breaking these restrictions, preferably with as much commotion as possible" ("Wisdom," 55). The image of a tiger loose in a quiet rural district creates a picture of wonderful chaos. Tyler's closing sentences reiterate her admiration for West's strong independence; in addition, they reiterate her position that feminists would do well to succeed within realistic goals rather than attempting to convert the world. It is not a position that the radical feminist will tolerate, but it is a statement that emphasizes the necessity of getting on with day-to-day living even though all the victories have yet to be won. Tyler reminds readers of West's position: "Never will woman be saved," West wrote, "until she realizes that it is a far, far better thing to keep a jolly public-house really well than to produce a cathedral full of beautiful thoughts" (quoted in "Wisdom," 56). And to West's stringent words Tyler adds, "Modern feminists might hope for some of her exuberance" ("Wisdom," 56). When Tyler praises West's trademarks as "a fierce social conscience, a wicked wit, and a stubborn refusal to accept the going fairy tale" ("Wisdom," 55), she identifies issues at the heart of continuing feminist concerns and rhetoric.

Other reviews indicate Tyler's stand. In 1977, for example, when she reviewed *The Goat, the Wolf, and the Crab*, by Gillian Martin, Tyler found that the two women characters failed "to engage us because each is a caricature of herself – submissive, quivering and misunderstood, and suddenly awakening to her condition in terms as sweeping and imprecise as if she'd been briefed by an article in a woman's magazine."[10] Consciousness-raising has been an inevitable step for many women, but if the process is "sweeping and imprecise" a new woman in unlikely to emerge. Tyler's sympathy has its limits, and her responses generally are as sharp as they are balanced. For example, when Tyler reviewed *The Letters of Jean Rhys* (1984) she found that from the "whining, raging, rationalizing, self-deprecating" Rhys comes across to the reader "as a charter member of the 'of course it rained school.' "[11] Excessive self-indulgence fails to elicit much sympathy, and the numerous incidents that Rhys discusses portray her as one utterly "singled out for these misfortunes by some personally vindictive and ironic fate" ("Poor Me," 30). With all this overindulgence Tyler is tempted to protest, she says, with a strong "Oh, good grief," but then in the midst of all Rhys's self-indulgence "there are moments when she comes through as so sad and anxious and fluttery, so desperate to be liked that it breaks your heart" ("Poor Me," 30).

It takes a sensitive and understanding reader to feel the need for sympathy in an excess of self-indulgence. More to Tyler's liking are the heroines in Gail Godwin's novels, who "are intelligent, independent, and ruefully humorous."[12] These women, Tyler goes on to note, may often make mistakes "in their relationships with men, but their lives never totally center on these men" ("Family," 39). A detail in her review of Robert and Jane Coles's *Women of Crisis II* (1980) marks Tyler's impatience with some women who want it all – independence, career, marriage, children. One of the Coleses' subjects was a former Student Nonviolent Coordinating Committee worker who spoke in "her harsh, trendy language, the woman executive whose dithering over whether to have a baby seems less than crucial when she solves it by hiring a full-time English Nanny."[13] Not many women can solve that age-old problem of the career mother by hiring an English nanny, and those who can may have difficulty relating to the economic stress of women who are single parents. Even this brief sampling of Tyler's reviews shows her preference for women who do not let themselves drift into a state of inaction but instead are sharp, independent, intelligent, and realistic.

In her review of Ellen Moers's *Literary Women: The Great Writers* (1976) Anne Tyler took issue with the book, wondering in particular if "the feminist jargon wasn't scribbled in between the lines just before the book went to press."[14] But Tyler's major complaint centered on the issue of gender. Women should, Tyler suggested, recognize and draw on an inner self "that goes beyond any question of anatomy" ("Separate," 21). In 1976 Tyler rejected the notion that gender was a critical condition for the writer and treats the issue at some length in her discussion of Moers's book: "In fact, the implication here is that women are increasingly informed by their femaleness – that it colors their every thought, vision, and creative effort at every moment of their lives" ("Separate," 21). Tyler declares that only a portion of her life – "and almost none of my writing life" – is affected by the sex she simply happens to be. "And," she continues, "I can't imagine that even that portion would be affected in the same way for everyone. But Ellen Moers appears to disagree" ("Separate," 21).

Many other feminist critics also disagree – as the literature of the past 20 years attests – declaring, as Elaine Showalter does, that "the feminist content of feminine art is typically oblique, displaced, ironic and subversive; one has to read between the lines, in the missed possibilities of the text."[15] In reviewing Moers's *Literary Women* Tyler doubtless irritated many feminist readers of the mid-1970s when she found the author's exclusion of men "strange at this point in history" and added that to justify the exclusion with the argument that women have long been left out of standard anthologies reminds Tyler of children forming a secret club when they are excluded from a secret club ("Separate," 21). At least two generations of feminist critics probably take issue, and take sharp issue.

Tyler rejects the imposition of political stands in literature and criticizes the preface that Pat Rotter provided for the fiction anthology *Bitches and Sad Ladies: An Anthology of Fiction by and about Women* (1975). Rather than assessing the stories on their literary merit, Rotter's preface emphasizes instead "their politics, so to speak – their heroines' anger or lack of it, aggressiveness or passivity, dependence on men or independence."[16] Tyler argues that it is not a matter of agreeing or disagreeing with the political position; rather, the point is "whether it is fair to burden a collection of short stories with this introduction" ("Bitches," 31). Tyler concludes her review by asking, "Shall we determine, finally, whether women do write differently from men? Whether there is some shared quality that sets their work apart from men? No, I'm happy to say; it can't be done" ("Bitches," 31). Perhaps androgyny is at the heart of Tyler's view. When she reviewed Paul Theroux's *Picture Palace* (1978) Tyler thought Theroux succeeded well "in adopting the voice of a first-person woman narrator – apparently working on the assumption that women aren't all that different from men, which seems reasonable enough to me."[17] "The gesture toward androgyny," Mary Jacobus says, "is millenial, like all dreams of another language or mode of being; but its effect is to remove the area of debate (and the trespass) from biological determination to the field of signs; from gender to representation ('words' not 'things')."[18]

In her important study *Toward a Recognition of Androgyny* (1964) Carolyn Heilbrun discusses Lytton Strachey's biographical work on those "eminent Victorians" and says about Strachey's portrayal of Florence Nightingale, "He at least understood that sweetness without intelligence and forcefulness is as powerless as masculine domination without the balance of femininity is destructive."[19] Tyler's female characters are not distinguished for their aggressive conquests, but they do learn to compromise, and most of them are strong; her male characters are often out of step with the stereotypic American success story, living lives, if not of quiet desperation, then certainly of disappointment and compromise. Ira Moran is denied his dream of medical school; Ian Bedloe must give up his youthful plans and raise three small orphaned children; Caleb Peck can fulfill his longing for life only by abandoning his family and city for a meager, if happy, life in New Orleans; Macon Leary *does* choose Muriel and a new life but senses as well the risks that life with her will bring. Perhaps neither the female nor the male characters in Tyler's novels reach the balance that Strachey found ideal, but some of her major characters are able to tap the feelings and responses more often associated with the opposite gender.

Doris Betts in "Tyler's Marriage of Opposites" takes up the issue of feminism and praises Tyler's characters who "survive and persist *beyond* crisis during their long, steady, three-meal-a-day aftermaths" (1990, 2).[20] Tyler's women characters do not rebel; they do not kite off for independent lives and careers; they generally appear singularly oblivious to the strong feminist issues of the day. At the conclusion of the novels Tyler's heroines are not, as Betts's allusions suggest, like the heroines of Ibsen, Kate Chopin, or Charlotte Perkins Gilman – "no rebellious Nora goes slamming out of her doll's house in these conclusions; no woman is swimming out to where horizon meets sea or going mad from seeing creatures swarm inside her yellow wallpaper" (Betts 1990, 11). Given those conclusions for her fictional women's lives, given Tyler's disinclination to take up political feminist issues in her fiction, given her dismissal of defined gender differences between writers, and given the absence of a strong protest against the patriarchy, it is indeed easy to exclude Tyler from those dedicated to and sympathetic with a strong feminist stand. Betts, however, sees that staying married and staying home may require far more courage than many care to admit. "Can we even call Anne Tyler by that capital-F word, *Feminist?*" Betts asks. "One conclusion I draw from *Breathing Lessons* is that Tyler understands the differences between the male and female consciousness more intimately than Gloria Steinem; but because Tyler's women often collaborate with the chauvinist enemy, and by staying married try to merge those opposites into one flesh, her heroines are seldom angry enough to star in the average Women's Studies syllabus" (1990, 3).

Among the subjects of Tyler's reviews are a number of children's books, including Anne Eliot Crompton's *A Woman's Place* (1978). The publisher recommends the book for 12-year-olds and up, but Tyler says it should appeal to teenagers and straight on through to adult readers. Crompton writes about an old farmhouse that dates back to 1750 and structures the book in five parts, each a 50-year span. Every event is, one way or another, shaped by a woman. The book's one weak section, Tyler finds, is the modern one, which, by comparison to the preceding 200 years, "seems thin and querulous compared to the others."[21] Tyler looks at the lives of women who take their turn with the restrictions, limitations, and possibilities that their particular generation imposes. "What seems to emerge from *A Woman's Place*," Tyler says, "is that life ran deeper and richer when there were fewer choices – when [the character] Mary Stone's only choice was how to save the children from starvation, and the blizzard outside was far too fierce for her to escape making a choice, even if the thought had occurred to her. In 1950, [the character] Lynne Cambridge has an infinity of choices and she dithers among them, irritated by her children, depressed by her cleaning chores, fractious with her husband" ("Farm," 69).

It is not particularly sophisticated today for fictional women to content themselves with home and fireside, and when those women *do* have choices they would be wise not to dither among them. "Tyler's feminism," Doris Betts says, "is of this less dramatic sort – she admires the people, often women, who have an abyss running right through their own backyards and still hang out the laundry" (1990, 13). High drama created through independence and success, change and rebellion, are certainly more exciting, but there is, as Betts suggests, a good bit to be said for the Pearl Tulls and the Mildred Vintons and the Maggie Morans, who have a backyard abyss and go right on with their version of the daily laundry.

Critical Attention

Anne Tyler has published novels at a steady pace since 1964, and her readership continues to grow. Appearances of her novels on the best-seller list and as Book-of-the-Month Club selections – as well as the film version of *The Accidental Tourist* – make her a successful and popular author. Critical attention has been less pervasive even though from the outset Tyler's books have been reviewed in major publications by prominent critics. In addition to dissertations and articles in scholarly journals, two full-length book studies have appeared: *Art and the Accidental in Anne Tyler* (1989), by Joseph C. Voelker, and *Understanding Anne Tyler* (1990), by Alice Hall Petry.[22] Both Voelker and Petry give thorough, insightful, and useful analyses of Tyler's novels in chronological order through *Breathing Lessons*, although Voelker chooses to omit *Morgan's Passing* from the Tyler canon because he finds the novel's symmetry marred by being linked "to a psychology so abstract and implausible that the story drifts off its anchor" (Voelker, 12).

It is probably inevitable that critics search for sources and connections between authors' works and, once finding them, sometimes overstate the presence of influence. Paula Gallant Eckard points out similarities in Tyler's *Dinner at the Homesick Restaurant* with characters and themes in Faulkner's *As I Lay Dying* (1930) and Carson McCullers's *Ballad of the Sad Café* (1951). Eckard's parallels between Tyler's Pearl Tull and Faulkner's Addie Bundren demonstrate that both women have the terrible mother characteristics, both women were orphaned spinsters who made relatively late marriages, and neither Pearl nor Addie had women friends – interesting and convincing parallels. Eckard suggests that Jenny Tull can be seen as a modern inversion of Dewey Dell Bundren. With her mother's death, Dewey Dell has no woman to turn to in her dilemma; when Jenny collapses, her mother, Pearl, finally stops the cycle of destructive ambivalence, comes to look after her daughter, and can at last love her again. Jenny deals with the recognizable aspects in herself of the Good Mother and the Terrible Mother; in the process she emerges as a woman able to cope with life's daily hazards and problems. When Eckard draws similarities between Cody Tull and Darl Bundren, however, she is less convincing, as is the case between Ezra Tull and McCullers's Miss Amelia (Eckard, 36, 37, 39, 40). Both Eckard and Mary J. Elkins give useful readings of Tyler's novel, but they also overemphasize the Faulkner influence. Years ago Flannery O'Connor surely spoke for southern writers when she said, "The presence alone of Faulkner in our midst makes a great difference in what the writer can and cannot permit himself to do. Nobody wants his mule and wagon stalled on the same track the Dixie Limited is roaring down."[23]

Alice Hall Petry in *Understanding Anne Tyler* notes Tyler's dislike of nineteenth-century writers, but then Petry argues that Tyler uses images and details from Hawthorne, Emerson, and Thoreau. Many of the examples Petry examines are tenuous connections. For example, Evie Decker's slashed forehead in *A Slipping-Down Life* is a gesture that recalls Hester Prynne's scarlet letter (especially since Evie lives on "Hawthorne Street"); in *The Clock Winder* the family name of Emerson may ironically reflect the family members' failure at self-reliance; and in *Celestial Navigation* Mary Tell's exodus from Baltimore with her children to take up life in the ill-equipped and woefully inadequate lake cabin is an act Petry interprets as "a kind of feminist rendering of Thoreau's stay at Walden Pond" (Petry, 116). Petry's analysis of Tyler's novels is most insightful, but the parallels to the nineteenth-century writers – especially to Thoreau's Walden Pond experience – are strained.

In "Anne Tyler's Accidental Ulysses" William K. Freiert reads *The Accidental Tourist* as "a witty and ironic inversion of Homer's *Odyssey*," seeing Macon Leary as a "readable and middle-brow Ulysses."[24] The mythic association here is interesting, but Tyler's novel does not, I think, even invite mythic echoes as, for instance, Eudora Welty's seven interlocking stories do in *The Golden Apples* (1947), where ambiguity, image, language, and character encourage the crossover with myth. The literary echoes – reverberations within reading memory of ancient myth or of a contemporary writer's story or novel – provide much pleasure. The connections and parallels can be interesting and rewarding, but to insist on close parallels and influences when the tone and the intent of works are radically different is risky. "Nothing puts writers on their guard faster than mention of 'influence,'" Tyler has written, " – the suggestion, in a review or critical essay, that their work bears the mark of someone else. Small wonder, too; for when critics use the word it often has a euphemistic ring. You can just picture a schoolteacher holding up two identical test papers and accusing one student of being 'influenced' by the other's answers."[25]

A far more convincing study is Carol Manning's "Welty, Tyler, and Traveling Salesmen: The Wandering Hero Unhorsed." Manning stresses the "similarities in the two authors' narrative techniques" and emphasizes these similarities more than influence. Both Welty and Tyler use the family as microcosm, and some in their fictional families wander and some are mired at home. These two authors also share "irony, humor, and keen observation of human nature" (110). Tyler is far more in tune with Welty's techniques and subject matter than with Faulkner's. Manning's excellent analysis of King MacLain in Welty's *The Golden Apples* and Beck Tull in Tyler's *Dinner at the Homesick Restaurant* – traveling salesmen-husbands – shows these two wayward men as more ordinary than not. Both Welty and Tyler, Manning suggests, make "the reader *see*, in contrast, the unspectacular man beneath the myth" (116).

Rather than claiming direct influence, it might be useful to point out an instance when a *situation* in a Tyler novel uses a deep human experience that has interested other quite different writers. The point is not whether one writer has read the other and thus is being influenced. It is simply that many of the same deep human experiences interest *many* writers. In *Dinner at the Homesick Restaurant* all three of the Tull children suffer because their father leaves them. But it is only the rough-edged Cody who expresses his great longing for the absent father and is haunted by guilt. Cody dreams about his father and wonders on waking why his father left. "Was it something I said? Was it something I did? Was it something I didn't do, that made you go away?" (*Dinner*, 47). This delicate trauma for the deserted child is universal and has found its way into the fiction of many. One thinks of Eugene MacLain's adult agony in Welty's "Music from Spain" when, living in San Francisco, he remembers his childhood home in Morgana, Mississippi, and thinks of his father, King MacLain, "the one who had never seen him or wanted to see him." Eugene's twin brother, Ran, who has remained in Morgana and is now middle-aged and disappointed in his life, cries out to his father and brother, "Father, Eugene! What you went and found, was it better than this?"[26] Or of Faulkner's young character, Colonel Sartoris Snopes, who, having been driven at last to desert his barn-burning father still in the end calls out "Father" to a man who rejects the son's inclination for the truth. These male characters are as different as can be, but they all have been pushed into the dire suffering of a child/man who longs for a father.

Comic Spirit and Dark Reality

While Tyler's novels and short stories are bright with excellent
humor, they consistently show forth the melancholy and often the
tragic whether it is the child who longs for the absent father, the
woman who senses she will never escape her unhappy home or
marriage, or the parent who suddenly finds the child he raised is a
disappointment. Sometimes the melancholy and tragic converge in
allusions to songs whose titles and lyrics often enrich the scene.
(Elizabeth Abbott's refusing to use the traditional Mendelssohn
wedding march, for instance, and replacing it with music from
Prokofiev's *Lieutenant Kije* is a blatant signal that this wedding will
take unexpected turns.) Tyler frequently alludes to song titles and
lyrics, and of course singing is pervasive in *A Slipping-Down Life*,
since Drumstrings Casey fancies himself a professional singer. At a
dark part of the novel when Drum is out of work and Evie is pregnant, he sits in their meager dwelling and sings, "reaching for notes
deep on the scale." Although Evie does not know much about music,
she knows that these particular songs are not "rock," and the titles
mirror the unsettled lives these two young people have entered:
"Trouble in the Mind," "Nobody Knows You When You're Down
and Out," and a song that Tyler will also use in *Searching for Caleb*,
"The St. James Infirmary Blues."

When Justine Peck in *Searching for Caleb* meets up with
Alonzo's Amazing Amusements, the merry-go-round of the small carnival company plays only one piece, "The St. James Infirmary Blues,"
a tune Justine cannot resist "because the music was so tinny and
sweet and sad and made her nostalgic for times before she was
born" (*Caleb*, 37). Alonzo is irresistibly drawn back to Justine periodically because he must have his fortune read again, and Justine is
drawn to Alonzo's Amazing Amusements. At the end of the novel
husband and wife have joined the carnival – Justine as the fortune-
teller, Duncan as mechanic and handyman. The fact that Tyler
alludes to "The St. James Infirmary Blues" in at least two of her novels may be nothing more than her liking the title – she may or may
not recognize the tune when it is played or know the lyrics. But the
presence of a concrete allusion allows at least a brief look at the
source of the allusion and its use within the text.

"The St. James Infirmary Blues" tells a sad, sad tale. James Leisy in *The Folk Song Abecedary* (1966) recounts that the song is sometimes called "The Gambler's Blues" and probably derived originally from a British street ballad "The Unfortunate Rake." It also bears kinship with "The Cowboy's Lament" (perhaps more familiar as "The Streets of Laredo") and "Wrap Me Up in My Tarpaulin Jacket." Although some claim Joe Primrose (a pseudonym for Irving Mills) as the author, Leisy insists many claims of authorship have been made since at least 1920 "with no one settling the matter yet."[27] *The Penguin Book of American Folk Songs* designates that the tempo for "St. James Inifrmary" should be "*Slow Blues, with intensity*" and notes that the song's origin, the British eighteenth-century stall ballad "The Unfortunate Rake," "celebrates the gaudy and bawdy funeral of a soldier who died of syphilis. American singers censored the song in creating from it the Western 'Streets of Laredo,' and the jazzy blues tune, 'St James Infirm'ry.'"[28] It is the jazzy tune to which Tyler alludes, a tune whose lyrics tell the tale of a man who goes down to St. James Infirmary where old Doctor Sharp tells him that his love will not recover; she will be playing a golden harp by six o'clock that evening. The man leaves, and the lyrics move to his giving precise instructions for his own burial, which, the chorus reiterates, will be caused by a woman. He ends his story, calls for another round of booze, and says to his listeners that, should anyone ask about him, they are simply to say that he has "The St. James Infirmary Blues."

There are many musical allusions in *Searching for Caleb*. Caleb Peck deserts his family and leaves his job to wander because the old Creole gardener, Lafleur Boudrault, had taught Caleb ragtime, "a disreputable, *colored* kind of music" (*Caleb*, 53). He lives the years in New Orleans working long hours so that he can play music when his daily work is over. In the proper Baltimore houses where the Pecks live, the young cousins dutifully hammer out "Country Gardens" – all, that is, except for the maverick Duncan, who has a dented Hohner harmonica on which he belts out "Chattanooga Choo-Choo" in a performance laced with "whistles and a chucka-chucka and a country-sounding twang that delighted the children and made the grownups flinch" (*Caleb*, 73). And Caleb's cold father, Justin, who had refused to allow Caleb to follow his inclination to music, lies on his sick bed listening by the hour to the wind-up Victrola "recordings of Caruso, Arturo Toscanini and Jan Kubelik on violin" (*Caleb*, 58-59). And the mournfulness of "The St. James Infirmray Blues" lingers in this novel that has its own share of loneliness, disappointment, death, and grief. Its tune is irresistible to Justine, and its lyrics tell a tale of loss, sadness, and death.

The comic spirit of Tyler's work endures but does not overshadow the suffering and grief that is the lot of her characters. If her fictional milieu is confined to the domestic and to the everyday life of characters, it is well to remember that Jane Austen also mined that subject matter. Austen knew well that "everyday domestic occurrences are silly *and* trivial and they are enormously interesting and significant."[29] Reviewing Andre Dubus's *Selected Stories* (1989) Tyler commented that Dubus "feels morally responsible for his characters, and it's this sense of responsibility that gives his work its backbone."[30] The same certainly can be said for Anne Tyler, whose characters are, like the author, interested in day-to-day endurance. If Tyler's retirement dream is to live in a small town where all of her characters dwell in houses on Main Street, the reader might consider moving there too. You at least know that the neighbors will be people to care about.

Tyler's novels are popular and they are appealing and they are readable – not necessarily the adjectives most readily applied to "great" literature. Writing about May Sarton's *Mrs. Stevens Hears the Mermaids Singing* (1965), Carolyn Heilbrun quotes W. H. Auden on reading and pleasure: "Though large sales are not necessarily a proof of aesthetic value, they are evidence that a book has given pleasure to many readers, and every author, however difficult, would like to give pleasure" (1990, 158). Recalling E. M. Forster's notion, Heilbrun says that "one tends to overpraise a long book because one has got through it, and one wonders if, in the academic world, the same does not also apply to books that make hard reading" (Heilbrun, 158).

Tyler's books are not *hard* reading, and she has bluntly said that she *wants* to be understood. If giving pleasure to the reader counts, Anne Tyler continues to do that and much more as she gives readers the stories of her characters' interesting, moving, and complicated lives. As long as Anne Tyler is there and writing, there just may be, as Daniel Peck declares, "no place better than Baltimore, Maryland."

Notes and References

Chapter One

1. Arthur E. Morgan and Grisom Morgan, "Notes from Memory on the Beginnings of the Celo Community in North Carolina," unpublished pamphlet, 7 October 1957; hereafter cited in text.

2. Phyllis Mahon Tyler, letter to author, November 1990.

3. Betty Hodges, interview with Anne Tyler, Durham, N.C., *Morning Herald*, 12 December 1982, D3, Anne Tyler Papers, Perkins Library, Duke University; hereafter cited in text.

4. "Still Just Writing," in *The Writer and Her Work*, ed. (with an introduction) Janet Sternburg (New York: Norton, 1980), 13; hereafter cited in text as "Writing."

5. Lucinda Irwin Smith, *Women Who Write: From the Past and the Present to the Future* (Englewood Cliffs, N.J.: Prentice-Hall, 1989), 139-40.

6. Reynolds Price, *Clear Pictures: First Loves, First Guides* (New York: Atheneum, 1989), 210.

7. Jorie Lueloff, "Authoress Explains Why Women Dominate in the South," in *Critical Essays on Anne Tyler*, ed. Alice Hall Petry (New York: G. K. Hall, 1992), 23; hereafter cited in text.

8. Wendy Lamb, "An Interview with Anne Tyler," *Iowa Journal of Literary Studies* 3 (1981): 63; hereafter cited in text.

9. "Youth Talks about Youth: Will This Seem Ridiculous?" *Vogue*, February 1965, 85.

10. Clifford Ridley, "Anne Tyler: A Sense of Reticence Balanced by 'Oh, Well, Why Not?'" *National Observer*, 22 July 1972, 23; hereafter cited in text.

11. Eudora Welty, *One Writer's Beginnings* (Cambridge: Harvard University Press, 1984), 12-13.

12. "The Fine, Full World of Eudora Welty," *Washington Star*, 26 October 1980, D1; hereafter cited in text as "Fine, Full World." In his article "The Necessary Balance: Distance and Sympathy in the Novels of Anne Tyler" (*Southern Review* 20 [1984]: 851-60) Frank Shelton notes the Tyler-Welty connection: "Anne Tyler has frequently acknowledged her debt to Eudora Welty for demonstrating how meaningful literature can be made of the small and seemingly insignificant" (851).

13. Fred Chappell, "An Idiom of Uncertainty: Southern Poetry Now," *Georgia Review* 44 (1990): 698-707; hereafter cited in text.

14. Julius Rowan Raper, "Inventing Modern Southern Fiction: A Postmodern View," *Southern Literary Journal* 22 (1990): 5; hereafter cited in text.

15. Eudora Welty, "Place in Fiction," in *The Eye of the Story: Selected Essays and Reviews* (New York: Random House, 1978), 116-33.

16. Donald R. Noble, "The Future of Southern Writing," in *The History of Southern Literature*, ed. Louis D. Rubin, Jr. (Baton Rouge: Louisiana State University Press, 1985), 578.

17. Quoted in Bruce Cook, "New Faces in Faulkner Country," *Saturday Review*, 4 September 1976, 39-41. "I actually don't consider myself Southern," she says, "though I suppose I'm that more than anything else. Because if I did consider myself Southern, then that would make me a Southern novelist – and I don't think there is any such thing" (40). In a rather uneven and careless review, Carol Iannone ("Novel Events," *National Review*, 1 September 1989) says that Tyler "sometimes goes for a Southern effect, but she is no more a Southern writer than her hometown of Baltimore is a Southern city. Basically what we hear when we're hearing anything is watered-down Welty, MacCullers [*sic*], or Faulkner. In *Celestial Navigation* (1974), for example, a bunch of middle-aged siblings reflect in separate sections on the death of their mother in an aimless imitation of *As I Lay Dying*" (47). Well, Baltimore is *not* Anne Tyler's hometown; it is Carson *McCullers*. And Alice Hall Petry (*Understanding Anne Tyler* [Columbia: University of South Carolina Press, 1990]) quotes Tyler in an interview as saying, "To the best of my knowledge, I've never read *As I Lay Dying*" (20; hereafter cited in text). Mary J. Elkins ("*Dinner at the Homesick Restaurant*: Anne Tyler and the Faulkner Connection," in *The Fiction of Anne Tyler*, ed. C. Ralph Stephens [Jackson: University Press of Mississippi, 1990], 133) claims that Tyler pays homage to Faulkner and in *Dinner* explores the family's psychological dynamics.

18. "Chocolates in the Afternoon and Other Temptations of a Novelist," *Washington Post Book World*, 4 December 1977, E3.

19. "Down in New Orleans," *New Republic*, 24 June 1985, 36-37; hereafter cited in text.

20. "The South without the Scent of Lavender," *New York Times Book Review*, 19 April 1981, 6, 15; hereafter cited in text.

21. "The Mosaic of Life," *New Republic*, 19 October 1982, 36.

22. "Writers Talk about Writing," *National Observer*, 11 September 1976, 19.

23. "The Mission," *New Republic*, 6 April 1987, 40, 41; hereafter cited in text.

24. "Stories within Stories," *New Republic*, 4 April 1983, 30; hereafter cited in text as "Stories."

25. "Manic Monologue," *New Republic*, 17 April 1989, 46.

26. "Everyday Events," *New York Times Book Review*, (9 March 1980): 10.

27. *Washington Post Book World*, 18 March 1979, E1.

28. *Dinner at the Homesick Restaurant* (New York: Knopf, 1982), 303; hereafter cited in text as *Dinner*.

29. Barbara Lazear Ascher, "A Visit with Eudora Welty," *Yale Review* 74 (1984): 149.

30. "Canadian Club," *New Republic*, 15 September 1986, 54.

31. "Stretching the Short Story," *National Observer*, 13 March 1976, 21.

32. "An Art of Distance," *New Republic*, 7 February 1981, 37; hereafter cited in text as "Art of Distance."

33. "Farewell to the Story as Imperiled Species," *National Observer*, 9 May 1977, 23.

34. "The Complexities of Ordinary Life," *New York Times Book Review*, 19 September 1982, 3.

35. "Kentucky Cameos," *New Republic*, 1 November 1982, 36.

36. "Apocalypse in a Teacup," *Washington Post Book World*, 18 September 1977, E3; hereafter cited in text as "Teacup."

37. Manuscript letter, Judith B. Jones to Anne Tyler, 8 November 1976, Anne Tyler Papers, Perkins Library, Duke University.

38. In "Because I Want More than One Life" (*Washington Post*, 15 August 1976) Tyler wrote, "I don't type because then I wouldn't hear my characters' voices; and besides, I often have the feeling that everything flows direct from my right hand" (G1; hereafter cited in text as "One Life").

39. "When the Novel Turns Participant, the Reader Switches Off," *National Observer*, 14 June 1975, 19; hereafter cited in text.

40. "Thought? Action? Or a Bit of Both?" *National Observer*, 19 April 1975, 25.

41. "Writers' Writers," *New York Times Book Review*, 4 December 1977, 70.

42. "Novels of Other Times and Places," *New York Times Book Review*, 23 November 1980, 45.

43. "A Breathless Dash through a Whirlwind Life," *National Observer*, 14 August 1976, 17.

44. Walter Sullivan, "The Insane and the Indifferent: Walker Percy and Others," *Sewanee Review* 86 (1978): 154.

45. *People*, 26 December – 2 January 1989, 76.

46. Virginia Schaefer Carroll, "The Nature of Kinship in the Novels of Anne Tyler," in *The Fiction of Anne Tyler*, 26.

47. Michiko Kakutani, "Books of the Times," *New York Times*, 28 August 1985, C 21.

48. John Updike, *New Yorker*, 6 June 1977, 130; hereafter cited in text.

49. Thomas M. Disch, "The Great Imposter," *Washington Post Book World*, 16 March 1980, 5.

50. Diane Johnson, "Southern Comfort," *New York Review of Books*, 7 November 1985, 17.

51. Susan Gilbert, "Private Lives and Public Issues: Anne Tyler's Prize-Winning Novels," in *The Fiction of Anne Tyler*, 137.

52. Laurie L. Brown, "Interviews with Seven Contemporary Writers," Contemporary Southern Writers: I. *Southern Quarterly* 21 (1983): 21.

53. J. D. Reed, "Postfeminism: Playing for Keeps," *Time*, 10 January 1983, 61.

54. Edward Hoagland, "About Maggie, Who Tried Too Hard," *New York Times Book Review*, 11 September 1988, 44; hereafter cited in text.

55. Walter Sullivan, "Gifts, Prophecies, and Prestidigitations: Fictional Frameworks, Fictional Modes," *Sewanee Review* 85 (1977): 121.

Chapter Two

1. Doris Betts, "The Fiction of Anne Tyler," *Southern Quarterly* 21 (1983): 36; hereafter cited in text.

2. "The Common Courtesies," *McCall's*, June 1968, 62; hereafter cited in text as "Courtesies."

3. *Archive* 72 (October 1959): 5.

4. Frederick Asals, *Flannery O'Connor: The Imagination of Extremity* (Athens: University of Georgia Press, 1982), 9.

5. "The Lights on the River," *Archive* 72 (October 1959): 5; hereafter cited in text as "Lights."

6. "Laura," *Archive* 71 (March 1959): 36; hereafter cited in text as "Laura."

7. "Average Waves in Unprotected Waters," *New Yorker*, 28 February 1977, 32; hereafter cited in text as "Waves."

8. "A Misstep of the Mind," *Seventeen*, October 1972, 118, 172; hereafter cited in text as "Misstep."

9. "Anne Tyler," *Current Biography Yearbook*, ed. Charles Moritz et al. (New York: H. W. Wilson, 1981), 431.

10. Joseph C. Voelker, *Art and the Accidental in Anne Tyler* (Columbia: University of Missouri Press, 1989), 111.

11. "The Tea-Machine," *Southern Review*, n.s. 3 (1967): 171; hereafter cited in text as "Tea."

12. "Outside," *Southern Review*, n.s. 7 (1971): 1134; hereafter cited in the text as "Outside."

13. *Earthly Possessions* (New York: Knopf, 1977), 9; hereafter cited in text as *Possessions*.

14. When this story was reprinted in the *Prize Stories 1969: The O. Henry Awards* Miss Lorna's ever-present "vanilla wafers" got a substitute: "Sunshine biscuits," the ordinary giving way to trade name. The *McCall's* illustration by Kim Whitesides features Miss Lorna in her youth singing away against a backdrop of a vanilla wafer box with a wicker chair dominating the foreground.

15. "As the Earth Gets Older," *New Yorker*, 29 October 1966, 63; hereafter cited in text as "Earth."

16. "A Knack for Languages," *New Yorker*, 13 January 1975, 33; hereafter cited in text as "Knack."

17. There is a group of Eastern students in *Saint Maybe*, but they function far more as a group and type rather than as distinct individuals.

18. "Your Place Is Empty," *New Yorker*, 22 November 1976, 45; hereafter cited in text as "Place."

19. "Uncle Ahmad," *Quest/77* 1 (November-December 1977): 76; hereafter cited in text as "Ahmad."

20. Doris Betts, "Tyler's Marriage of Opposites," in *The Fiction of Anne Tyler*, 4; hereafter cited in text.

21. "With All Flags Flying," *Redbook*, June 1971, 89; hereafter cited in text as "Flags."

22. "Linguistics," *Washington Post Magazine*, 12 November 1078, 38-40, 43-46.

23. "Under the Bosom Tree," *Archive* (Spring 1977): 76.

24. "Laps," *Parents' Magazine*, August 1981, 130.

25. "Some Sign That I Ever Made You Happy," *McCall's*, October 1975, 132; hereafter cited in text as "Sign."

Chapter Three

1. Manuscripts of the three unpublished novels are part of the Anne Tyler Papers, Perkins Library, Duke University.

2. Doris Betts, review of *If Morning Ever Comes, Raleigh News and Observer*, 29 November 1964, sec. 3, p. 5.

3. Jonathan Yardley, review of *The Clock Winder, New Republic*, 13 May 1972, 29. Orville Prescott called *If Morning Ever Comes* "an exceedingly good first novel" and Tyler's touch "deft, her perceptions . . . keen, her ear for the rhythms and wild irrelevancies of colloquial speech . . . phenome-

nal. Her people are triumphantly alive" (*New York Times*, 11 November 1964, 41). Sara Sprott Morrow wrote in the Nashville *Tennessean* that "this is a splendid novel by a young writer; it would be a good novel by any writer" (14 November 1965; newspaper clipping, Anne Tyler Papers, Perkins Library, Duke University).

4. Quoted in Marguerite Michaels, "Anne Tyler, Writer from 8:05 to 3:30," *New York Times Book Review*, 8 May 1977, 43.

5. Judith B. Jones, letter to Anne Tyler, 18 May [1981], Anne Tyler Papers, Perkins Library, Duke University.

6. Sara Kenney, review of *If Morning Ever Comes*, *Hartford Courant*, 8 November 1964; newspaper clipping, Anne Tyler Papers, Perkins Library, Duke University; hereafter cited in text.

7. *If Morning Ever Comes* (New York: Knopf, 1964), 209-10; hereafter cited in text as *Morning*.

8. Reynolds Price, "The Fare to the Moon," in *Three Stories: The Foreseeable Future* (New York: Atheneum, 1991), 47.

9. Carol S. Manning, "Welty, Tyler, and Traveling Salesmen: The Wandering Hero Unhorsed," in *The Fiction of Anne Tyler*, 114; hereafter cited in text.

10. Diane Hobby, review of *If Morning Ever Comes*, *Houston Post*, 14 October 1964; newspaper clipping, Anne Tyler Papers, Perkins Library, Duke University.

11. Robert Tower, review of *Morgan's Passing*, *New Republic*, 22 March 1980, 28.

12. In her excellent dissertation, "Anne Tyler's Treatment of Managing Women" (1985), Dorothy Faye Sala Brock raises these same feminist concerns, noting in particular the sign Jenny's third husband, Joe, places in her office: "Dr. Tull Is Not a Toy" suggests that Jenny does not take her profession seriously.

13. David Marion Holman, "James Agee," in *The History of Southern Literature*, ed. Louis B. Rubin, Jr., et al. (Baton Rouge: Louisiana State University Press, 1985), 478.

14. *The Tin Can Tree* (New York: Knopf, 1965), 211; hereafter cited in text as *Tree*.

15. In her review of *The Tin Can Tree* Millicent Bell ("Tobacco Road Updated," *New York Times Book Review*, 21 November 1965) commends Tyler's depiction of this episode: "she makes use of a nice specificity of local detail and neatly captures the casual and yet complex movement of Southern rural speech with its indirections and interruptions, its reticences and awkwardnesses which manage to express emotion" (77).

Chapter Four

1. John Updike, *New Yorker*, 28 October 1985, 111.

2. "Male and Lonely," *New York Times Book Review*, 31 July 1983, 22; hereafter cited in text as "Lonely."

3. "Two Sets of Bleak Lives," *New York Times Book Review*, 29 July 1979, 13; hereafter cited in text as "Bleak Lives."

4. "He Did It All for Jane Elizabeth Firesheets," *New York Times Book Review*, 15 June 1986, 9; hereafter cited in text as "Firesheets."

5. "In the 'Wood,' Mere Flashes of a Wicked Mind," *Detroit News*, 27 April 1980, F4; hereafter cited in text as "Wicked Mind."

6. "Her World of Everyday Chaos," *Detroit News*, 19 March 1978, G3; hereafter cited in text as "Chaos."

7. "The Wit and Wisdom of Rebecca West," *Saturday Review*, April 1982, 55-56; hereafter cited in text as "Wisdom."

8. *New Republic*, 26 May 1979, 36; hereafter cited in text as Spark review.

9. "Clothes Make the Man," *Washington Post Book World*, 15 June 1980, 5.

10. *Searching for Caleb* (New York: Knopf, 1976), 190-91; hereafter cited in text as *Caleb*.

11. *A Slipping-Down Life* (New York: Knopf, 1970), 179; hereafter cited in text as *Life*.

12. *The Clock Winder* (New York: Knopf, 1972), 149; hereafter cited in text as *Clock*. In "The Individual in the Family: A Critical Introduction to Anne Tyler" (Ph.D. diss., Louisiana State University, 1979) Stella Ann Nesanovich notes that the original title for *The Clock Winder* was "The Button Mender." When Knopf expressed dissatisfaction with the title, someone there proposed in its place "A Help to the Family," a title Tyler resisted, Nesanovich says, because it sounded like "a first-aid book for beginning babysitters" (110).

13. *Breathing Lessons* (New York: Knopf, 1988), 67; hereafter cited in text as *Lessons*.

14. *Saint Maybe* (New York: Knopf, 1991), 120; hereafter cited in text as *Saint*.

15. Mary Gordon, *Good Boys and Dead Girls and Other Essays* (New York: Viking, 1991), 92; hereafter cited in text.

16. *Celestial Navigation* (New York: Knopf, 1974), 31; hereafter cited in text as *Navigation*.

17. *The Accidental Tourist* (New York: Knopf, 1985), 190; hereafter cited in text as *Tourist*.

18. Justin Kaplan, "In Search of That Great Good Place," *New York Times Book Review*, 12 May 1991, 7.

19. Constance Rourke, *American Humor: A Study of the National Character* (1931; New York: Anchor, 1953), 232.

Chapter Five

1. Susan Friedman, "Women's Autobiographical Selves: Theory and Practice," in *The Private Self: Theory and Practice in Women's Autobiographical Writings*, ed. Shari Benstock (Chapel Hill: University of North Carolina Press, 1988), 40.

2. Kathleen Woodward, "Simone de Beauvoir: Aging and Its Discontents," in *The Private Self*, 111.

3. Margaret Atwood, "That Certain Thing Called the Girlfriend," *New York Times Book Review*, 11 May 1986, 39.

4. Ellen Moers, *Literary Women: The Great Writers* (1976; New York: Oxford University Press, 1985), 72. Tyler reviewed Moers's book in the *National Observer*, 10 April 1976, 21.

5. Margaret Morganroth Gullette, *Safe at Last in the Middle Years: The Invention of the Midlife Progress Novel: Saul Bellow, Margaret Drabble, Anne Tyler, John Updike* (Berkeley: University of California Press, 1988), xii-iii.

6. Wendy Martin, *An American Triptych: Anne Bradstreet, Emily Dickinson, Adrienne Rich* (Chapel Hill: University of North Carolina Press, 1984), 180.

7. Nina Auerbach, *Romantic Women and Other Glorified Outcasts* (New York: Columbia University Press, 1985), 50.

8. Linda Wagner-Martin, "'Just the doing of it': Southern Women Writers and the Idea of Community," *Southern Literary Journal* 22 (1990): 32.

9. Quoted in Carolyn G. Heilbrun, "Non-Autobiographies of 'Privileged' Women: England and America," in *Life/Lines: Theorizing Women's Autobiography*, ed. Bella Brodzki and Celeste Schenck (Ithaca, N.Y.: Cornell University Press, 1988), 72.

10. Ellen Cronan Rose, "Through the Looking Glass: When Women Tell Fairy Tales," in *The Voyage In: Fictions of Female Development*, ed. Elizabeth Abel, Marianne Hirsch, and Elizabeth Langland (Hanover: University Press of New England, 1983), 215.

11. Blanche H. Gelfant, "Revolutionary Turnings: *The Mountain Lion* Reread," in *The Voyage In*.

12. Quoted in Heilbrun, "Non-Autobiographies of 'Privileged' Women," 72.

13. In the story "I Stand Here Ironing" Tillie Olsen records the mother-narrator's despair for her daughter who was "thin and dark and foreign-looking at a time when every little girl was supposed to look or

thought she should look a chubby blonde replica of Shirley Temple" (in *Tell Me a Riddle* [New York: Dell, 1960], 7).

14. Evan S. Connell published *Mrs. Bridge* in 1959, its companion *Mr. Bridge* in 1969. In *Mrs. Bridge* James D. Hart notes that Connell presents the "humorous, ironic, and sad series of sketches about a suburban society matron who lives a life of quiet desperation" (*The Oxford Companion to American Literature* [New York: Oxford University Press, 1983] 160). The same quiet desperation can certainly be said of Mrs. Emerson. (*Mr. and Mrs. Bridge* presents Mrs. Bridge in precisely this manner.)

15. Karen E. Rowe, "Fairy-born and Human-bred: Jane Eyre's Education in Romance," in *The Voyage In*, 69-89.

16. Carolyn G. Heilbrun, "Marriage Perceived: English Literature, 1873-1944," in *Hamlet's Mother and Other Women* (New York: Columbia University Press, 1990), 115; hereafter in text.

17. "Three Novels," *New York Times Book Review*, 28 August 1977, 7.

18. "A Solitary Life Is Still Worth Living," *New York Times Book Review*, 3 February 1985, 31.

19. Sandra M. Gilbert and Susan Gubar, *No Man's Land: The Place of the Woman Writer in the Twentieth Century*, vol. 1, *The War of the Words* (New Haven: Yale University Press, 1988), 73.

20. "An Affair to Remember," *Washington Post Book World*, 3 September 1978, E1; hereafter cited in text as "Affair."

21. *Morgan's Passing* (New York: Knopf, 1980), 189; hereafter cited in text as *Passing*.

22. "Mirage of Love Past," *Washington Post Book World*, 26 November 1978, E5.

Chapter Six

1. Brad Leithauser, "Just Folks," *New York Review of Books*, 16 January 1992, 54.

2. Benjamin DeMott, "Funny, Wise and True," *New York Times Book Review*, 14 March 1982, 1.

3. Stella Ann Nesanovich, "The Individual in the Family: Anne Tyler's *Searching for Caleb* and *Earthly Possessions*," *Southern Review* 14 (1978): 172.

4. Paula Gallant Eckard, "Family and Community in Anne Tyler's *Dinner at the Homesick Restaurant*," *Southern Literary Journal* 22 (1990): 44; hereafter cited in text. See also Mary J. Elkins, "*Dinner at the Homesick Restaurant*: Anne Tyler and the Faulkner Connection," in *The Fiction of Anne Tyler*.

5. "Of Different Feathers," *Washington Post*, 16 February 1979, D8.

6. "Even in the Frenzy of the 90's, Dinner Time Is for the Family," *New York Times*, 5 December 1990, A1, C6; hereafter cited in text as *NYT*.

7. M. F. K. Fisher, *An Alphabet for Gourmets* (1949; San Francisco: North Point Press, 1989), 37-38; hereafter cited in text.

8. "Down in New Orleans," *New Republic*, 24 June 1985, 38.

9. Margaret Visser, *The Rituals of Dinner: The Origins, Evolution, Eccentricities, Rituals, and Meaning of Table Manners* (New York: Grove Weidenfeld, 1991), 97; hereafter cited in text.

10. "Meg and Hannah and Elaine," *New York Times Book Review*, 31 July 1977, 14.

11. "Poor Me," *New Republic*, 10 September 1984, 30; hereafter cited in text as "Poor Me."

12. "All in the Family," *New Republic*, 17 February 1982, 39; hereafter cited in text as "Family."

13. "Finding the Right Voices: No Writer's Skill Can Beat Real People's Stories," *Detroit News*, 22 June 1980, E2.

14. "Women Writers: Equal but Separate," *National Observer*, 10 April 1976, 21; hereafter cited in text as "Separate."

15. Elaine Showalter, "Towards a Feminist Poetics," in *Women Writing and Writing about Women*, ed. Mary Jacobus (London: Croom Helm Ltd. / Oxford University Women's Studies Committee, 1979), 35; hereafter cited in text.

16. "Of Bitches, Sad Ladies, and Female 'Politics,' " *National Observer*, 22 February 1975, 31; hereafter cited in text as "Bitches."

17. "The Artist as an Old Photographer," *New York Times Book Review*, 18 June 1978, 10.

18. Mary Jacobus, "The Difference of View," in *Women Writing and Writing about Women*, 30.

19. Carolyn G. Heilbrun, *Toward a Recognition of Androgyny* (1964; New York: W. W. Norton, 1982), 142.

20. A different view of Tyler's feminist position appears in Frank W. Shelton, "Anne Tyler's Houses," in *The Fiction of Anne Tyler*. Shelton notes the obvious fact that Gilbert and Gubar approach their critical books "with a particularly feminist perspective; Anne Tyler, on the other hand, has few if any feminist intentions" (40). In an unsympathetic piece on Tyler, Carol Iannoe notes that some reviewers have placed Tyler among the best women writers publishing in America. Iannoe adds, "Still, she is no feminist. Her female characters do not flirt with ideas of independence but usually come to stitch themselves rather firmly back into the familial fabric from which they were beginning to unravel" ("Novel Events," 43).

21. "Generations on a Farm," *New York Times Book Review*, 10 December 1978, 69.

22. In addition, two critical essay collections have been published: *The Fiction of Anne Tyler* (1990), ed. C. Ralph Stephens, and *Critical Essays on Anne Tyler* (1992), ed. Alice Hall Petry.

23. Flannery O'Connor, *Mystery and Manners: Occasional Prose*, selected and edited by Robert and Sally Fitzgerald (New York: Farrar, Straus & Giroux, 1969), 45.

24. William K. Freiert, "Anne Tyler's Accidental Ulysses," *Classical and Modern Literature* 10 (1989): 71-79.

25. "Varieties of Inspiration," *New Republic*, 12 September 1983, 32-33.

26. Eudora Welty, *The Golden Apples* (New York: Harcourt, Brace, 1949), 180, 160.

27. James F. Leisy, *The Folk Song Abecedary* (New York: Hawthorne, 1966), 293.

28. *The Penguin Book of American Folk Songs*, compiled and edited with notes by Allen Lomax; piano arrangements by Elizabeth Poston (Baltimore: Penguin Books, 1964), 134; hereafter cited in text.

29. Deborah Kaplan, "Representing Two Cultures: Jane Austen's Letters," in *The Private Self*, 222.

30. "Master of Moments," *New Republic*, 6 February 1989, 41.

Selected Bibliography

PRIMARY WORKS

Novels

If Morning Ever Comes. New York: Knopf, 1964.
The Tin Can Tree. New York: Knopf, 1965.
A Slipping-Down Life. New York: Knopf, 1970.
The Clock Winder. New York: Knopf, 1972.
Celestial Navigation. New York: Knopf, 1974.
Searching for Caleb. New York: Knopf, 1976.
Earthly Possessions. New York: Knopf, 1977.
Morgan's Passing. New York: Knopf, 1980.
Dinner at the Homesick Restaurant. New York: Knopf, 1982.
The Accidental Tourist. New York: Knopf, 1985.
Breathing Lessons. New York: Knopf, 1988.
Saint Maybe. New York: Knopf, 1991.

Short Stories

"Laura." *Archive* 71 (March 1959): 36-37.
"The Lights on the River." *Archive* 72 (October 1959): 5-6.
"I Never Saw Morning," *Archive* 73 (April 1961): 11-14.
"The Baltimore Birth Certificate." *The Critic: A Catholic Review of Books and the Arts* 21 (February-March 1963): 41-45.
"I Play Kings." *Seventeen*, August 1963, 338-41.
"Nobody Answers the Door." *Antioch Review* 24 (1964): 379-86.
"Dry Water." *Southern Review*, n.s. 1 (Spring 1965): 259-91.
"As the Earth Gets Older." *New Yorker*, 29 October 1966, 60-64.
"The Genuine Fur Eyelashes." *Mademoiselle*, January 1967, 102-3, 136-38.
"The Feather behind the Rock." *New Yorker*, 12 August 1967, 26-30.
"The Tea-Machine." *Southern Review*, n.s. 3 (Winter 1967): 171-79.
"The Common Courtesies." *McCall's*, June 1968, 62-63, 115-16.
"With All Flags Flying." *Redbook*, June 1971, 88-89, 136-39, 140.
"Outside." *Southern Review*, n.s. 7 (Autumn 1971): 1130-144.

"A Misstep of the Mind." *Seventeen*, October 1972, 118-19, 170, 172.
"A Knack for Languages." *New Yorker*, 13 January 1975, 32-37.
"The Geologist's Maid." *New Yorker*, 28 July 1975, 29-33.
"Your Place Is Empty." *New Yorker*, 22 November 1976, 45-54.
"Average Waves in Unprotected Waters." *New Yorker*, 28 February 1977, 32-36.
"Uncle Ahmad." *Quest/77* 1 (November-December 1977): 76-82.
"The Country Cook: A Story." *Harper's*, March 1982, 54-62.
"Rerun." *New Yorker*, 4 July 1988, 20-32.

Miscellaneous Biographical Pieces

"Youth Talks about Youth: Will This Seem Ridiculous?" *Vogue*, 1 February 1965, 85, 206.
"Because I Want More than One Life." *Washington Post*, 15 August 1976, G1, 7.
"Writers' Writers: Gabriel García Márquez." *New York Times Book Review*, 4 December 1977, 70.
"Chocolates in the Afternoon and Other Temptations of a Novelist." *Washington Post Book World*, 4 December 1977, E3.
"Please Don't Call It Persia." *New York Times Book Review*, 18 February 1979, 3, 34-36.
"Still Just Writing." In *The Writer and Her Work: Contemporary Women Writers Reflect on Their Art and Situation*, edited by Janet Sternburg, 3-16. New York: W. W. Norton, 1980.
"The Fine, Full World of Eudora Welty." *Washington Star*, 26 October 1980, D1.
"A Visit with Eudora Welty." *New York Times Book Review*, 2 November 1980, 33-34.
"Why I Still Treasure the Little House." *New York Times Book Review*, 9 November 1986, 56.

SECONDARY WORKS

Bibliographies

Nesanovich, Stella Ann. "An Anne Tyler Checklist, 1959-1980." *Bulletin of Bibliography* 38, no. 2 (1981): 53-64. Contains brief introduction and a valuable listing of Tyler's novels through 1980, including all editions, translations, and abridged versions; of short stories, including first publication citations and later appearances in anthologies or collections; of Tyler's miscellaneous articles and reviews in national publications and newspapers. Secondary sources consist primarily of reviews of Tyler's novels and biographical entries on Tyler in standard resource books.

Gardiner, Elaine, and Catherine Rainwater. "A Bibliography of Writings by Anne Tyler." In *Contemporary American Women Writers: Narrative Strategies*, edited by Catherine Rainwater and William J. Scheick, 142-52. Lexington: University Press of Kentucky, 1985. Covers 1959 to 1984.

Criticism

Baum, Rosalie Murphy. "Boredom and the Land of Impossibilities in Dickey and Tyler." *James Dickey Newsletter* 6 (1989): 12-20. Attempts to draw connections between the protagonists in Dickey's *Deliverance* and Tyler's *The Accidental Tourist*.

Betts, Doris. "The Fiction of Anne Tyler." Special Issue. Contemporary Southern Writers: I. *Southern Quarterly* 21 (Summer 1983): 23-37. A fellow southern novelist, Betts continues to be the most insightful reader and critic of Anne Tyler's work. This essay also appears in *Women Writers of the Contemporary South*, edited by Peggy Whitman Prenshaw. Jackson: University Press of Mississippi, 1984.

_____. "Tyler's Marriage of Opposites." In *The Fiction of Anne Tyler*, edited by C. Ralph Stephens, 1-15. Jackson: University Press of Mississippi, 1990.

Bond, Adrienne. "From Addie Bundren to Pearl Tull: The Secularization of the South." *Southern Quarterly* 24 (Spring 1986): 64-73. Sees Tyler as free to use William Faulkner "for a model as Joyce was to use Homer." Focuses on similarities between Addie Bundren and Pearl Tull; on the Calvinistic presence in Faulkner's *As I Lay Dying* and in *Dinner at the Homesick Restaurant* the absence of Calvinistic imposition in its more secular world; and on the failure of language to communicate reality.

Bowers, Bradley R. "Anne Tyler's Insiders." *Mississippi Quarterly* 42 (Winter 1988-89): 47-56. Discusses *Dinner at the Homesick Restaurant* and, like Mary F. Robertson, focuses on failed communication.

Brock, Dorothy Faye Sala. "Anne Tyler's Treatment of Managing Women." Ph.D. diss., University of North Texas, 1985. A most useful examination of Tyler's strong women characters, some of whom are strong *and* can adapt while others are strong *and* find it virtually impossible to change or adapt.

Brooks, Mary Ellen. "Anne Tyler." In *The Dictionary of Literary Biography*. Vol. 6: *American Novelists since World War II*, 336-45. Detroit: Gale Research, 1980. Good biographical survey and especially valuable because of quotations from correspondence with Tyler.

Brown, Laurie L. "Interviews with Seven Contemporary Novelists." Special Issue. Contemporary Southern Writers: I. *Southern Quarterly* 21 (Summer 1983): 3-22. Brown posed questions to Lisa Alther, Ellen

Douglas, Gail Godwin, Shirley Ann Grau, Mary Lee Settle, Elizabeth Spencer, and Anne Tyler about their respective writing processes, their reconciling their writing life with their social and family responsibilities, and their being influenced or not by readers, critics, and other writers.

Carson, Barbara Harrell. "Complicate, Complicate: Anne Tyler's Moral Imperative." *Southern Quarterly* 31 (Fall 1992): 24-34. Suggests that Tyler's heroes are those characters who "achieve authentically complex lives" as they show concern toward others while maintaining their own independent nature.

Crane, Gwen. "Anne Tyler." In *Modern American Women Writers*, edited by Lea Baechler and A. Walton Litz, 499-510. New York: Charles Scribner's Sons, 1991. Useful discussion of Tyler's novels through *Breathing Lessons*. Includes a selected bibliography.

Eckard, Paula Gallant. "Family and Community in Anne Tyler's *Dinner at the Homesick Restaurant*." *Southern Literary Journal* 22 (1990): 33-44. Discusses *Dinner at the Homesick Restaurant* and its similarities with William Faulkner's *As I Lay Dying* and Carson McCullers's *Ballad of the Sad Café*. The connections drawn between Pearl and Addie are useful as is the claim that Jenny Tull is a modern inversion of Dewey Dell Bundren. Much less convincing is the similarity suggested between Cody Tull and Darl Bundren and between the plights of Ezra Tull and McCullers's Miss Amelia.

Elkins, Mary J. "*Dinner at the Homesick Restaurant*: Anne Tyler and the Faulkner Connection." *Atlantis: A Women's Studies Journal* 10 (Spring 1985): 93-105. Presses the similarities between Tyler's novel and William Faulkner's *As I Lay Dying*. Sees *Dinner at the Homesick Restaurant* ending with "optimism limited but unmistakable." (Reprinted in *The Fiction of Anne Tyler*, edited by C. Ralph Stephens, 119-35. Jackson: University Press of Mississippi, 1990.)

Freiert, William K. "Anne Tyler's Accidental Ulysses." *Classical and Modern Literature* 10 (1989): 71-79. Interesting reading but overstates the parallels between Tyler's contemporary novel and Homer's epic.

Gibson, Mary Ellis. "Family as Fate: The Novels of Anne Tyler." *Southern Literary Journal* 16 (1983): 47-58. Attributes Tyler's slow critical popularity (as of this date) to her novels not being stereotypically southern and her stories not presenting successful "upwardly mobile suburbanites." Sees Tyler's fiction as "an intricate commentary on the nature of fate and on the importance of family to individual understanding of fate and responsibility."

Gullette, Margaret Morganroth. *Safe at Last in the Middle Years: The Invention of the Midlife Progress Novel: Saul Bellow, Margaret Drabble, Anne Tyler, John Updike*. Berkeley: University of California Press, 1988. Excellent argument that favors the midlife novel as a positive view of life rather than an automatic time of disminishing. (Chapter 5, "Anne Tyler: The Tears [and Joys] Are in the Things," appears in *The Fiction of Anne Tyler*, edited by C. Ralph Stephens, 92-109. Jackson: University Press of Mississippi, 1990.)

Johnston, Sue Ann. "The Daughter as Escape Artist." *Atlantis: A Women's Studies Journal* 9 (Spring 1984): 10-22. Explores the heroines in Margaret Atwood's *Lady Oracle*, Margaret Drabble's *Jerusalem the Golden*, and Anne Tyler's *Earthly Possessions* who "leave home, hoping to create themselves anew" but instead realize "not that they cannot go home again, but that they have never left." Johnston argues that these three protagonists must all emerge from too close identification with their mothers.

Jones, Anne G. "Home at Last, and Homesick Again: The Ten Novels of Anne Tyler." *Hollins Critic* 23 (April 1986): 1-14. Jones argues that "Tyler's texts concern themselves, through the metaphor of home and wandering, with the issue of personal psychic growth. Her characters travel from homes where everything stays the same to homes that admit change, and surprise; they move from (false) Eden to (real) earth."

Lamb, Wendy. "An Interview with Anne Tyler." *Iowa Journal of Literary Studies* 3 (1981): 59-64. Lamb quotes Tyler's comments that express her dissatisfaction now with her early novels. A question/answer format provides useful information about Tyler's life and work.

Linton, Karin. "The Temporal Horizon: A Study of the Theme of Time in Anne Tyler's Major Novels." *Studia Anglistica Upsalicensia* 68 (1989). Linton draws on the French psychologist Paul Fraisse and his concept of time as a means of interpreting Tyler's characters and their ability to adapt to change (examines *Celestial Navigation*, *Searching for Caleb*, *Dinner at the Homesick Restaurant*, and *The Accidental Tourist*). Contains an excellent bibliography through 1988.

Lueloff, Jorie. "Authoress Explains Why Women Dominate in the South." Baton Rouge *Morning Advocate*, 1 February 1965, sec. A, p. 11. One of the earliest interviews with Tyler. Especially useful for Tyler's view on the South and southern writers. (Reprinted in *Critical Essays on Anne Tyler*, edited by Alice Hall Petry, 21-23. New York: G. K. Hall, 1992.)

Manning, Carol S. "Welty, Tyler, and Traveling Salesmen: The Wandering Hero Unhorsed." In *The Fiction of Anne Tyler*, edited by C. Ralph Stephens, 110-18. Jackson: University Press of Mississippi, 1990. Draws parallels between Eudora Welty's character Snowdie MacLain and Tyler's Pearl Tull as both women endure the problems caused by the wandering habits of their husbands. Both women suffer and do so silently, keeping their own counsel.

Michaels, Marguerite. "Anne Tyler, Writer from 8:05 to 3:30." *New York Times Book Review*, 8 May 1977, 13, 42-43. Conveys the daily problem

Tyler (and many women writers) face to balance their responsibilities as mothers/wives and their work as writers.

Nesanovich, Stella Ann. "The Individual in the Family: A Critical Introduction to Anne Tyler." Ph.D. diss., Louisiana State University, 1979. One of the earliest studies of Tyler, this dissertation continues to be a most useful analysis, of the episodes involving the strong women who populate Tyler's novels.

Petry, Alice Hall. "Bright Books of Life: The Black Norm in Anne Tyler's Novels." *Southern Quarterly* 31 (Fall 1992): 7-13. Notes Tyler's shift in the depiction of blacks from somewhat stereotypic characters to complex individuals. In her more recent fiction Tyler is concerned "with the capacity of blacks to survive and thrive in a hostile world" (12).

_____. *Understanding Anne Tyler*. Columbia: University of South Carolina Press, 1990. Provides excellent analysis of Tyler's novels through *Breathing Lessons*. Of particular importance are the discussion of popular culture in *A Slipping-Down Life* and the direct references from interview material with Tyler. By far the most useful resource on Tyler to date.

Reed, J. D. "Postfeminism: Playing for Keeps." *Time*, 10 January 1983, 60-61. Argues that the recent work by Ann Beattie, Joyce Carol Oates, Gail Godwin, Anne Tyler, Fran Lebowitz, Joan Didion, and Ursula LeGuin is "characterized by less dogmatic treatment of men and women" to produce what the New York literary agent Lynn Nesbit calls "postfeminist writing."

Ridley, Clifford. "Anne Tyler: A Sense of Reticence Balanced by 'Oh, Well, Why Not?'" *National Observer*, 22 July 1972, 23. Useful biographical information.

Robertson, Mary F. "Anne Tyler: Medusa Points and Contact Points." In *Contemporary American Women Writers: Narrative Strategies*, edited by Catherine Rainwater and William J. Scheick, 119-52. Lexington: University Press of Kentucky, 1985. Emphasizes the important theme of communication and connection in Tyler's fiction.

Shelton, Frank W. "The Necessary Balance: Distance and Sympathy in the Novels of Anne Tyler." *Southern Review* 20 (Autumn 1984): 851-60. Sees Tyler's fiction deepening with the publication of *The Clock Winder*. Focuses on Tyler's exploring "the vexing relationship between distance and sympathy or, in other terms, disengagement and engagement" within her characters' lives and relationships. Finds that almost every novel has a scene where family happiness/reconciliation can occur if "her characters overcome their detachment and disengagement to make the effort to reach out to others."

Smith, Lucinda Irwin. *Women Who Write: From the Past and the Present to the Future*. Englewood Cliffs, N.J.: Prentice-Hall, 1989. Includes useful biographical material about Tyler.

Stephens, C. Ralph, ed. *The Fiction of Anne Tyler*. Jackson: University Press of Mississippi, 1990. Although uneven in quality, this is the first collection of essays published on Tyler. Especially valuable are the essays by Doris Betts, Carol Manning, and Margaret Gullette. Stephens's introduction points out areas of Tyler's work that have not received adequate attention: humor, influences of Quaker values, dream imagery, the theme of feeding, and the relation both to southern and Russian writers.

Town, Caren J. "Rewriting the Family during Dinner at the Homesick Restaurant." *Southern Quarterly* 31 (Fall 1992): 14-23. Argues that *Dinner at the Homesick Restaurant* allows family members to create for themselves "a fictional family" in which no traditional voice of authority speaks for the family.

Voelker, Joseph C. *Art and the Accidental in Anne Tyler*. Columbia: University of Missouri Press, 1989. Analyzes Tyler's novels through *Breathing Lessons* but omits *Morgan's Passing* because he sees it attached to a psychology so abstract and implausible that the plot "drifts off its anchor." Moves from Tyler's first three novels to the "middle period" of the 1970s.

Wagner-Martin, Linda. " 'Just the doing of it': Southern Women Writers and the Idea of Community." *Southern Literary Journal* 22 (1990): 19-32. Excellent discussion of several southern women writers and the tradition of a female line of ancestry that creates "a true community of women."

Zahlan, Anne R. "Anne Tyler." In *Fifty Southern Writers after 1900: A Bio-Bibliographical Sourcebook*, edited by Joseph M. Flora and Robert Baines, 491-504. New York: Greenwood Press (1987). Provides a most useful resource for biographical data, major themes (through *The Accidental Tourist*), and survey of criticism on Tyler.

Index

The Author

Elizabeth Evans received her Ph.D. in English from the University of North Carolina at Chapel Hill. She is the author of *Eudora Welty* (1981), *Thomas Wolfe* (1984), and *May Sarton Revisited* (1989). Retired from the Georgia Institute of Technology where she taught English, Evans now lives in the mountains of western North Carolina.